Interactive Artifacts and Furniture Supporting Collaborative Work and Learning

COMPUTER-SUPPORTED - LEARNING

VOLUME 10

The *Computer-Supported Collaborative Learning Book Series* is for people working in the CSCL field. The scope of the series extends to 'collaborative learning' in its broadest sense; the term is used for situations ranging from two individuals performing a task together, during a short period of time, to groups of 200 students following the same course and interacting via electronic mail. This variety also concerns the computational tools used in learning: elaborated graphical whiteboards support peer interaction, while more rudimentary text-based discussion forums are used for large group interaction. The series will integrate issues related to CSCL such as collaborative problem solving, collaborative learning without computers, negotiation patterns outside collaborative tasks, and many other relevant topics. It will also cover computational issues such as models, algorithms or architectures which support innovative functions relevant to CSCL systems.

The edited volumes and monographs to be published in this series offer authors who have carried out interesting research work the opportunity to integrate various pieces of their recent work into a larger framework.

Pierre Dillenbourg • Jeffrey Huang
Mauro Cherubini
Editors

Interactive Artifacts and Furniture Supporting Collaborative Work and Learning

 Springer

Editors
Pierre Dillenbourg
CRAFT-Ecole
Polytechnique Fédérale de Lausanne
Switzerland
pierre.dillenbourg@epfl.ch

Jeffrey Huang
CRAFT-Ecole
Polytechnique Fédérale de Lausanne
Switzerland
jeffrey.huang@epfl.ch

Mauro Cherubini
Multimedia scientific group
Telefónica Research
Spain
mauro@tid.es

ISBN:978-0-387-77233-2   e-ISBN: 978-0-387-77234-9
DOI: 10.1007/978-0-387-77234-9

Library of Congress Control Number: 2008931139

Printed on acid-free paper

springer.com

Acknowledgements

First of all, we thank the École Polytechnique Fédérale de Lausanne (EPFL) for providing the necessary founds for organizing the CAIF workshop where the idea of this book was first sketched.

We thank all participants of the Collaborative Artefacts and Interactive Furniture workshop (CAIF) held on the 20th, 21st, and 22nd of June 2005 in Château D'Oex, Switzerland: Edith K. Ackermann, Anders-Petter Andersson, David Aymonin, Maribeth Back, Waltraud Beckmann, Jan Borchers, Giovanni Cannata, Birgitta Cappelen, Dana Cho, Régine Debatty, Fabien Girardin, Christophe Guignard, Jean-Baptiste Haué, Jaana Hyvarinen, Tom Igoe, Patrick Jermann, Frédéric Kaplan, Osamu Kato, Karen Johanne Kortbek, Jean-Baptiste Labrune, Saadi Lahlou, Sara Ljungblad, Christophe Marchand, Stefano Mastrogiacomo, Takashi Matsumoto, Mark Meagher, Scott Minneman, Gaelle Molinari, Lira Nikolovska, Nicolas Nova, Chris O'Shea, Amanda Parkes, Thorsten Prante, Roger Ibars, Anural Sehgal, Andrew Sempere, Chia Shen, Ranjan Shetty, Frank Sonder, Peggy Thoeny, Cati Vaucelle, Nicolas Villar, Kevin Walker, Rachna Argawal, Satyendra Nainwal.

Additionally, we thank all anonymous reviewers for providing their feedback to an initial draft of this book.

Finally, we thank Kamni Gill for proofreading the chapters of this book written by authors whose main language is not English.

Contents

Contributors

Edith K. Ackermann is an Honorary Professor of Developmental Psychology, University of Aix-Marseille, currently Visiting Scientist at the Massachusetts Institute of Technology School of Architecture in Cambridge, MA. She teaches graduate students, conducts research, and consults for companies, institutions, and organizations interested in the intersections between learning, teaching, design, and digital technologies. http://www.media.mit.edu/~edith

Khaled Bachour has a master's degree in Computer Science from the American University of Beirut. He is currently a Ph.D. student at the Swiss Federal Institute of Technology in Lausanne (EPFL) in the Center for Research and Support for Training and Its Technologies (CRAFT). He is developing, under the supervision of Pierre Dillenbourg and Frederic Kaplan, an interactive table for supporting casual collaborative learning. He is studying different ways of displaying real-time information about the collaborative process to the participants, and is investigating the effect of such shared visualizations on group behaviour.

Maribeth Back is a senior research scientist at the FX Palo Alto Laboratory; prior to that she was a senior research scientist at Xerox PARC. Her current research focuses on the intersection of real and virtual environments, with a bit of ubiquitous computing mixed in. She holds a doctorate from the Harvard Graduate School of Design in computational design, and has a background in professional audio as a recording engineer and theatrical sound designer. Research areas she has worked in include smart environments (real and virtual), multi-modal interface design, ubiquitous computing, new forms of reading and writing, and interactive audio systems design and engineering.

John Boreczky is a member of the Smart Environments project at FXPAL. He has over 16 years of experience in video and related multimedia technology. He received a B.S. and an M.S. degree in Computer Science from the University of Michigan, and is an ABD (all but dissertation) at the University of California at Berkeley. He has authored journal and conference papers in the areas of automotive human factors, computer interface design, and multimedia systems.

Mauro Cherubini is a researcher at Telefonica Research and Development (TID), multimedia group, in Barcelona, Spain. He received a B.A. in Education from the University of RomaTre, in Rome, Italy, and an M.A. in Education from St. Patrick's College, in Dublin, Ireland. He holds a doctorate from the Computer Science School of the Swiss Federal Institute of Technology in Lausanne. He is interested in tangible interfaces to support learning. http://www.i-cherubini.it/mauro/

Patrick Chiu is a senior research scientist at the FX Palo Alto Laboratory. His general research interests lie in multimedia, smart spaces, human–computer interaction, machine learning, visualization, and mathematics.

Pierre Dillenbourg a former teacher in elementary school, graduated in educational science (University of Mons, Belgium). He started his research on learning technologies in 1984. He obtained a Ph.D. in Computer Science from the University of Lancaster (UK), in the domain of artificial intelligence applications for educational software. He has been assistant professor at TECFA, University of Geneva. He joined EPFL in November 2002. His current interests concern computer-supported collaborative learning (CSCL): the design and experimentation of interactive furniture; the effects of awareness tools on group performance and mutual modelling; the authoring of CSCL scripts; the use of eye tracking method for predicting interaction patterns. P. Dillenbourg has been consultant for companies in Switzerland and Europe. He is the editor of the Kluwer Series "Computer-Supported Collaborative Learning" and former president of the International Society for Learning Sciences. http://people.epfl.ch/pierre.dillenbourg

Son Do-Lenh is currently a Ph.D. student at Swiss Federal Institute of Technology in Lausanne (EPFL). He obtained his B.Sc. and M.Sc. degree in Computer Science at University of Natural Sciences, Vietnam National University in HoChiMinh City (HCM-UNS) in 2003 and 2007, respectively. During this period, he was also involved in teaching activities at the same school as a teaching assistant and then lecturer. He spent 1 year as a research intern at CRAFT, a HCI and CSCL lab in EPFL, implementing a real-time multi-fingertip detection algorithm for the Docklamp, a portable interactive projector-camera system. His research interests include human–computer interaction and computer-supported collaborative learning. His Ph.D. is about inventing and evaluating new generation of interactive furniture that can be exploited for collaborative learning. http://people.epfl.ch/son.dolenh

Alan Esenther is a user interface software developer in the Technology Lab at Mitsubishi Electric Research Laboratories. His research interests include human–computer interaction, finding the right digital tool for the job, and, lately, making multi-user, multi-touch, and large touch surface interactions and development much easier. Alan has an M.S. in Computer Engineering from Boston University. http://www.merl.com/people/esenther/

Katherine Everitt is a Ph.D. student in Computer Science at the University of Washington. Her research interests include tabletop interfaces, computer supported cooperative work, and multimodal interfaces. She has an M.S. in Computer Science from the University of California, Berkeley. http://www.cs.washington.edu/homes/everitt

Jonathan Foote spent a number of years as a senior research scientist at FXPAL, and is now a consultant in the area of media analysis and interaction. Dr. Foote has more than 60 publications and 15 patents in this area. Dr. Foote's inventions include the TreeQ nonparametric density estimator, Video Manga video summaries, "similarity matrix" media segmentation, the "beat spectrum" method of rhythm analysis, and innovative applications such as automatic music video creation and the first query-by-content search engine for digital music.

Clifton Forlines is a researcher at Mitsubishi Electric Research Laboratories. His research interests include the design and evaluation of novel user interfaces, including digital video presentation; collaborative tabletops; multi-user, multi-display workspaces; and hand-held projectors for augmented reality. Forlines has a Masters of Human-Computer Interaction and a Masters of Entertainment Technology from Carnegie Mellon University and is pursuing a Ph.D. in Computer Science at the University of Toronto. http://www.cliftonforlines.com

Graduated in digital design from l'Ecole de design Nantes Atlantique, **Clément Gault** discovered the research field through a work with Frédéric Kaplan on tangible interfaces for robot programming and gestual grammar for multi-finger interfaces. Recently, he designed the interface and movements of Wizkid, a robotic screen which was introduced at the MoMA of New York. He is now working for Orange Labs and beginning a Ph.D. in computer science at Institut de Recherche et de Communication et de Cybernétique de Nantes (IRCCyN) about design and methodology for creating tangible interfaces.

Mark Hancock is a Ph.D. candidate in computer science at the University of Calgary. His research interests include interaction on large display surfaces, with a specific focus on 3D tabletop interaction. Hancock has an M.Sc. in Computer Science from the University of British Columbia. http://markhancock.ca

Jean-Baptiste Haué has worked on various projects in a human-centred-design approach. His Ph.D., at the R&D department of EDF (Electricité de France), focused on the formalization of ethnographic knowledge into computer model, within the "Course of Action" framework that was developed by his supervisor Jacques Theureau. During his post-doctoral position at ICLab and the HCI/D-Cog labs (University of California San Diego) with David Kirsch, James Hollan and Ed Hutchins, he worked on collaborative work and studied car driving from a distributed cognition perspective. In the Interactive Table project at EPFL led, he initiated the design of innovative furniture and investigated on collaborative processes, as reported in this volume. Jean-Baptiste Haué is currently leading R&D at Yuseo, a small French company realizing qualitative and quantitative usability studies of computer interfaces. http://jbh.lautre.net/

H. Ulrich Hoppe holds a professorship for "Cooperative and Learning Support Systems" in the Department of Computer Science and Applied Cognitive Science of the University of Duisburg-Essen, Germany. With an original background in mathematics and educational technology (PhD from Tübingen University in 1984),

Ulrich Hoppe has been working for about ten years (1984–95) in the area of intelligent user interfaces and cognitive modelling of human–computer interaction, before he re-focused his research on intelligent support in educational systems and distributed collaborative environments. Ulrich Hoppe has been engaged in several European projects in the area of advanced computational technologies in education. He has served as programme co-chair of AIED 2003 in Sydney (Australia) and CSCL 2003 in Bergen (Norway). His current research interests comprise integrated teaching/learning technologies for face-to-face classroom environments, community support tools, as well as learning process modelling. http://www.collide.info

Jeffrey Huang is the Director of the Media and Design Laboratory and a Full Professor at the Faculty of Computer and Communications Sciences (I&C), and at the Faculty of Architecture, Civil and Environmental Engineering (ENAC). His research focuses on the intersection of architecture and information systems. His interests include data visualization and the design of digital spaces (three-dimensional navigation interfaces), the integration of physical computing (sensors, actuators, RFID, LEDs, etc.) into architecture and cities, and more generally, design-centred approaches to human–computer interaction (design thinking). http://people.epfl.ch/jeffrey.huang

Gloria Yi-Ming Kao received her master degree in Computer Information and Science (2001) from National Chiao-Tung University in Taiwan. After she received her M.S., she worked as a research and development engineer in the wireless networking department of BenQ Corporation for 2 years. In 2007, she participated in research on interactive furniture at CRAFT, a laboratory of the Ecole Polytechnique FÈdÈrale de Lausanne (EPFL). She is a Ph.D. candidate in Computer Science department of National Chiao-Tung University and is currently working on research projects concerning e-learning, creativity, concept maps, agent-assisted learning, and digital game culture. http://gloriakao.googlepages.com/overview

Frédéric Kaplan graduated as an engineer of the Ecole Nationale Supérieur des Télécommunications in Paris and received a Ph.D. degree in Artificial Intelligence from the University Paris VI. After 10 years of research at the Sony Computer Science Laboratory in Paris, he supervises now research on interactive furniture and robotic objects at CRAFT, a laboratory of the Ecole Polytechnique Fédérale de Lausanne (EPFL). In his research, he has been exploring technologies permitting to endow objects with a personal history so that they become different as we interact with them and to learn from one another, thus creating an ecosystem in perpetual evolution. In parallel with his investigations in artificial intelligence, he collaborates with developmental psychologists, ethologists, neuroscientists and designers. His researches are published in international scientific journals of these different fields and some of his machines and robots have been exhibited in museums around the world, including the Museum of Modern Art in New York and the Centre Pompidou in Paris. He also authored two popular science books in French "La naissance d'une langue chez les robots" (the birth of a language among robots) (Hermes, 2001) and

"Les machines apprivoisÈes: comprendre les robots de loisir" (Tamed machines: understanding entertainment robots) (Vuibert, 2005). http://www.fkaplan.com

Don Kimber is a senior research scientist at FXPAL, working with sensor network systems, mixed reality, and virtual environments. Before coming to FXPAL he was a member of the research staff at Xerox PARC.

Saadi Lahlou is a social psychologist, he worked on social representations, text mining and consumer behaviour. For the last 15 years, he has been analyzing the determinants of human behaviour in real settings and "natural experiments" in industry, with protocols using digital ethnography and video, including the subcam, a miniature video-camera worn at eye-level by users. Saadi Lahlou heads the Laboratory of Design for Cognition at EDF R&D, and is associate research director at CNRS-EHESS/IIAC/ Centre for Transdisciplinary Studies. He is the scientific director of the Cognitive Technologies research program at Fondation Maison des Sciences de l'Homme since 1998. http://www.iiac.cnrs.fr/cetsah/

Surapong Lertsithichai is a designer and professor at Silpakorn University in Bankok, Thailand. He holds a doctorate from the Harvard Graduate School of Design where his dissertation focused on tangible interfaces and tools for computer-aided design.

Qiong Liu received his Ph.D. degree in computer science from the University of Illinois at Urbana-Champaign (UIUC) in 2001. He received his M.S. in precision instruments from Tsinghua University, Bejing, and his B.S. in biomedical engineering and instrument science from Zhejiang University, Hangzhou, China. Now, he is a senior research scientist at the FX Palo Alto Laboratory in the Immersive Conferencing and Interactive Media teams. His current research interests include immersive conferencing, image/video/audio processing, multimedia, computer vision, machine learning, human–computer interaction, and robotics.

Takashi Matsumoto is a designer working in a Ph.D. course at Keio University Media Design. His research field is an integrated design of tangible objects and ubiquitous computing. He has been designing unique digital gadgets for a network era.

Meredith Ringel Morris is a researcher in the Adaptive Systems and Interaction group at Microsoft Research. She earned her Ph.D. in Computer Science from Stanford University, and her Sc.B. in Computer Science from Brown University. Her main research interests are human–computer interaction and computer-supported cooperative work. More details about Merrie's research can be found at http://research.microsoft.com/~merrie

Lira Nikolovska is an interaction designer and architect. She works at Autodesk in the Revit Emerging Products and Technologies team. She has worked for the Strategic Design department at Philips Design in The Netherlands and taught at RISD Furniture and Textiles departments. She holds a Ph.D. in Computation from MIT Architecture and is SIGGRAPH 2008 Chair of Curated Art. http://liranikolovska.com

Nicolas Nova is a User Experience and Foresight researcher at the LIFTlab think tank. His work is about studying how people use various technologies and turn them into insights, ideas, prototypes or recommendations to inform design and foresight. He is interested in various fields such as mobility, urban environments, digital entertainment and new interfaces. He is also part of the near future laboratory. http://www.liftlab.com/think/nova/

Kathy Ryall is currently a principal research scientist at BAE Systems Advanced Information Technologies (AIT). Prior to joining AIT she has held positions at MERL, Xerox, DEC, AT & T Bell Laboratories, Harvard University and the University of Virginia. Her main research interests are in human–computer interaction, computer-supported cooperative work, and information visualization. Ryall earned a Ph.D. in computer science from Harvard University and is a senior member of both the IEEE and the ACM. Contact her at ryall@acm.org

Chia Shen is a Senior Research Scientist at MERL in Cambridge, MA, where she served as Associate Director of the Research Lab from 2003 to 2006. She currently is also a Visiting Senior Scientist at the IIC@Harvard. DiamondSpin (http://www.diamondspin.org), developed at MERL under her direction during 2001–2003, is the first open toolkit made available to the tabletop research community for the construction of experimental multi-user tabletop applications. Her co-authored paper on the PDH (Personal Digital Historian), a tabletop story-sharing system, has been ranked as the most cited paper for the 2002 ACM CSCW. She was Conference Chair of the 20th ACM UIST 2007. Dr. Shen is on the Editorial Board of ACM Computers in Entertainment, as well as the Steering Committee of the IEEE Workshop on Tabletop and Interactive Surfaces.

Masanori Sugimoto received B.Eng., M.Eng., and Dr.Eng. degrees from University of Tokyo, Japan, in 1990, 1992, and 1995, respectively. He is an associate professor in the Department of Frontier Informatics, Graduate School of Frontier Sciences, University of Tokyo. His research concern is related to human–computer interaction, especially mixed reality, mobile and ubiquitous computing, human–robot interaction, computer supported collaborative work/learning, and so on. Dr. Sugimoto is a member of ACM, IEICE, ISLS, IEICE, JSAI, IPSJ, VRSJ, and JCSS. http://www.itl.t.u-tokyo.ac.jp/

Edward Tse is an Alberta Ingenuity R&D Associate and Project Research Leader at Smart Technologies. His Ph.D., from the University of Calgary, specialized in natural interaction over large digital displays where he collaborated with researchers at Smart Technologies and Mitsubishi Electric Research Laboratories. His research interest is supporting the speech and gesture actions that people naturally do when working together over large surfaces. For more information visit http://www.EdwardTse.com

Frédéric Vernier is an assistant professor in the Department of Computer Science, University of Paris Sud in France working at the LIMSI-CNRS laboratory. His research interests include Human-Computer Interaction and Interactive Visualization.

Frèdèric Vernier has a Ph.D. in computer science from the University of Grenoble. Contact him at frederic.vernier@limsi.fr

Daniel Wigdor is a senior interaction designer on the surface project at Microsoft. He earned his Ph.D. in Computer Science from the University of Toronto while working as part of the DiamondSpace project at Mitsubishi Electric Research Labs. His research interests include multi-surface interactive spaces, shared tabletop interaction, and interaction with mobile devices. More details on Daniel's work can be found at http://www.wigdor.com/daniel

Mike Wu is a Ph.D. candidate in computer science at the Dynamic Graphics Project at the University of Toronto. He is also a Health Care, Technology, and Place Fellow. His current research interests include assistive technologies and tabletop user interfaces. Wu has an M.Sc. in Computer Science from the University of Toronto. http://www.dgp.toronto.edu/~mchi/

Introduction
Why Would Furniture Be Relevant for Collaborative Learning?

J. Huang, M. Cherubini, N. Nova, and P. Dillenbourg

Keywords Framework, Roomware, Noise–sensitive table, Embeddedness, RFID

This books presents research into "collaborative artifacts and interactive furniture", (CAIF), i.e., interfaces embedded in everyday objects, such as tables, chairs, lamps, especially with a view to support collaborative learning.

For the first two decades since the birth of the personal computer, the development of hardware has been driven by the vision of "bringing a computer to every desktop" expressed by Bill Gates, founder of Microsoft, in the late 1970s. Following this vision, hardware designers and computer manufactures ordinarily constrained the form of computing to standardized flat or tower (often beige) boxes, suitable for placement on every desktop, and serving the primary function of running a wide variety of desktop software applications. In the 1990s, a trend towards miniaturization meant that smaller devices emerged, including notebooks, laptops, PDAs and other hand-held mobile devices. The advent of cell phones and mobile Internet has also led to the "mobile learning" paradigm, namely systems that engage in learning across contexts and learning with mobile devices. Recently, there has been a new shift towards what is called "roomware" (Streitz et al. 1998): the integration of technologies into everyday artefacts, ranging from tables to walls or kitchen furniture, with interactive tables and tabletops being a particular focal point for such efforts. Roomware appears as a parallel track of research to mobile learning that sometimes that sometimes has complementary affordances; the phone can, for example, be employed as a means of inputting data to interact with furniture or interactive architectures.

Within the Computer Supported Collaborative Learning (CSCL) and the Ubiquitous computing (Ubicomp) community, interest in this trend towards embedding collaborative technologies into furniture is growing. Researchers explore the elements that make up interactive spaces and the role of interactive, and effects these spaces have on collaboration. Different approaches have been implemented to support group work with adapted office spaces and room elements, but so far, at this early stage of development, none of these approaches alone offers a consistent solution to the question of how to integrate technologies in objects and environments in a way to support collaboration.

P. Dillenbourg et al. (eds.), *Interactive Artifacts and Furniture Supporting Collaborative Work and Learning*,
DOI: 10.1007/978-0-387-77234-9_1, © Springer Science + Business Media, LLC 2009

The present book is a compilation of papers presented in a workshop called "Collaborative Artifacts Interactive Furniture" that we organized in Château d'Oex, Switzerland, in June 2005.[1] Our motivation for this workshop was to bring together researchers, architects, psychologists, and computer scientists interested in collaboration and how new kinds of environments can support it. It aimed at sharing experiences and discussing research results in this area with the ultimate goal of defining emergent research questions and future research directions. A secondary motivation was a new project being planned on our campus: the construction of the EPFL Rolex Learning Center.[2] One of the Learning Center's main objectives is to optimize access to information by providing the necessary infrastructure, services and skills to the academic community. This new building provided a concrete application platform for thinking about, testing and put into action some of the interactive furniture and collaborative artefacts discussed here, serving as a reality check for our conversations.

1   Interactive Furniture

There are various reasons for the surging interest in augmented interactive furniture in conjunction with collaboration and collaborative learning.

The first reason is that it is a general trend in the larger research area of human-computer interaction (HCI), in which area computer supported work and learning is situated. The new sub area typically referred to as "ubiquitous" or "pervasive" computing is a logical extension of HCI research, once it has moved beyond the desktop. Research in this area is derived from recent advancements in three interrelated fields: tangible user interfaces (which involves explicit contact with hands and bodies as described in Ishii and Ullmer 1997), ubiquitous computing (in which one person have multiple devices available in his or her environment and computational power is available everywhere as envisioned by Weiser 1991) and augmented reality (the result of overlaying and adding digital information to real objects or integrating computational power into them as described in Feiner et al. 1993).

The general promise at the convergence of these three areas is that by building tangible interaction environments with ubiquitous computing facilities that adapt to the needs of the people working in them, we might enhance, augment, and facilitate more natural interaction within face-to-face collaboration. The rationale is to move beyond the desktop computing paradigm with more natural affordances: table or wall interactions are more intuitive and direct as opposed to the desktop metaphor.

A second reason coming from the professional community is that this paradigm shift in human-computer interaction opens up new areas for engineers and designers

---

[1] Workshop website:http://craftsrv1.epfl.ch/~cherubini/caif, last accessed March 2008.
[2] Project website: http://learningcenter.epfl.ch/, last accessed April 2008.

to either develop new artefacts or augment existing ones. In this context, furniture, as everyday objects, is a natural candidate for interactivity. Furniture is flexible, omnipresent, socially already adapted and integrated. Moreover, the roles of furniture and operations in different contexts are well understood, at least intuitively. In this paradigm, the computer disappears and objects take advantage of computational capabilities to support new usage scenarios. This has the following implications on design practice: artefacts in the world are becoming interfaces for information spaces and collaboration among people. This is a shift from seeing objects and furniture as containers or pedestals for computing, to a view of furniture as communication vectors. Along the same lines, the rooms where interactive furniture is located are being transformed, since computing affects not only the objects themselves but also what happens between and among them. Architects and interior designers are asking: what is the role of rooms in the emerging society of interactive furniture? This merger of software, hardware and rooms leads to collaboration between space designers and information technology researchers in a new a research area where the design and the evaluation of computer-augmented room elements like walls, furniture, tables and chairs with integrated information and communication technology are explored.

Finally, a third, psychological, reason for the rising interest in interactive furniture links interactive furniture cognitively to spatial organization and co-presence. Furniture has important affordances: objects, tools and information on a table/wall have a specific organization. Human beings organize information spatially so as to simplify perception and choice (Kirsh 1995), or they modify their environments to help them solve problems (Kirsh and Maglio 1994). The spatial environment is hence used as an external representation employed to solve the problem they are working on. The location of artefacts in the environments is an important source of information (e.g., Dix et al. 1993). By their positions, orientations, and movement, artefacts can show the state of people's interaction with them. For example, the observatory work of traditional tabletop collaboration described by Scott et al. (2004) has shown how collaborators have different sorts of "territories". They indeed found that participants employed three types of tabletop territories to help coordinate their interactions within the shared tabletop workspace: personal, group, and storage territories. In the context of collaboration, furniture is particularly well suited to supporting collocated collaboration and providing a means of indicating co-presence. According to researchers, co-presence matters for:

(1) Having a feeling of presence (Lombard and Ditton 1997). Co-presence is thus the psychological sense of "being together" in such an environment. It can be defined as a form of human co-location where the participants can see each other. Co-presence is the cornerstone of collaboration since it is the subjective experience of being together with other participants and building trust between people.

(2) Carrying out joint activities through awareness of others' reactions: the effect of close proximity in work settings is that it helps maintaining task and group awareness.

(3) Monitoring eye gazes: Mutual gaze plays a powerful role in face-to-face conversation: regulating the conversation flow, monitoring if the addressee has understood what the contributor meant, communicating facially evident emotion, communicating the nature of the interpersonal relationship, communicating the status, preventing distraction and information overload, signalling interest and attention and coordinating turn-taking during the interaction (Argyle and Cook 1976).

Furniture elements (be they interactive or not) are hence thought of as pertinent artefacts in supporting collaborative interactions through the augmentation of the co-present phenomena described above.

2   Collaborative Learning

This book belongs to a series entitled "computer-supported collaborative learning" (CSCL). However, the interactive furniture elements presented in this book are quite different from the environments usually referred to in CSCL such as on-line forums or shared simulations. To elaborate about the relevance of these artefacts for CSCL, let us analyze the four words that compose this title.

The first part of this introduction carries a specific message regarding to the first "C" of CSCL, which refers to computers. This book illustrates the fact that technologies for educational practices are not only these ugly boxes that we refer to as computers, but a variety of artefacts enhanced with digital technologies, an evolution of CSCL that has been initiated by Ulrich Hoppe (Chap. 4). We should indeed refer to "computing" instead of "computers" to cover the range of artefacts now being investigated as means of supporting collaborative learning.

As a result, the readers may wonder about the "L" of CSCL: most technologies reported here could fit in living rooms, office or bars more easily than in traditional classrooms. We did not want to restrict the workshop or the book to a narrow educational definition. Except in Chaps. 2 and 4, the relevance of the different artefacts for supporting learning is far from obvious. This is not an accidental drift in the scope of the series, but instead an intentional move: we hypothesize that technologies that do not have an obvious educational intent might actually have a greater chances of being adopted for classrooms than those that are obviously designed for school practices. Let us consider teachers in western European schools. They book low cost airline tickets or concert tickets on the Internet simply because it is the only way to do it. They upload their holiday photos on the computers and share them with friends over the Internet. They exchange SMS and download music for their MP3 players. In other words, they cope well with our technology-rich environment until… it comes to using computers for teaching. As soon as we address educational computing, they often explain the various practical constraints that justify why they use computers more outside the classroom than inside. We reached the point where the low deployment of learning technologies cannot simply be explained by the teachers' lack of computer skills. What would be alternative explanations for the fact that technologies are still moderately exploited in classrooms while they are pervasive outside classrooms? One explanation – among others – could be that the educational label attached to e-learning environments, questions the teachers' role. If the designer starts with the question "how could a computer support the learning process", the designed software or environment will inevitably interfere with the activities the teacher is supposed to carry out. Even if his interference is supposed to be positive, i.e., if it helps teachers trigger learning mechanisms, the new software or environment redefines of the educator's role. Other innovative technologies that do not have any educational terms in their names, such as sticky notes, CD players or digital cameras, do not encounter similar resistance. These informal observations raised the hypothesis that technologies with an educational label are more easily adopted by teachers than those that have an explicit educational function. Let us admit that this is only a wild hypothesis and that we are far from having a strong empirical evidence for it.

A more pragmatic question regarding to the "L" of CSCL is whether the type of interactive furniture presented in this book will ever enter into learning places. The answer varies according to the educational context. In Switzerland, primary schools actually have a diverse geographical structure that often includes 5 zones: the standard table and chairs area, a more open area in front of the whiteboard where kids may sit on the ground for informal but collective activities (e.g., reporting their week-end story), a corner with a sofa or pillows where they can borrow and read books, a corner with a computer and finally an area where kids store and retrieve exercises sheets for their individualized work plan. This rich and diverse environment offers multiple opportunities for innovative pieces of furniture and requires that type of spatial flexibility that Lahlou addresses in Chap. 5. At the other end of the educational chain, many universities complement their traditional lecturing theatres with rooms where students may work individually or in teams, as well as enjoying life (e.g., watching a movie using the available projectors). We mentioned that fact that our university (EPFL) is constructing an ambitious learning centre: since it takes several years to build such a centre, we had to create multiple smaller learning places in the interim to accommodate an urgent need for places purposely designed for team learning. Similar needs have also emerged in corporate training. These dedicated workplaces offer many opportunities for the type of innovative furniture presented in this book. The time structure and the curriculum of secondary education do not seem to provide the same range of opportunities that primary and tertiary education do for interactive technologies.

Let us now consider the second "C" of CSCL, which stands for "collaborative". It is interesting to notice that in the label "CSCW", the second "C" stands for "cooperative". There is no point here in arguing long about the difference between these words in terms of division of labour (Dillenbourg 1999). The key point here is that empirical studies have shown that positive learning outcomes do not result simply because students are asked to collaborate or to cooperate. Learning occurs to the extent to which students engage into rich verbal interactions such as the co-construction of elaborated explanations, the resolution of epistemic conflicts through argumentation and negotiation of meanings and the elicitation of mutual regulation processes. Hence, the main purpose of CSCL technologies is not necessarily what is usually presented as collaboration (mainly coordination) functionalities (e.g., awareness tools, dialogue history), but the fact that they favour the emergence of interactions that are known to produce learning. The range of artefacts presented in this book are not all "collaborative" in the strictest sense of the term, but they do have in common is that they each create some kind of affordances for social interactions. Do the tables and other artefacts presented favour any kind of social interactions, or do they specifically foster the categories of verbal interaction that generate knowledge (explanation, argumentation, regulation)? This question leads us to analyze the "S" of CSCL, by asking how does technology shapes social interaction in a favourable way?

For a subset of CSCL environments, the "S" actually means an "M": the computer supports collaboration simply because it enables on-line communication at a distance as in "computer-mediated communication". This book addresses co-present team-work, not remote collaboration. This is not new for the field of CSCL where some of initial work of Roschelle (1992) on physics simulations or Suthers on graphical argumentation (Suthers et al. 1995) was about co-present collaboration. However, in these CSCL applications, even if the students are sitting next to each other, the technology was only concerned by their interaction within a digital representation or virtual space on the computer display. The physicality of co-presence was not integrated in the design of such environments. It was introduced in CSCL by scholars working on multiple-input devices, such as computers with two mice (Inkpen et al. 1999) or single-display groupware (Zanella and Greenberg 2001). This book goes one step further in considering the physicality of collaborative work. It addresses the affordances and constraints of the physical space in which students learn together, not only in their immediate interactions with artefacts or between students, but also with the surrounding space.

In current CSCL environments, the "S" is often interpreted as "scaffolding", – the fact that the technology will favour the emergence of rich social interactions. "Favor" covers a range of more or less intrusive ways ranging from interface cues (e.g., a graphical palette that includes a "counter-evidence" box) to direct prompts (e.g., "Please provide counter-evidence to the claims made by your partner") and learning scenarios or scripts (Dillenbourg and Jermann 2007). This book clearly focuses on the less intrusive, less didactic ways of shaping social interactions, although the Reflect table (this volume, Chap. 8) nonetheless conveys a rather normative model of what effective collaboration should be.

In summary, two decades of CSCL research have led to one key lesson: collaboration can be "designed", and team processes shaped by the software tools used by the team. This lesson is extended in this book by the fact that interactions are also influenced by hardware, by the physicality of interacting with artefacts as well as the spatial properties of the immediate surroundings.

3   Precedents

Prior to "roomware" and the introduction of digital technologies into the world of furniture and objects, the idea of "augmenting" furniture through interactivity was already present in ancient history, in the practices of traditional furniture makers, and has been an integral part of furniture design. Indeed, the existence of augmented furniture in which the interactive component goes beyond common affordances, e.g., opening and closing a door or drawer, or changing the height of table legs, can be traced back across different times and cultures.

Examples of furniture where the interactive component has become integral part of the very furniture type (and not merely of some instances of a furniture type) include the French "secrétaire", the British "maritime desk", or the American "lazy susan".

The French secrétaire is high-standing hybrid furniture originally created in the 16th century as a salon piece for writing letters and journals that can morph from an armoire to a desk. The furniture includes multiple drawers for stationary and documents, and, as the name suggests, features one or multiple "secret" compartments, which, depending on the skills and ingenuity of the furniture maker, were more or less well hidden, and only accessible through the exact performance of a combination of interactive movements such as lifting, pulling and sliding.

A different category of furniture uses interactivity not to hide objects but to make the furniture itself more adaptable. Examples of this type of augmented furniture include maritime furniture used by sea captains of the British fleet: light-weight yet weatherproof mahogany desks and cabinets, easily foldable, and reconfigurable, ideally suited to accommodate the captains' lifestyles which were often divided between land and sea. Furniture had to be transportable and rapidly configurable for different (usually tight) spaces.

Yet another type of interactive furniture was developed to enhance sharing. A good example in this category is the "lazy susan" whose invention is generally attributed to Thomas Jefferson around 1800. The lazy susan, a rotating tray placed on top of a table, augments the table by giving it an interactive turning platform, helping users to share and move food and condiments around.

These examples augment furniture mechanically, and serve as precedents to the digitally augmented interactive furniture discussed here.

4　Interactive Furniture Framework

Researchers have approached the topic of interactive furniture from different points of view. Research foci range from the development of basic technologies and software platforms for building interactive furniture to application of the technologies in real settings and usage studies of interactive furniture in different environments. The types of furniture investigated vary. Here we propose how the different variations could be classified.

The variation of existing interactive furniture types can be roughly classified along three dimensions: geography of interaction (where), input/output (how), and purpose (what for).

4.1 Geography of Interactions

There is a long list of built interactive furniture examples, ranging from tables, walls, chairs, curtains, and picture frames. A preliminary way to organize interactive furniture types is along their geographical context or where they are employed in space. Where in architectural space is the furniture located? This question can be further broken down into how the furniture is oriented. For example, is there a difference in horizontality and verticality as in. a tabletop or an interactive wall? Researchers have discussed the differences between a horizontal and a vertical surface with regards to what would be preferable for supporting collaboration (Shen et al. 2004). Each orientation has its own advantages and drawbacks and encourages different types of collaborative interaction. For example, Rogers and Lindley (2004) showed how people can work more collaboratively when seated next to each other as opposed to standing. Another consideration tied to orientation is the interaction or viewing angle: when people stand or sit at different positions around a horizontal display they will be viewing the contents from different angles. The classical problem occurs when two people are seating opposite each other and operate on the same, shared textual document. One of the participants will inevitably be obliged to read the document upside down (See also Streitz et al. 2001 and Tandler et al. 2001). This problem is often solved by specific software that "reorients" objects so that a given individual can view the content the right way (Shen, this volume Chap. 7). Kruger et al. (2004), however, have argued how this software solution may be too simplistic because the orientation of objects has specific affordances and "proves critical to how individuals comprehend information, how collaborators coordinate their actions, and how they mediate communication. The coordinating role of orientation is evident in how people establish personal and group spaces and how they signal ownership of objects. In terms of communication, orientation is useful in initiating communicative exchanges and in continuing to speak to individuals about particular objects and work patterns as collaboration progresses…"

What is also interesting about geographical context is the combined use of various devices that connect a personal interface (the desktop or one interactive table) to multiple devices distributed in space: the geographic fragmentation of interaction. The simplest example is the combination of one table plus laptops, PDA and augmented objects (with RFID for example).

This is the case in the UbiTable developed by Mitsubishi Electronic Research Lab, described in Chap. 7: users can walk up to the UbiTable and connect laptops, cameras, and other USB devices to the table to share, manipulate, exchange, and mark up their contents with each other on a large tabletop surface. At the same time, each user can still maintain explicit control over the accessibility and interactability of his/her own documents displayed on the tabletop.

The geographic position of the furniture also has an effect on the level of attention required. Furniture that attracts little attention (or now commonly known as ambient furniture) is placed at the periphery of the user's daily flow of activities (e.g., a clock), furniture that demands a high level of attention (or immersive furniture) typically occupies the centre; they so to speak operate "in your face" (e.g., the doorbell). Some designers proposed the concept of "informative art" as a way to integrate information visualization in the everyday human environment. "Interactive wallpaper" (Huang and Waldvogel 2005) or the "Weather by Mondrian" project (Holmquist and Skog 2003) are relevant examples. The Mondrian project used a composition similar to the style of an abstract painter, Piet Mondrian, to show current weather conditions in picture frames, geographically located high on the wall, where they do not demand a lot of attention and thus do not distract the user from his/her main activity while still providing information.

4.2   Input/Output

We can also look at interactive furniture by examining what their input and output is.

A. *Input* Here we can distinguish between input of information into interactive furniture from other digital devices such as a laptop or PDA, through USB or Bluetooth connections, and input directly from human interaction. In the latter category, fall touch or multi-touch input interfaces which received increased attention recently with Jef Han's multi-touch table[3] and Microsoft's Surface interface. [4] Tangible input existed in several custom products before, such as in the Onomy Tilty Table, designed by Onomy Labs, in Menlo Park, California. The Tilty Table was designed for specific interactions in museum settings, and uses, as the name suggests, a tilting interface. Images on the screen move when the table is tilted, as though some imaginary gravity force pulled them down. Other senses have been employed as input with a view to make interaction more natural. Acoustical interfaces have had an especially long research trajectory, yet the perfect text recognition interface seems still elusive. More playful interactive tables that deploy acoustical input exist, however. Examples of playful acoustical interfaces include musical furniture, such as Onomy's drumming table where the common drumming-on-the-edge-of-a-table gesture is converted into something more musical (Back et al. 2001), or noise-sensitive tables (Karahalios and Bergstrom, 2006), where the table acts as a mirror reflecting the dynamics of a group conversation by visually discriminating the contribution of individual group members in discussions around the table (see Chap. 8).

B. *Output* The most frequent output interfaces in interactive furniture are probably high-resolution displays (VGA or XGA) using integrated LCD/DLP projectors, or flat screens (LCD or plasma screens). The degree of embeddedness (the level at which the output is integrated into the furniture) is an interesting differentiation factor, ranging from low embeddedness (e.g., a LCD screen placed on top of an

---

[3] http://cs.nyu.edu/~jhan/ftirtouch/index.html, last accessed March 2008.
[4] http://www.microsoft.com/surface, last accessed March 2008.

existing table) to a complete symbiosis of output device and furniture. An example for the latter can be found in MIT Media Lab's CounterActive project (Selker 2003). The project focuses on interactive furniture in the kitchen. A computer, stored under the counter, is connected to a projector over the kitchen doorway that projects a tri-part image onto a portion of the kitchen counter. It can show step-by-step recipe instructions, playing the steps aloud and with images and videos. The project combines visual output with sound output. Other projects focus on audio output only. An early example is Laurie Anderson's "handphone table" which allows people to listen to sounds by putting their elbows on the table and covering their ears with their hands. In this example, bone conduction allows the conveyance of sounds

Between the input and output variations, there are, as one can imagine, almost limitless combinatorial possibilities. An interesting example that elegantly exploits combinatorial opportunities is the "Reactable" designed at the Music Technology Group UPF in Barcelona.

The Reactable combines tangible input (moving and rotating physical objects on a table) with audio output to generate music. This interactive furniture was successfully used by the popular artist Bjork as an instrument during her "Volta" tour in 2007.

4.3   Purpose

Finally, interactive furniture can be categorized according to what their purpose is. Typical purposes for interactive furniture includes brainstorming, negotiation, document sharing (text documents or sharing and sorting photos), information visualization, and background awareness. Furniture can also enable new functions rather than only supporting existing ones. An interactive table developed by FX PAL enables the storing and sharing of digital documents with participants' mobile devices (Chiu et al. 2007). The noise-sensitive table (Chap. 8) augments collaboration through group involvement features such as the social mirroring of the group activity and tools to regulate and structure turn taking.

Furniture can also allow the inclusion of new users, as in furniture that enables remote participation in an interaction. The interactivity of the furniture is then meant to augment remote collaboration by allowing a mix of the digital and the physical space.

Clearly, interactive furniture is being developed along exciting dimensions, for different geographic contexts, using different input and output modalities, and for different purposes. Yet outside of research labs, interactive furniture is rarely seen or used. Why? The inflexibility of interactive furniture may be one of the reasons that would explain this situation: input interaction techniques can be too specific to let the table be used in other contexts, orientation issues of documents are often problematic as is the control of interactive features (display control, data inputs).

The integration of existing artefacts (PDA, cell phones) into furniture is often difficult and requires the use of additional systems and software. In addition, one of the general difficulties of roomware is that it generally requires users to adjust their practices. Therefore, it will take some time to develop new habits of use for interactive furniture. Yet over 3,000 years of furniture history,[5] this transitional period of a couple of years that the use of digitally enhanced interactive furniture appears to be negligible. We are in a transitional period, at the very beginning of discovering what the real opportunities, affordances and dangers of interactive furniture might be, and we hope with this initial compilation to give a snapshot of the current research in this field, and provide a platform for future work.

5 Book Overview

The essays collected in this book have been selected from workshop presentations. They cover different aspects regarding the design and use of interactive furniture in conjunction with collaboration support.

In the second chapter, Masanori Sugimoto presents three systems to support collaborative learning in an elementary school. The core idea of these interactive table applications is to enhance face-to-face interaction through the physical manipulation of objects. The paper describes the various steps in the design process, from determining learning requirements to different design iterations.

The chapter by Haué and Dillenbourg reports an empirical study of people working around a table with their laptops. It illustrates the complementarity of qualitative and quantitative methods.

The fourth chapter about collaborative learning, by Ulrich Hoppe, is an account of how the disappearing computer propelled by ubiquitous computing technologies leads to "integrated classrooms", which eventually enable new production of learning material. Hoppe articulates his visions and the problem about such an approach based on his experience in an integrated classroom.

In Chap. 5, Saadi Lahlou presents empirical studies conducted within an energy provider company in order to augment meetings. They were using shared interactive boards and videoconferencing systems embedded in walls and on mobile trolleys. The next chapter, by Maribeth Back et al. shows how a conference room podium could be augmented for supporting different interaction tasks, including authoring, presenting, and supporting telepresence. In the next chapter, Chia Shen describes the main issues regarding the design of collaborative tabletop applications through prototypes developed at Mitsubishi Electric Research Labs. She raises the issue that direct-touch tables are an emerging but immature user interface.

The eighth chapter, by the EPFL team, develops a design framework that articulates a model of self-regulation in collaborative learning with the design of a noise-sensitive table that displays interaction patterns.

In the last chapter, Lira Nikolovska and Edith Ackermann raise the importance of taking into account the physical, relational and cultural qualities of the objects

---

[5] See http://en.wikipedia.org/wiki/Furniture, last accessed May 2008.

to be augmented as "interactive furniture". They speculate about the need to use new design methods through two examples, exploring the poetics of everyday objects.

6 Synthesis

This book does not provide a synthetic account of how interactive furniture might enhance collaborative learning. On the one hand, the picture is still fragmentary and lack of empirical evidence. On the other hand, it opens a different way to think about the role of technologies for supporting collaborative learning. We strongly believe that, beyond the "gadget" dimension of existing examples, this new role will initiate a paradigm shift in the field of technology-enhanced learning.

References

Argyle, M., and Cook, M. (1976) *Gaze and Mutual Gaze*. Cambridge: Cambridge University Press.

Back, M., Cohen, J., Gold, R., Harrison, S., and Minneman, S. (2001) Listen Reader: An Electronically Augmented Paper-Based Book. In Beaudouin-Lafon, Michel and Jacob, Robert J. K. (Eds.), *Proceedings of the ACM CHI 2001 Human Factors in Computing Systems Conference,* Seattle, Washington, USA, March 31–April 5, 2001 (pp. 23–29). ACM Press.

Chiu, P., Lertsithichai, S., and Liu, Q. (2007) Interaction Models for Multi-Display Slideshows. *Pervasive 2007* Invited Demo, May 13, 2007.

Dillenbourg, P. (1999) What Do You Mean by Collaborative Learning? In P. Dillenbourg (Ed.), *Collaborative-Learning: Cognitive and Computational Approaches* (pp. 1–19). Oxford: Elsevier.

Dillenbourg, P., and Jermann, P. (2007) Designing Integrative Scripts. In F. Fischer, H. Mandl, J. Haake, and I. Kollar (Eds.), *Scripting Computer-Supported Collaborative Learning – Cognitive, Computational, and Educational Perspectives* (pp. 275–301). Computer-Supported Collaborative Learning Series, New York: Springer.

Dix, A., Finlay, J., Abowd, G., and Beale, R., (1993) *Human-Computer Interaction.* Prentice-Hall, Harlow, England.

Feiner, S., MacIntyre, B., and Seligmann, D. (1993) Knowledge Based Augmented Reality. *Communication of ACM*, 36 (7), 53–62.

Holmquist, L.E., and Skog, T. (2003) Informative Art: Information Visualization in Everyday Environments. In *Proceedings of 1st International Conference on Computer Graphics and Interactive Techniques in Australia and Southeast Asia* (2003) (pp. 229–235).

Huang, J., and Waldvogel, M., (2005) Interactive Wallpaper. In *SIGGRAPH Electronic Arts and Animation Catalog (EAAC), SIGGRAPH 2005*, Los Angeles.

Inkpen, K., Ho-Ching, W., Kuederle, O., Scott, S.D., and Shoemaker, G. (1999) This Is Fun! We're All Best Friends and We're All Playing: Supporting Children's Synchronous Collaboration. In *Proceedings of CSCL*, Stanford (pp. 252–259).

Ishii, H., and Ullmer, B. (1997) Tangible Bits: Towards Seamless Interfaces between People, Bits and Atoms. In *Proceedings of Conference on Human Factors in Computing Systems CHI '97*, Atlanta, March 1997 (pp. 234–241), ACM Press.

Karahalios, K., and Bergstrom T. (2006) Visualizing Audio in Group Table Conversation. In *Proceedings of Horizontal Interactive Human-Computer Systems,* IEEE (pp. 131–134).

Kirsh, D. (1995) The Intelligent Use of Space. *Artificial Intelligence*, 73 (1–2), 31–68.

Kirsh, D., and Maglio, P. (1994) On Distinguish Between Epistemic from Pragmatic Action. *Cognitive Science*, 18, 513–549.

Kruger, R., Carpendale, M. S. T., Scott, S. D., and Greenberg, S. (2004) Roles of Orientation in Tabletop Collaboration: Comprehension, Coordination and Communication. *Journal on Computer Supported Cooperative Work,* 13 (5–6), 501–537.

Lombard, M., and Ditton, T. (1997) At the Heart of it All: The Concept of Presence. *Journal of Mediated Communication*, 3 (2).

Rogers, Y., and Lindley, S. (2004) Collaborating Around Vertical and Horizontal Displays: Which Way is Best? *Interacting With Computers;* 16 (4), 1133–1152.

Roschelle, J. (1992) Learning by Collaborating: Convergent Conceptual Change. *Journal of the Learning Sciences*, 2, 235–276.

Scott, S.D., Carpendale, M.S.T., and Inkpen, K.M. (2004) Territoriality in Collaborative Tabletop Workspaces. In *Proceedings of CSCW 2004* (pp. 294–303).

Selker, T. (2003): Fostering Motivation and Creativity for Computer Users. In *Proceedings of the Tenth International Conference on Human-Computer Interaction* 2003 (pp. 1303–1307).

Shen, C., Vernier, F. D., Forlines, C., and Ringel, M. (2004) DiamondSpin: An Extensible Toolkit for Around-the-Table Interaction. In Dykstra-Erickson, Elizabeth and Tscheligi, Manfred(Eds.), *Proceedings of ACM CHI 2004 Conference on Human Factors in Computing Systems*, Vienna, Austria, April 24–29, 2004 (pp. 167–174).

Streitz, N., Geißler, J., and Holmer, T. (1998) Roomware for Cooperative Buildings – Integrated Design of Architectural and Information Spaces. In Streitz(Ed.), *Proceedings of the International Workshop on Cooperative Buildings* (CoBuild'98). Springer, LNCS.

Streitz, N., Tandler, P., Mller-Tomfelde, C., and Konomi, S. (2001) Roomware: Towards the Next Generation of Human-Computer Interaction based on an Integrated Design of Real and Virtual Worlds. In J. A. Carroll (Ed.), *Human-Computer Interaction in the New Millenium* (pp. 551–576). Addison Wesley.

Suthers, D., Weiner, A. Connelly J., and Paolucci, M. (1995) Belvedere: Engaging Students in Critical Discussion of Science and Public Policy Issues. In J. Greer (Ed.), *Proceedings of the International Conference in Artificial Intelligence in Education*, Washington, August 16–19 (pp. 266–273).

Tandler P., Prante, T., Mller-Tomfelde, C., Streitz, N., and Steinmetz, R. (2001) ConnecTables: Dynamic Coupling of Displays for the Flexible Creation of Shared Workspaces. In *Proceedings of the 14th Annual ACM Symposium on User Interface Software and Technology* (UIST'01), Orlando, Florida, USA, November 11–14, 2001, CHI Letters 3(2), ACM Press.

Weiser, M. (1991) The Computer for the 21st Century. *Scientific American*, 265 (3), 94–104.

Zanella, A. and Greenberg, S. (2001) Reducing Interference in Single Display Groupware Through Transparency. In W. Prinz, M. Jarke, Y. Rogers, K. Schmidt, and V. Wulf (Eds.), *Proceedings of the Seventh Conference on European Conference on Computer Supported Cooperative Work* (ECSCW), Bonn, Germany, September 16–20, 2001 (pp. 339–358). Norwell, MA: Kluwer Academic Publishers.

Design of Systems for Supporting Collaborative Learning Augmented with Physical Artefacts

Masanori Sugimoto

In this chapter, the design process of systems for supporting collaborative learning is described. We have developed the collaborative learning support systems called Epro, Epro2, and CarettaKids and evaluated through educational practices in elementary schools. Based on our experience with these systems, lessons related to the design issues of tangible or tabletop interface systems for supporting children's collaborative learning are discussed.

Keywords Collaborative learning, Tabletop interface, Environmental learning, Elementary school children, Sensing board, PDA

1 Introduction

We have been developing systems to support collaborative learning (Koschmann 1996) in elementary school education. The underlying philosophy of our research project is that learners should be regarded as active creators, rather than passive recipients, of information and knowledge (Fischer 1998). Therefore, the role of computational media should be to support learners' active participation in the learning process.

Many computational systems or media used in school education support learning by allowing children to access and to explore virtual information spaces, to search Internet resources for information related to their learning and to have synchronous or asynchronous discussions with other children in separate locations. The proposed systems in this chapter, on the other hand, integrate physical and virtual spaces to enhance active learning. Children can experience, in virtual space, visual feedback of their interactions with physical artefacts in a physical space.

The systems are designed to enhance learning about environmental problems through simulations and discussions. Each system allows children to construct a model town in a physical space and view the environmental impact of their actions simulated in the virtual space. With these systems, a group of children can verify knowledge they acquired from their schoolteachers or textbooks. Therefore, the

P. Dillenbourg et al. (eds.), *Interactive Artifacts and Furniture Supporting Collaborative Work and Learning,*
DOI: 10.1007/978-0-387-77234-9_2, © Springer Science + Business Media, LLC 2009

systems are more effective at augmenting children's learning experiences, raising their learning motivation and supporting their participation than systems that allow them to interact only within a virtual space.

In this chapter, we discuss the design processes of the systems. As users of the systems are elementary school children and their teachers, the author's group first asked them to use a paper-based prototype system, to identify requirements of systems to be designed through interviews with children and teachers and analyses of their behaviours. The designed systems have evolved through the evaluations of educational practices in elementary schools. This chapter describes three systems called Epro, Epro2, and CarettaKids, respectively, and the issues raised in their evaluations. Based on our experiences with these systems, recommendations related to the design of tangible or tabletop interface systems for supporting children's collaborative learning are given.

2   Key Issues Collaborative Learning in Designing Systems for Supporting Children's Collaborative Learning

When we think of learning support technologies, we can take various approaches or systems based on different learning theories. The underlying conceptual and theoretical premise of our project is that people learn through interactions with others by participating in a learning community (Lave and Wenger 1991, Fischer and Sugimoto 2006, Resnick 1991). They are also related to theories of social constructivism (Steffe and Gale 1995). Based on these learning theories, we investigate how learning support systems should be designed, utilizing information and communication technologies to enable the systems to enhance learners' experiences. Our basic strategies for designing systems for supporting collaborative learning are as follows.

2.1   Designing User Interfaces That Allow Physical Manipulations

In many conventional systems for supporting learning, learners stay in a fixed position, such as sitting in front of a computer, using it with a keyboard and a mouse and viewing a display. However, when we think of our daily lives, we interact naturally with other people and manipulate real-world artefacts. Therefore, we believe that user interfaces of systems for supporting collaborative learning should allow learners to conduct physical manipulations. Moreover, as users of our systems are children who are not always good at using computers, we have to design computational media that allow children to conduct an intuitive manipulation to promote their participation in learning situations.

2.2 Designing Computational Media That Enhance Interactions Between Learners

In school education, children have traditionally learned by absorbing knowledge provided by their teachers and textbooks, that is, they have been passive recipients of knowledge. Recently, some schools have begun to try different learning/teaching approaches: children actively discuss topics with each other and construct knowledge by themselves (Scardamalia and Bereiter 1996). One effective way to support such knowledge construction through discussions and interactions between children, is to design computational media integrated with physical media that allows children to manipulate and share concepts in the physical world (Arias et al. 2000).

2.3 Introducing a Sense of Play for Learners' Engagement

A sense of game or play is useful for raising the level of learners' engagement and excitement (Kafai 1996). Learning through playing is one of the most effective approaches because it provides learners with an easy starting point for learning and immerses them in their activities. If learners' play activities are smoothly linked to authentic learning, they will learn by themselves while retaining high levels of motivation.

A solution that satisfies the issues raised above is a tabletop and tangible interface system that allows learners to manipulate physical artefacts and share them with each other. However, the design requirements for such a system enhancing children's collaborative learning were not clear when the author's group started their project. Therefore, a prototype system for investigating the requirement was first developed.

3 Prototype System for Identifying Design Requirements

3.1 Overview

The system to be designed was used for supporting children's collaborative learning about environmental problems. The functions first thought to be necessary were:

- The system should automatically and rapidly recognize types and locations of objects manipulated by learners.
- Based on the arrangement of the objects, the system should calculate environmental changes and visualize them through simulations.

The first function relates to the design of the hardware, and several existing methods for object recognition – such as sensors or image processing – were applicable. The second function relates to the software and user interface design. The author's group decided to investigate the hardware design first, because hardware would take longer to develop and because – in contrast to software – changing hardware is difficult and costly once implementation has begun.

3.2   A Prototype System: Paperboard and Software

To understand the requirements of users (teachers and children), "Wizard of Oz" experiments were conducted. The following prototype system was brought to classrooms:

- Paperboards: Several paperboards were created and used not only to find suitable size and number of grid cells, but also to identify how children behave while using them. Figure 1 shows an example of a paperboard.
- Simulation and visualization software: From discussions with teachers, and from a textbook used in lessons, the knowledge with which to construct a simulation model of the software was extracted. The teachers requested that the simulation model should not be complicated, enabling the children to guess the relationship between cause and effect. Therefore, three types of pieces (a house, a factory, and a tree, each of which represents people, industry, and nature, respectively) to be directly manipulated on the paperboards by the children were created, and five parameters describing environmental changes in a town were selected.

Elementary school children (fifth graders aged 10–11) participated in the experiments. The prototype system could not automatically identify the pieces on the paperboard. When children put a piece on the paperboard, one of the experimenters would manually input the type and location of the piece into a personal computer.

Fig. 1 An example of a paperboard for clarifying design requirements and children's behaviours

Then the computer started the simulation and created a visualization of the results. Through these experiments, post-experimental interviews with the children, analyses of their behaviours, and discussions with teachers, the following issues were clarified:

- While using the system, children pushed and pulled the paperboard so that they could easily place a piece on it. They sometimes leaned over the paperboard to place a piece on it.
- As the system must be designed to be used in one class period, the time to construct a town on the board needed to be less than 50 min. However, for all the children in one group to have sufficient opportunities for manipulating pieces and to make the results of computer simulation educationally meaningful, more than 200–300 pieces should be placed on the board.
- The system must be large enough for four to eight children to sit around it.
- As the system would be used in an elementary school classroom, not in a university laboratory, special equipment requiring remodelling of the room cannot be used. The system design must secure children's safety and also allow for their unpredictable movements and behaviours.
- It is desirable that children be able to independently set up and dismantle the system.
- Although the simulation model was simple, it effectively stimulated children's thinking. For example, they discussed the factories on the board that should be removed or where trees should be placed to reduce the level of CO_2 density. They also considered the level of noise in residential areas (where many houses were placed).

Based on these findings and from discussions with the teachers, the design requirements for the system were formulated as follows:

- For object recognition, a method using image-processing technology (e.g., Underkoffler and Ishii 1999) or a touch-sensitive display (e.g., Arias et al. 2000) is not suitable for this project and a sensor-based method is preferable.
- The system should be more than 60 cm × 60 cm, and large enough for four to eight children to sit around it.
- The system should simultaneously accept the input from about 500 objects and rapidly recognize their types and locations.
- The system should be as light and simple as possible, allowing children to use it independently.

A design decision at that time (Spring 1999) was not to use image-processing technology or a touch-sensitive display for object recognition. To use image-processing technology, a camera must be installed over or below a desk. Installation requires very tall, large or heavy special equipment that may be difficult to use without remodelling the classroom. The camera must be calibrated before using the system, which is not an easy task for children to perform. Another problem with image-processing technology is related to occlusions that happen when children hide pieces with their hands, heads or bodies. Moreover, processing time for object

recognition is also significant. Children become frustrated if feedback is not immediately given after manipulation of pieces. At that time, stable recognition of
hundreds of different pieces within a sufficiently short period (e.g., a tenth of a
second) seemed very difficult. Touch-sensitive displays are single input devices and
are not suitable for applications required to recognize multiple pieces quickly.

In experiments with the prototype system, a suitable size for a piece was also
investigated, because children would have difficulty manipulating pieces that were
too big or too small. The size was chosen by asking children to grasp pieces of
differing sizes in the palm of their hand, place them on the paper-based board, and
move them by picking them up with their fingers.

4   How Designs of the Systems Evolved

4.1   Design of Sensing Board

Through these investigations, we decided to use a sensor-based technology called
RFID (Radio Frequency Identification) technology, and developed a board-type
multiple input device (we call it a "sensing board"). RFID (Omron V720 series in
this study) is a non-contact object identification and data transfer technology. The
RFID system consists of two components: an antenna (with a transceiver and
decoder) and a tag as shown in Fig. 2.

The performance of data transmission between tag and antenna is stable, and a
tag is small enough to be invisible once embedded in a piece. However, the data
transmission speed between a reader and a tag is not very fast (10 ms–20 ms). This
may cause serious communication delays; for example, it will take one to two

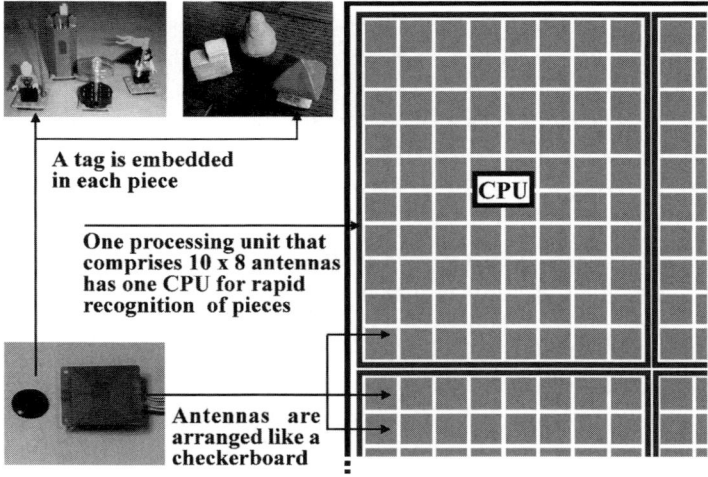

Fig. 2 A sensing board and pieces that utilize RFID technology

seconds to identify a hundred pieces. We devised a method that reduces the processing time for data transmission. In the current implementation, one central processing unit (CPU) (Hitachi H8 16 MHz microcomputer unit) is attached to a unit comprising 10 × 8 squares as shown in Fig. 2. When the sensing board receives a command for detecting the arrangement of pieces on it from the attached personal computer, it first simultaneously sends a read command to all CPUs through the interface CPU. Then, the CPU of each unit sequentially activates and controls 80 antennas in its unit, enabling each to activate a tag and read its data. Finally, the sensing board sends the tag data from the CPUs through the interface CPU. The architecture of the sensing board enables parallel processing of communication between tags and readers, and makes the communication time theoretically independent of the number of units, or the size of the board. The time taken to acquire the arrangement of pieces on the current version of the sensing board is less than 0.05 s. The merits of this architecture are as follows:

- Multiple users can simultaneously place or move multiple pieces on the sensing board.
- By changing the number of units, the sensing board can be freely extended or reduced without increasing response time.

Slits are aligned on the surface of the sensing board, allowing users to recognize a checkerboard-like grid. A tag embedded in a piece is placed inside a grid cell, and a reader is embedded in the board under each cell. The current version of the sensing board (Sugimoto et al. 2001), has 20 × 24 cells with sides of three centimetres (the size of the board: 60 cm × 90 cm). The board can be separated into two parts whose weights are about 4 kg and 3 kg, respectively. The sensing board is not light enough to be portable, but one or two children can easily set it up once they learn how. The setup involves assembling the parts and connecting a personal computer and the sensing board through their RS-232C interfaces. Then the sensing board is ready to start object recognition on its surface.

4.2 Epro: Integrating Physical and Virtual Spaces to Enhance Children's Interactions

The author's group developed their first generation system called Epro (Kusunoki et al. 1999, 2002; Sugimoto et al. 2002) based on the design requirements and lessons gained through the prototype system. The sensing board was used to identify objects manipulated by children. In designing Epro's software, the simulation model and the visualization of simulation results in the prototype system were modified: To enhance the effects on children's learning, a simulation model was developed based on lessons given by the teachers and textbook material. Through further discussions with the teachers, the following input and output parameters were chosen:

- Input parameters: house, tree, factory (input by placing pieces on the sensing board).
- Output parameters: noise, distribution of CO_2 and NO_x/SO_x, finance, population, water pollution, garbage.

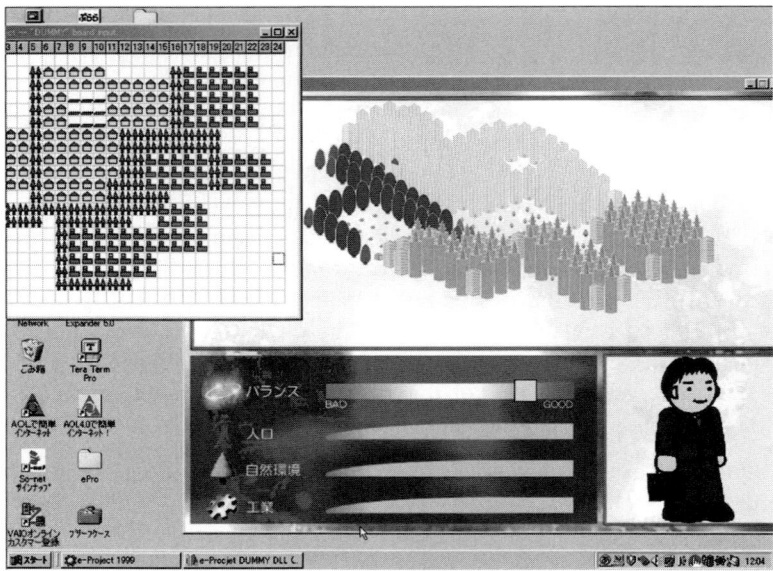

Fig. 3 An example of visualized simulation results

Figure 3 shows an example of visualized simulation results. When individual children conduct their manipulation on the sensing board, the simulation software calculates the current status of the town based on the arrangement of pieces and updates the visualized results on a computer display. Horizontal bars that appear on the lower middle of the figure represent the status of the town, such as its population, natural environment, and industry based on how many houses, factories, and trees are in the town: children are requested to change the number of the pieces and their locations on the sensing board and to have as high a score as possible by keeping the values of the bars balanced. By using characters (at the lower left corner), Epro makes children intuitively understand what happens as their town is being designed.

Figure 4 shows how children used Epro in their classroom. Three-year evaluations with fifth and sixth graders in elementary schools indicated that (1) Epro allowed children to easily test and understand knowledge acquired through textbooks or teachers, (2) children who were not good at using a computer (by mouse or keyboard) could participate in collaborative learning, and (3) by sharing artefacts (a physical board and pieces), children could actively externalize their own opinions and discuss them with others.

4.3   Epro2: Supporting Collaborative Learning by Integrating Face-To-Face and Networked Environments

Epro proved to effectively support children's collaborative learning in elementary schools. However, through analyses of children's behaviours and comments from schoolteachers, the following issues emerged:

Fig. 4 Children use Epro in their classroom

1. Does a sense of play really support children's learning?

A sense of play was useful for supporting children's participation in a learning situation, and raising the level of their engagement and excitement. However, evaluations of Epro indicated that some children were interested in the system as a game, but were not as motivated to learn with it. For example, when children reviewed bad simulation results given by Epro, they did not think deeply about the reasons for such results by using their knowledge, nor did they intensively discuss how they should change the situation. They often tried to improve the results by moving pieces randomly.

2. How should children's learning be contextualized?

Learners are engaged in their learning when they realize that their practice is situated in the real world, and is meaningful and authentic (Jonassen et al. 1997, Roussou 2004). On the other hand, when children learn about environmental issues in a classroom only through textbooks or Epro, they may not feel that their learning activities are related to problems in the real world.

These findings drove the research project to the next step. The author's group first examined how a system with a sense of play could support authentic learning by children. Then the second generation system called Epro2 (Sugimoto et al. 2003) was developed by retaining the sense of play of Epro and extending its functions for raising the level of authenticity in learning about environmental issues. The author's group also collaborated with schoolteachers to develop a new curriculum. What follows describes our approach.

- Epro2: a system for supporting group learning in face-to-face and networked settings.

In dealing with environmental issues, we need to not only use scientific knowledge, but also to reach a certain agreement through negotiations with different stakeholders. In Epro, discussions and negotiations between children in a face-to-face setting were supported. Epro2, on the other hand, was designed to support discussions and negotiations in face-to-face and networked settings. In Epro2, multiple sensing boards are located in different places and connected through a computer network. Like Epro, a group of children sits around a sensing board and constructs a town by manipulating physical pieces in a face-to-face setting. Epro2, however, makes these physically distant towns virtually contiguous and executes environmental and financial simulations based on the arrangement of pieces on the boards. Therefore, these towns are mutually affected by the other town's activities. Epro2 visualizes the environmental and financial status of a town on each board and the influences received from another town. By reviewing the visualized results, a group of children can negotiate with children in a different place through a chat system.

The author's group extended the system from a standalone system (Epro) to a networked system (Epro2) because, on several occasions, problems occurring in the real world have to be solved through negotiations between people separated by distance or who do not know each other. Moreover, through the evaluations, we found that learning with Epro in a face-to-face setting was not always appropriate, because some children who were leaders among their classmates seized the leadership role and the other children often followed without discussion or consideration of the arguments. Therefore, to avoid as much as possible the influences of interpersonal relationships in daily lives on children's activities with Epro2, and to activate discussions and negotiations between them (Sproull and Kiesler 1991), communications between groups were carried out using a chat system with anonymity; the name of a child in one group could not be identified by children of the other group.

- Design of a curriculum to enhance authentic learning with the system.

To contextualize children's learning, fieldwork in the neighbourhood of the children's elementary school was introduced into the curriculum. Investigating and experiencing for themselves what happens in the real world gave children opportunities for discovering, in collaboration with other children, their own problems (Boud and Feletti 1997). After the fieldwork, children used Epro2 to solve the problems. To enhance the continuity between children's learning in the fieldwork and with Epro2, its simulation software was designed to accept geographical or meteorological features of their fieldwork sites as simulation conditions.

Figure 5 shows the configuration of Epro2. Epro2 is composed of a server computer and multiple sets of sensing boards, a simulation client, an LCD projector, and a chat client. A group of children constructs a town on each sensing board in a face-to-face setting. A personal computer for the chat client is placed next to each sensing board and is used by the group of children to discuss and negotiate with the other groups at different sites.

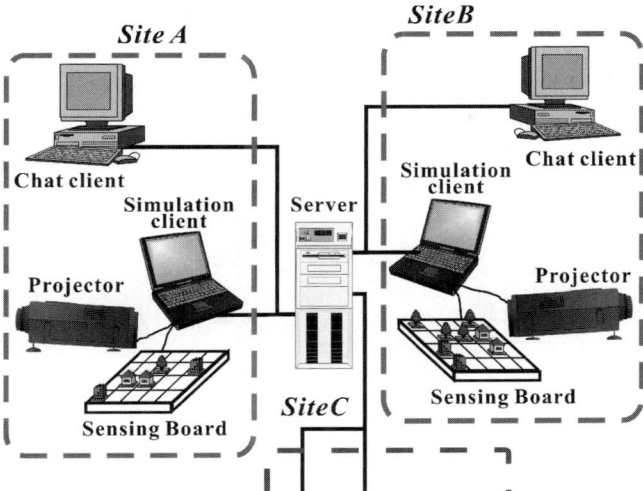

Fig. 5 System configuration of Epro2

The server computer receives piece arrangement information on the sensing board from each client and broadcasts it to all the clients. Each client computer executes environmental and financial simulations based on the data sent by the server, and provides children with graphical simulation results. The arrangement data of the pieces are updated periodically (in the current implementation, every 0.1 s). In Epro2, there are four different types of pieces: a house, a tree, a factory, and one "whatever" piece. The roles and functions of the "whatever" piece (e.g., a school) are given by schoolteachers based on the curriculum or on the children's learning tasks. In the evaluations reported here, this "whatever" piece was taken to be a shopping mall.

Epro2 displays the simulation results as shown in Fig. 6 and provides them to the children. In the case of Fig. 6, two sensing boards placed in physically different locations are virtually placed next to each other: A river flows from one sensing board (the upstream board) to another (the downstream board). This means that the environment of the downstream town is damaged by water polluted by the upstream town. Figures 6a and b show the arrangement of pieces on the upstream and downstream boards, respectively, and Fig. 6c shows the simulation results for the town on the upstream board. In the right part of Fig. 6c, distribution maps of six parameters (CO_2, NO_x/SO_x, noise, water pollution, amount of disposed garbage, and population) are displayed. Each grid cell of a map corresponds to that of a sensing board, and a different colour is assigned to a cell based on its value (for example, the level of noise or pollution). By viewing these maps, children are aware of the circumstances of the town as they are being constructed on the sensing board.

The upper left part of Fig. 6c shows the wind direction (from southwest to northeast). This causes heavier air pollution (CO_2, NO_x/SO_x) in the north eastern area of the town. The toggle buttons in the middle left of the figure are used to

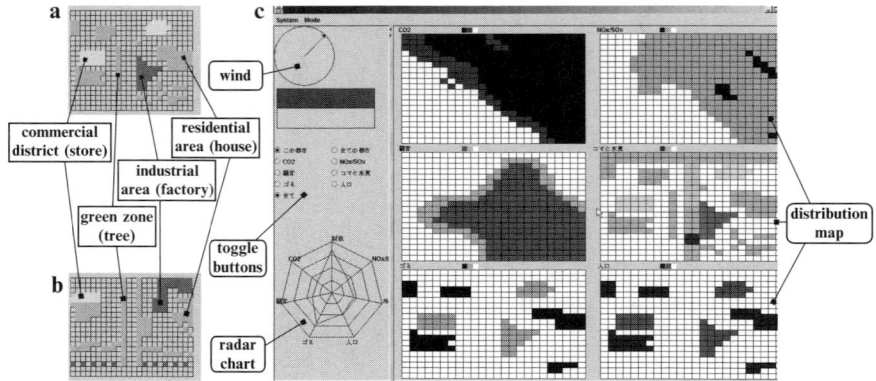

Fig. 6 (a) Piece arrangement on the upstream board, (b) piece arrangement on the downstream, and (c) an example of visualization of the upstream town

Fig. 7 Epro2 in use (upstream and downstream boards). The group of children pictured in the right figure has constructed a downstream town on a sensing board and used a chat system

switch towns (local or remote) or parameters to be visualized as distribution maps. A radar chart in the lower left of Fig. 6c shows the evaluations of the town being visualized: when a red polygon becomes bigger, the conditions of the town are desirable in terms of parameters related to its living environment and finances. (In this example, the radar chart shows that the town has a good financial position, but is faring poorly in terms of the other parameters).

In the evaluations of Epro2, fifth and sixth graders who had used Epro participated in classes that integrated fieldwork and the use of Epro2. They formed groups of seven to eight and a pair of groups simultaneously constructed a town on the upstream and downstream sensing boards, as shown in Fig. 7. The post-experimental interviews of the children and the video analyses on their usage of Epro2 indicated that children who manipulated pieces as they would play a game, intensively discussed within their group and negotiated with the other group: Based on their own knowledge and simulation results, children had to explain the reasons for their manipulation not only to the others in the same group, but also to children in a remote place to convince them to change the design of their town. Therefore, Epro2 could more successfully support children's learning than Epro by retaining a sense of play in contextualized settings.

5   Carettakids: Face-To-Face Collaborative Learning by Integrating Personal and Shared Spaces

Through the evaluations of Epro and Epro2, we have found several problems in supporting collaborative learning. The following two are especially critical:

- When multiple children manipulated pieces on the sensing board at the same time, they were not always able to understand how their individual manipulations on the board changed the simulation results. This was because their manipulations were simultaneously visualized along with the simulation results and children could not easily find the relationship between each manipulation and the corresponding simulation result.
- Some children with a reserved nature or who were not confident of their own idea often hesitated in manipulating pieces on the sensing board. They did not want to represent the idea on the board visibly to all children.

The problems mentioned above are related to those in Single Display Groupware systems (Stewart et al. 1999) that accept simultaneous inputs by multiple users. To solve the problems described above, the author's group developed a third generation system called CarettaKids (Sugimoto et al. 2004) that integrates personal and shared workspaces for supporting face-to-face collaborative learning. In CarettaKids, a sensing board is used for the shared workspace and a personal digital assistant (PDA) is used for each child's personal workspace, as shown in Fig. 8. The followings are important features of Carreta:

- Based on the arrangement of pieces, CarettaKids executes computer simulations and visualizes the simulation results using an overlay on the physical pieces. Using augmented reality technologies, CarettaKids not only increases the level of visibility of the children's actions, but also creates an immersive environment that enhances their learning experiences and raises the level of awareness (Dourish and Bellotti 1992) among children.
- CarettaKids allows children to conduct tasks on their own PDA: children can arrange (virtual) pieces on their own display and execute personal simulations without being disturbed or seen by other children.
- The shared workspace and personal workspaces are linked: children can easily display the results of their tasks conducted in the shared workspace on their own PDA, and project their personal tasks from their own PDA into the shared workspace. This allows children to work seamlessly in both personal and shared workspaces. To support children's seamless use of the shared and personal workspaces, an intuitive method for supporting children's smooth transition between the workspaces was developed.

Fig. 8 Overview of CarettaKids

Figure 9 shows the shared workspace of CarettaKids. A group of children, with PDAs in their hands, surrounds the shared workspace. They manipulate physical pieces such as houses, stores, or factories, to redesign a town. When CarettaKids identifies changes to the piece arrangement in the shared workspace, it starts computer simulations, and updates the simulation parameters and the visualization overlaid onto the workspace. Some simulation parameters shown in the upper right corner of Fig. 9 are related to the status of the whole town, such as the town's revenue and expenditure, population, etc.

Figure 10 depicts a personal workspace in CarettaKids that supports children's individual tasks. The arrangement of the pieces in this figure is the same as that in the shared workspace shown in Fig. 9. By themselves, children can freely redesign the town and test their ideas in their personal workspace – for example, by adding new pieces, or by removing or moving existing pieces. When children individually change the arrangement in their personal workspace, the visualization and values of simulation parameters in the workspace are immediately updated by computer simulations. Results of the simulations given to the children relate to both the whole town and their residential area shown in their personal workspace (for example, the level of convenience based on the distance from, and the number of working places such as factories). By viewing these simulation parameters, children can evaluate

Fig. 9 A shared workspace in CarettaKids. In the upper right of the figure, several simulation parameters are displayed

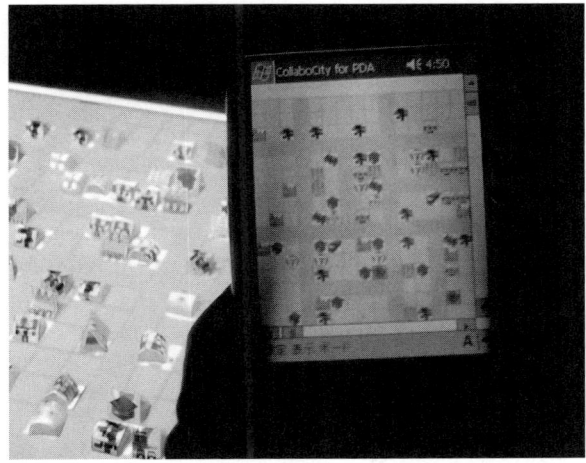

Fig. 10 A personal space in CarettaKids. A user can freely add, move, or remove pieces for personal simulation

their own ideas for designing the town. To support children in learning collabora-tively in the shared workspace, and individually in their personal workspaces, CarettaKids has several functions:

• Manipulating the shared workspace through a personal workspace.

Children's PDAs can be used to manipulate pieces in the shared workspace. For example, when children discuss where a highway should be constructed, they can draw it on the shared workspace using their own PDAs. This function is useful for

Fig. 11 By bringing a PDA near an area of interest in the shared workspace, the corresponding area appears on the personal workspace

placing virtual objects that are more difficult to place than physical pieces (for example, a bus service route, or physical items that are easier to draw than place physically, such as a railway).

- Transition from the shared workspace to personal workspaces.

When children collaboratively conducting design tasks in the shared workspace want to test their own ideas personally, they have to display the working area in the shared workspace on their personal workspaces. Children have to scroll through a small screen of their PDAs, and have difficulty in finding the corresponding area of the shared workspace. CarettaKids, therefore, provides children with an intuitive transition method from the shared workspace to their personal workspace. When children bring their PDAs close to an area of interest on the shared workspace (Fig. 11), the corresponding area immediately appears on their PDA screens. By using this method, children are liberated from the irritating task (scrolling through a small display to find an area of interest), and smoothly and intuitively transition to their personal workspaces.

- Copying a personal workspace to the shared workspace.

When children want to propose an idea for designing their town that has been examined individually in their own personal workspace, they can copy their personal workspace to the shared workspace. When children copy their idea over, the differences between their personal workspace and the shared workspace (such as piece arrangement, remarkably changed simulation parameters) are highlighted on the shared workspace. This function helps individual children easily propose their idea to other children, and helps them understand what will happen if their idea is adopted.

- Backtracking to reflect collaborative learning.

CarettaKids allows children to change design ideas previously decided in the shared workspace, or to look back over their design processes after they have completed their collaborative task. While backtracking, CarettaKids lets children know where pieces were placed by causing their corresponding locations to blink. Using this function, children can restart their collaborative tasks from any point in their design process.

CarettaKids was implemented using the sensing board, a simulation and database server, an LCD projector, and PDAs as shown in Fig. 8. Data communication between the PDAs and the server is through a wireless LAN. To support smooth transitions from the shared workspace to children's personal workspaces, an RFID tag is attached to each child's PDA. When a PDA is brought near the surface of the sensing board, the PDA's location on the sensing board is identified. Then, the visualization of the PDA is updated and the corresponding area of the shared workspace appears on its screen.

Recent PDA models have considerable computational capability, but remain insufficient to rapidly complete computer simulations. Therefore, we implemented CarettaKids to execute the simulations for each PDA on the server: when a PDA receives a request for a simulation from a child, the request is sent to the server. The server generates a thread for the simulation, and returns the simulation results to the PDA. However, from the viewpoint of children, the simulation seems to be executed on their PDA, and they need not pay attention to the server while conducting tasks on their PDAs.

The evaluations of CarettaKids with school children indicate that (1) children can participate in their learning by using personal and shared workspaces interchangeably, and (2) children can easily show their ideas devised on their own personal workspaces to other children by displaying them on the shared workspace. Then, the children collaboratively improved the ideas through discussions on the shared workspace. However, (3) children often concentrated on tasks in their personal workspaces, and did not always pay attention to the shared workspace. Fewer interactions and discussions between children happened in CarettaKids than in systems without personal workspaces (Deguchi et al. 2006). More intensive analyses will be conducted to investigate how CarettaKids supports children's externalization and reflection by integrating their shared and personal workspaces.

6 Discussion

So far, the author's group has been designed, developed and evaluated the systems discussed in the chapter. The followings are lessons learned through the experiences:

- Knowing the constraints of the setting in which the proposed systems will be used.

Adapting a system originally used in a laboratory setting to a school classroom is sometimes difficult, because remodelling for special equipment is usually not allowed, and children's safety must be considered. As shown in the design process of the sensing board, even if utilizing several existing technologies was possible, abandoning them and devising a different technology or method of implementation was necessary. Therefore, being familiar with the constraining features of settings in which the system will be used before commencing the design is important.

- Observation of children's behaviour.

Children's requirements could not be adequately known from just interviews because they often did not or could not clearly articulate their needs or preferences. Therefore, children's behaviours were observed by using a prototype system (paperboard and simple software) at the start of the project. Analyses of children's behaviour and utterances while using Epro and Epro2 clarified their potential problems and clues for developing the next version of the systems (Epro2 and CarettaKids, respectively). The information learned through evaluations in classrooms provided the author's group with very useful information and insight for designing the proposed systems.

- Participation of stakeholders in the design process (Schuler and Namioka 1993).

The design of the hardware and software in Epro, Epro2, and CarettaKids was conducted in collaboration with developers, schoolteachers, and their children. For example, in the development of the sensing board, children were asked to grasp different shapes and sizes of pieces to confirm their preference and ease of manipulation. To contextualize children's learning and raise the level of its authenticity, their teachers designed the curriculum through discussions with the project members and decided on the kind of scientific knowledge to embed in the simulation software of Epro, Epro2 and CarettaKids. Although tabletop or tangible interface systems were effective for attracting children's interest and attention, designing systems in collaboration with different stakeholders was critical to increasing the level of motivation and engagement in children's learning.

- Tabletop interface systems for collaboration: group or individual.

Various tabletop systems for supporting collaboration were developed (e.g., Field et al. 2002). One problem with this type of system is related to how it can support users in working/learning collaboratively and individually, because a workspace in tabletop systems is shared with and visible to multiple users, and a trade-off inherently exists between a group and an individual in supporting collaborative tasks (Gutwin and Greenberg 1998). Several systems were proposed to simultaneously support group and individual activities (e.g., Zanella and Greenberg 2001, Shoemaker and Inkpen 2001). CarettaKids is an example of such a system. We believe that additional investigation for supporting groups and individuals in collaboration processes must be conducted by fully utilizing mobile and ubiquitous computing technologies.

7 Conclusion

This chapter discussed the design processes of systems for supporting children's collaborative learning. The systems are used for learning about urban planning and environmental issues in school education. Although numerous tabletop and tangible interface systems have been proposed in HCI research areas, the author's group started investigations for identifying design requirements of the systems using a paper-based prototype system. Three systems called Epro, Epro2, and CarettaKids were developed based on the requirements gained through the investigations and issues raised through their evaluations.

In this research project, the design of the systems was conducted in collaboration with different stakeholders, such as developers, teachers, and children. The author believes that the lessons gained through the project, such as "Knowing the constraints of the setting in which the proposed systems will be used" or "collaboration support for group and individual", are consistent with designing not only learning support systems but also other types of interactive systems.

Acknowledgements The author thanks Professor Hiromichi Hashizume (National Institute of Informatics, Professor Shigenori Inagaki (Kobe University), Professor Fusako Kusunoki, Professor Etuji Yamaguchi, Professor Akiko Deguchi, and Dr. Atsushi Yoshikawa, who contributed to the design and implementation of the systems described in the chapter and their evaluations. The research is sponsored by a Grant-in-Aid for Scientific Research by the Japanese Ministry of Education, Science, Culture, Sports and Technology.

References

Arias, E., Eden, H., Fischer, G., and Scharff, E., 2000, Transcending the Individual Human Mind – Creating Shared Understanding Through Collaborative Design, *ACM Transactions on Computer–Human Interaction*, 7(1):84–113.

Boud, D., and Feletti, G., 1997, *The Challenge of Problem-Based Learning (2nd Edition)*. Kogan Page.

Deguchi, A., Yamaguchi, E., Inagaki, S., Sugimoto, M., Kusunoki, F., Tachibana, S., Yamamoto, T., Seki, T., and Takeuchi, Y., 2006, CarettaKids: A System for Supporting Children's Face-to-Face Collaborative Learning by Integrating Personal and Shared Spaces, in *Proceedings of Interaction Design and Children (IDC'06)*, Tampere, Finland, pp. 45–48.

Dourish, P., and Bellotti, V., 1992, Awareness and Coordination in Shared Workspaces, in *Proceedings of ACM CSCW'92*, Toronto, Canada, pp. 107–114.

Field, M., Lauche, K., Bichsel, M., Voorhorst, F., Krueger, H., and Rauterberg, M., 2002, Physical and Virtual Tools: Activity Theory Applied to the Design of Groupware, *Computer Supported Cooperative Work*, 11(1–2):153–180.

Fischer, G., 1998, Beyond "Couch Potatoes": From Consumers to Designers, in *Proceedings of 3rd Asia Pacific Computer Human Interaction Conference*, Kanagawa, Japan, pp. 2–9.

Fischer, G., and Sugimoto, M., 2006, Supporting Self-Directed Learners and Learning Communities with Sociotechnical Environments, *Journal of Research and Practice in Technology Enhanced Learning*, 1(1):31–64.

Gutwin, C., and Greenberg. S., 1998, Design for Individuals, Design for Groups: Tradeoffs Between Power and Workspace Awareness, in *Proceedings of CSCW'98*, Seattle, WA, pp. 207–216.

Jonassen, D., Peck, K., and Wilson, B., 1997, *Learning with Technology: A Constructivist Perspective*. NJ: Prentice-Hall.

Kafai, Y., 1996, *Minds in Play: Computer Game Design as a Context for Children's Learning*. Lawrence Erlbaum Associates.

Koschmann, T., 1996, Paradigm Shifts and Instructional Technology: An Introduction, in *CSCL: Theory and Practice of an Emerging Paradigm*, Koschmann, T. (ed.). Lawrence Erlbaum Associates, pp. 1–23.

Kusunoki, F., Sugimoto, M., and Hashizume, H., 1999, A System for Supporting Group Learning That Enhances Interactions, in *Proceedings of CSCL'99*, Stanford, CA, pp. 323–327.

Kusunoki, F., Sugimoto, M., and Hashizume, H., 2002, A Group Learning Support System Enhancing the Externalization of Thinking, *Systems and Computers in Japan*, 33(6):93–100.

Lave, J., and Wenger, E., 1991, *Situated Learning: Legitimate Peripheral Participation*. Cambridge University Press.

Resnick, L., 1991, Shared Cognition: Thinking as Social Practice, in *Perspective on Social Shared Cognition*, American Psychological Association, pp. 1–12.

Roussou, M., 2004, Virtual Reality and Interactive Theaters: Learning by Doing and Learning through Play: An Exploration of Interactivity in Virtual Environments for Children, *Computers in Entertainment*, 2(1):1–23.

Scardamalia, M., and Bereiter, C., 1996, Student Communities for the Advancement of Knowledge *Communications of the ACM*, 39(4):36–37.

Schuler, D., and Namioka, A. (Eds.), 1993, *Participatory Design: Principles and Practices*. Lawrence Erlbaum Associates.

Shoemaker, G., and Inkpen, K., 2001, Single Display Privacyware: Augmenting Public Displays with Private Information, in *Proceedings of CHI2001*, Seattle, WA, pp. 522–529.

Sproull, L., and Kiesler, S., 1991, *Connections: New Way of Working in the Networked Organization*. MIT Press.

Steffe, L., and Gale, J., 1995, *Constructivism in Education*. Lawrence Erlbaum Associates.

Stewart, B., Bederson, B., and Druin, A., 1999, Single Display Groupware: A Model for Co-present Collaboration, in *Proceedings of CHI'99*, Pittsburgh, PA, pp. 286–293.

Sugimoto, M., Kusunoki, F., and Hashizume, H., 2001, E2board: An Electronically Enhanced Board for Games and Group Activity Support, in *Proceedings of the International Conference on Affective Human Factors Design*, Singapore, pp. 238–245.

Sugimoto, M., Kusunoki, F., and Hashizume, H., 2002, Design of an Interactive System for Group Learning Support, in *Proceeding of DIS2002*, London, UK, pp. 50–55.

Sugimoto, M., Kusunoki, F., Inagaki, S., Takatoki, K., and Yoshikawa, A., 2003, Design of a System and a Curriculum to Support Group Learning for School Children, in *Designing for Change in Networked Learning Environments*, Kluwer Academic Publisher, pp. 303–312.

Sugimoto, M., Hosoi, K., and Hashizume, H., 2004, Caretta: A System for Supporting Face-to-Face Collaboration by Integrating Personal and Shared Spaces, in *Proceedings of CHI2004*, Vienna, Austria, pp. 41–48.

Underkoffler, J., and Ishii, H., 1999, Urp: A Luminous-Tangible Workbench for Urban Planning and Design, in *Proceedings of CHI'99*, Pittsburgh, PA, pp. 386–393.

Zanella, A., and Greenberg, S., 2001, Reducing Interference in Single Groupware through Transparency, in *Proceedings of ECSCW2001*, Bonn, Germany, pp. 339–358.

Do Fewer Laptops Make a Better Team?

Jean-Baptiste Haué and Pierre Dillenbourg

This study explores how the number of laptops within a team working around a table influences their collaborative processes. Complementary quantitative and qualitative analyses have been performed with eight groups of four participants who had to carry out a travel planning task with two, three or four laptops. The quantitative analysis of subjects' gaze locations for each dialogue utterance shows that laptop owners look at their display for 65% of coded events. This ratio is quite independent of the number of laptops in the group. Consequently, the higher the number of participants with laptops, the less attention is available for dealing with coordination. The qualitative analysis of the interaction between participants showed that if more laptops foster parallel individual searches, they are "cognitive attractors". Participants indeed have difficulty getting away from their laptops. More specifically, their verbal communication often takes place while keeping an eye on their screen, i.e., with only partial attention. The lack of full attention hampers the production of critical thinking about strategic issues, which appears detrimental not only for performance but also for learning. These findings seem to indicate that collaborative learning could be more effective with an asymmetrical layout, i.e. with fewer laptops than team members. This might scaffold the emergence of roles and foster social interaction: team members with no personal displays tend to regulate the activities of others or at least pay more attention to group interaction. Due to our qualitative methodology, we present these as provisional results.

Keywords Tabletop, Laptop, CSCW, CSCL, Dialogue analysis, Gaze location

1 Introduction

The difficulty of collaborating at distance, through computer-supported collaboration tools, compared to the fluidity of face-to-face collaboration led to the emergence of tabletop systems during recent years. These tabletops either have been developed for very specific tasks (e.g., Shen et al. 2002, Underkoffler and Ishii

P. Dillenbourg et al. (eds.), *Interactive Artifacts and Furniture Supporting Collaborative Work and Learning*,
DOI: 10.1007/978-0-387-77234-9_3, © Springer Science+Business Media, LLC 2009

1999, Buxton et al. 2000) or embedded in sophisticated and proprietary components (e.g., Shen et al. 2003, Prante et al. 2004). No affordable, generic and reliable system has been developed so far. Therefore, very few studies of real tabletop supported collaboration have been carried out outside the field of games (e.g., Ryall et al. 2006). In the best cases, systems have been tested with students in a university which also restricts the generalisability of results (e.g., Sundholm et al. 2004).

Our team is conducting research on mid-tech interactive tables intended to enhance collaboration and learning. By "mid-tech" we mean that these pieces of furniture embed interactive devices (LEDs, microphones …) but do not look like computers (with keyboard, large displays …). Prototypes have been developed and are reported in another chapter of this book (Kaplan et al., this volume, Chap. 8). The idea of embedding computational power in a table could appear silly since students often bring their own laptop to carry out group assignments. The influence of laptops on teamwork is, however, ambivalent. On the one hand, allowing people to use their laptop brings more resources to the group (laptop as private space and tabletop as public space), but, on the other hand, the fact that people somewhat disappear behind their display may hinder social interaction. The challenge of tabletop design is to benefit from the computational augmentation while maintaining the richness of face-to-face situations. Surprisingly, our community has poor knowledge of the role of laptops on co-present team members compared to the vast literature on computer-mediated collaboration. We can for instance find studies on gaze analysis in videoconferencing (Vertegaal 1999) but not in co-present collaboration with laptops.

This study uses data from an experiment initially designed for evaluating an interactive table but during which we became increasingly aware of the importance of the laptops in collaborative processes. After the presentation of the theoretical perspective (part 1), measures of users' gaze locations are compared for different conditions (part 2). A qualitative analysis is then provided to shed some light on the influence of laptops and team strategy (part 3) before the final discussion (part 4).

2   Related Work

This section presents existing studies relevant to our topic: working collaboratively, around a table, with some technological augmentation.

2.1   Tabletop Systems

The tabletop approach relies on the postulate that collaboration is more fluid when people are around a flat surface than when it occurs via computer mediation (Bly 1988, Tang 1991). Not only do face-to-face conditions allow a higher degree of workspace awareness (Tang 1991) and therefore more fluid coordination, but computers themselves may hinder collaboration. Desktops and laptops have been built for a one-user/one-computer paradigm (Stewart et al. 1999). Only one user has access to the input devices. For visual output, multiple users have to sit very close to each other to be within the range of perception of the screen. The audio outputs can more easily reach multiple users but they have so far not been exploited for that purpose.

Many tabletop systems have been developed to integrate computing facilities within a horizontal surface. Most prototypes are based on a computer display, which is top-projected on a traditional table from a beamer fixed on the ceiling or rear-projected from below the table (Patten et al. 2001, Scott et al. 2002, Shen et al. 2002). More elaborate systems embed a flat display in the table. Interaction with the display is achieved by cameras in top projection or the use of touch screens. Prante et al. (2004) present a system connecting large tactile display components with smaller individual components, where fine grain conflict detection allows true synchronous object edition. DiamondTouch is a large tactile display that can detect the hand gestures of two users and identify which user is performing the gesture (Dietz and Leigh 2001). DiamondSpin is a Java tool kit that manages the interactions between multiple users and the tabletop, including reorientation mechanisms (Shen et al. 2004).

Several systems combine a shared tabletop with connected laptops, which then create personal and public spaces, raising issues such as ownership and right of access. The Augmented Surface system (Rekimoto and Saitoh 1999) allows the connecting of personal laptops to public displays. Content can be "hyperdragged" from one space to another through direct manipulation, by, for instance, sending the laptop pointing device "across" the limit of the laptop screen. The UbiTable (Shen et al. 2003) offers a transitional personal space that is displayed both on the bottom of a laptop screen and on the corner of the table. Documents in this transitional space are visible to the other people around the table but can be accessed by them only when their owner moves them to the public space.

Despite 10 years of great prototypes and even commercial products, tabletop environments are still far from being widespread. The main reasons are probably that they are based on proprietary software and/or expensive hardware. Another explanation could be that the key problems that have been addressed by these artefacts, such as moving documents across private and public spaces or changing the orientation of the shared displays, are less critical for collaboration than some basic issues. What is the effect of having a personal display such as a laptop while interacting with co-located team-mates? Relatively few studies have made observations on the effect of introducing personal devices within a collaborative task performed around a table.

Gubman et al. (2004) compared the performance of a group of three persons in two conditions: around a unique laptop or around the MapNews table, which is specifically designed to geographically browse information about countries of the world. The results of the evaluation questionnaire showed a preference for their table (in the context of this specific task). More interestingly, they have also made observations about collective laptop usage. It appeared that a laptop provides a narrow social focus since users had to gather closely together to share the same view. Pointing was easier (due to proximity) but less precise (due to the laptop's small screen) than on the table. Moreover, only one person had control of the laptop, even if backseat users could use gestures or vocal commands.

Sundholm et al. (2004) presented qualitative observations of groups using an interactive environment, which was composed not only of wide horizontal and vertical collective surfaces but also of connected personal displays. This study focused on how ideas were constructed and negotiated in relation to the artefacts and the layout of the room. These authors showed that many different kinds of transitions between personal and public spaces were spontaneously used (showing personal material to the others, getting shared content to work on it, etc.). Moreover, they noticed that the different roles shown on the display (e.g., showing VS listening) were taken on by different people over time, even if personal preferences were observable (e.g., some people were stayed in their personal display).

Tabletop design guidelines (Scott et al. 2003) offer hints about possible positive (+) and negative (−) effects of personal displays:

- *Interpersonal Interaction* (−): As personal displays are not visible to everyone, laptops can hamper communicative gestures, such as pointing.
- *Transition between activities* (±): (−) The operations required to move content from a personal to a public display can slow down collaboration. (+) The computer interactivity allows users to move content quickly between software applications either on their personal display or the public one (if projected).
- *Transition between tabletop collaboration and external work* (+)*:* As a mobile device, the laptop provides a link between places and activities. A user can access the content of his emails, files or bookmarks at anytime and almost anywhere.
- *Simultaneous user actions* (+)*:* multiple laptops allow simultaneous work on objects through shared editors and parallel work on duplicated or complementary contents.

The reviewed work illustrates the fact that personal displays have positive and negative effects on collaboration. To better understand these effects, we need to zoom on their impact on the collaborative processes.

2.2   Collaborative Processes

In the field of collaborative learning, scholars have tried to predict team outcomes by manipulating variables such as group composition (group size, group heterogeneity, gender) or task features (convergent/divergent, procedural/declarative). Decades of studies revealed that too many factors interact in too complex ways; collaboration cannot be treated as a black box. Instead, scholars have to zoom in the collaborative process to understand how collaborative settings influence social interactions and how these interactions produce cognitive effects (Dillenbourg et al.

1996). Several types of interactions have been studied such as the quality of explanations (Webb 1991), mutual regulation (Blaye 1988), argumentation (Baker 1999), conflict resolution (Doise et al. 1975). What these various types of interactions have in common is that they lead students to verbalize knowledge that would otherwise remain tacit. In the same perspective, identifying the effects laptops around a tabletop requires looking at the social interactions that they support, hinder or modify.

A middle-grained description of the processes occurring during ideas construction within a group is proposed by Sundholm et al. (2004). Their model of how ideas are collectively constructed and negotiated consists of a loop of four phases that correspond to different group configurations: (1) discussion; (2) individual work; (3) interruption of individual work by a participant; (4) the participant presents his individual work to the others.

Scott et al. (2004) have studied how the organization of territories emerged during group activity and supported group interactions. In the case of the tabletop, they defined territories as a mix of spatial and computational properties that are delimited with little or no verbal negotiation and that support coordination mechanisms. They identified three kinds of territories:

- Group territories are spaces used to perform collective activity or to assist others. As these spaces have to be accessed by everyone, they are located in the centre of a tabletop. Ambiguity of responsibility was observed when different participants had an equivalent actual access to a group territory.
- Storage territories are areas dedicated to unused material, such as personal belongings or items not currently useful.
- Individual territories are safe places when one can disengage from the group activity. These frontiers may vary according to the person and the available space and they can take advantage of visible barriers. A laptop offers a perfect individual space, until it is ostensibly shown to others.

In some studies, gaze patterns are used as indicators of group dynamics. Argyle and Cook (1976) estimated that about 60% of conversation in **dyadic groups** involve gaze and about 30% involve mutual gaze. The different frequency of gaze observed during listening phases (75%) compared to speaking phases (41%) was explained by Kendon (1967) by the fact that the speaker is looking more intensely at the beginning of his utterance (to check attention) and at the end (preparing to give the floor). Fewer gazes were observed in face-to-face conditions when the topic was difficult, as it required more concentration (Vertegaal, 1999). In remote teamwork, participants established eye contact (mutual gaze) through the video channel when they were engaged in activities such as joking or discussing about strategy (Joiner et al. 2002), which both require more social feedback. Besides regulation of the flow of conversation, other functions of gaze patterns were identified (Joiner et al. 2002):

- Monitoring how others react to one's utterances and actions;
- Communicating emotion and relationship;
- Avoiding distraction by restricting visual inputs.

In larger groups (more than two people), gaze patterns are of course more complex and various. The ambiguity of who is addressed has to be considered. The 75/41 ratio of gaze observed during listening versus speaking time, that we reported for pair discussion, becomes 47/70 for multi-party discussions, denoting that the speaker has to show whom he is addressing (Vertegaal and Ding 2002). Moreover, gaze has a function of regulating the arousal within the group, where individuals manage their level of intimacy or public appearance (Vertegaal and Ding 2002): people who look more at others are more looked at in return. Good lecturers know how to use their gaze to sustain the attention of their audience!

Gaze is only one way of regulating conversation. In videoconferencing, since mutual gaze is usually not available, it is replaced by explicit addressing (Isaacs and Tang 1993), i.e., mentioning the name of the addressee. In chat environments, other conventions, such as using "…" to indicate that the sentence will be continued in the next text entry, take the place of gaze. Moreover, gaze patterns change dramatically when people are not only talking to each other but also acting together: for instance, gaze frequency drops from 77% to 6% of conversation time when subjects interact about a map (Argyle and Graham 1977).

Another field of research that is relevant for the laptop/tabletop debate is the study of shared representations in teamwork. A basic principle for shared editors is "what you see is what I see" (WYSIWIS). The different users edit the same document, which is permanently updated by the modifications performed by any team member. This shared representation provides the team with a shared referential space that, in addition to previous communication and group initial common grounds, helps to achieve interpersonal communication (Clark and Wilkes-Gibbs 1986, Clark 1996, Fussell et al. 2004). Because this co-constructed representation is more persistent than the dialogues, it often becomes the group working memory, i.e., a representation of the state of the problem to be solved (Dillenbourg and Traum 2006). However, the WYSWIS principle does not hold when there are multiple users or complex tasks for which it is necessary to distribute sub-problems among team members. In this case, scholars developed so-called WISIWIS-relaxed interfaces that enable different partial views of the document but which, nonetheless, sustain coordination with "workspace awareness tools" (Gutwin and Greenberg 1999). Awareness tools inform team members of what their team-mates are doing, what they are looking at, and where they are located. The use of laptops in teamwork lies at the heart of this tension between supporting coordination space while enabling individual actions.

3   Questions

The design of collaborative environments requires a better understanding of the use of laptops in teamwork. Our target situation is a session in which three to four students gather around a table in order to collectively do some project. Our general research question was: *Are laptops beneficial to teamwork around a table?* Since most tasks require at least a laptop, this question does not concern the presence or absence or laptops but the number of laptops on the team. Our hypothesis is that the number of laptops influences role distribution and patterns of communication as well as gaze patterns. More specifically, we hypothesized that more laptops would lead to more individual work and fewer collective discussions.

4   Methods

This contribution reports side-observations of a quasi-experiment carried out by our master students for evaluating an early prototype of the REFLECT table (see Kaplan et al., this volume). This table captures conversations with microphones and displays participation patterns with a matrix of 128 LEDs embedded in the table. In the earlier prototype used in this experiment, the matrix of coloured points was actually projected by a beamer located on the ceiling. The tables included an adhesive whiteboard in the centre onto which the matrix was beamed or on which the users could draw anything they wanted to. The experiments were conducted with a variety of tables having different shapes and dimensions. The independent variable was the presence and absence of the beamed matrix on this whiteboard. The experiments revealed that the participants did not pay much attention to this matrix. The first reason for this lack of attention was that the visibility of the matrix was too low under normal lightening conditions. The second and more interesting reason was this central space competes with individual laptops for capturing the users' attention. While the first reason has trivial implications, the second triggered our interest and raised the previously mentioned research question. The experiment was conducted with teams of three or four students using two to four laptops. This variety of conditions, which would be detrimental to a proper experimental study, gave us the opportunity to study the role of laptops in a broad range of situations.

4.1   Task

Each group of participants had to plan an air journey for two people, including multiple flights. They had to research flights on Internet websites (a list was provided) in order to maximize the length of the whole journey. The journey had to satisfy the following constraints: (1) No return to a country previously visited, (2) a stay between two and four days at each stop (therefore doing only direct flights) (3) avoidance of transits between airports of a same city, (4) a total ticket cost below CHF 75,000 for two people. The participants had 30 min. The last constraint, the budget, was not highly coercive, as most teams did not manage to spend all money within 30 min. This task required team members to coordinate flight searches while keeping track of locations and dates.

4.2   Participants

The participants were EPFL students. No specific constraints (age, gender) were imposed. Instead of paying each participant, we decided that four randomly selected participants would win a travel voucher for CHF 100. Altogether, 24 sessions were run and recorded. These experiments yielded a rich data set that presents an important diversity of collaborative styles and performance. We restrict our analysis to 13 sessions with four people talking in English or French.

4.3   Analysis

This contribution was built on two complementary forms of analysis. We started with an *extensive analysis* that focused on five elements: (1) use of the laptops, (2) use of the whiteboard, (3) problem solving strategy, (4) respect of the task rules, (5) mechanisms for coordinating location and dates. This analysis revealed that the number of laptops was a key factor to understand the dynamic of this collaborative task. Consequently, six experiments were more deeply analyzed. This *intensive analysis* was run on two experiments with a team having two laptops, two for three laptops and two for four laptops. For each condition, we selected one group that was performing well and one that was performing rather poorly.

As previously mentioned, the conditions of these experiments were not equivalent: the table shape, the laptops positions and even the rigor of the master students who performed the experiments vary. Hence, we did not proceed to a statistical comparison of team performance, but analyzed the emergence of group phenomena such as the team strategy or the type of leadership.

4.4   Coding and Counting

Our scheme for coding participants' visual attention contains five gaze locations:

- One's personal laptop.
- Paper sheet with instructions or to write down the results.
- Whiteboard on the table.
- Other participants' laptop.
- Other participant.

The main location of each participant's gaze was coded for each verbal message. We manually transcribed gaze location from the video even for participants who were not involved in a communication episode (e.g., C's gaze is recorded even if A speaks to B). The dialogues have been segmented into messages based on two criteria: speaker changes and topic changes. This segmentation and coding of gaze location is subjective but we did not proceed to dual coding as we were not aiming to produce statistics. We defined an episode as "collective discussion" when at least three (out of four) participants were looking at each other during dialogue.

This coding does not provide a duration measure for gaze locations but counts co-occurrences between verbal messages and gaze location. Only the main gaze location during a verbal message is counted. Short gazes within a longer visual fixation were not written down. This gaze analysis constitutes a medium-grained description of visual attention during verbal communication that appeared relevant to our research questions and appropriate to the amount of data to be processed.

4.5   Qualitative Analysis

For each group, the transcription of verbal exchanges and gaze location was enriched from further examination of the video in order to identify patterns of interaction among participants. The qualitative analysis was inspired by the Course of Action framework (Theureau 2003), even though it was only very loosely applied. Episodes of collaboration were identified, as moments of stable coordination between participants' individual activities. These episodes and the overall group collaborative style were systematically described according to the following criteria:

- Which strategy is used by the group; which roles emergence?
- Which tools are used and how?
- How does information circulate between people and tools?
- What is group performance?

5   Quantitative Results: How Much Laptops Attract Visual Gaze

Figure 1 compares the distribution of gaze towards the different locations. The average number of verbal communications with gaze directed toward other participants appears to be quite constant, whatever the number of laptops in the group is: from 25%, with 4 laptops, to 31%, with 3 laptops. Obviously, when the number of laptops is higher, the average ratio of gaze toward one's own laptop increases as it includes fewer participants without laptops. In reaction, the frequency of gaze toward the instruction sheet and whiteboard or toward other's laptop decreases.

If the average frequency of gaze toward one's own laptop increases in Figure 1, it is actually constant (Fig. 2), if one counts the proportion of gazes on one's own laptop only for those having a laptop (between 61 and 69%). Since gaze locations are counted every time a message is emitted, this means that a laptop owner spends approximately 2/3 of verbal exchanges with his gaze on his own laptop display. Considering that laptop owners tend to keep their gaze

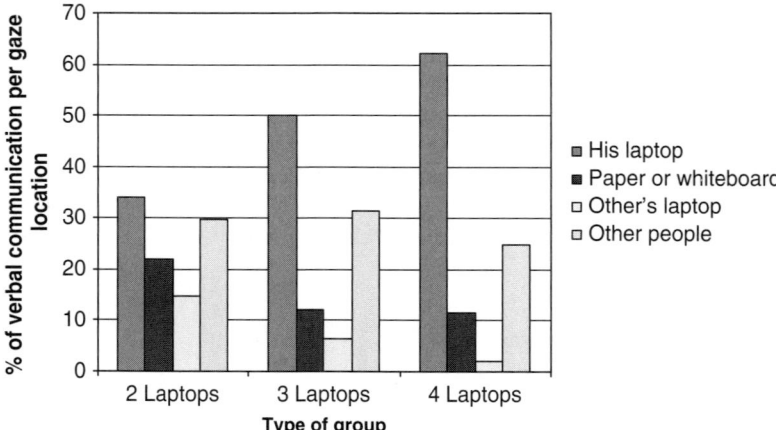

Fig. 1 Gaze distribution between groups, according to the number of laptops

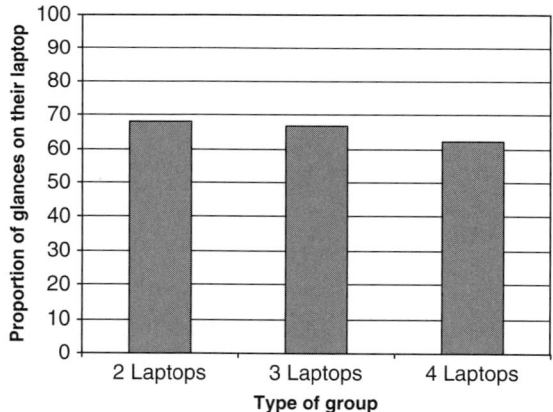

Fig. 2 Proportion of gazes of laptop owners on their own laptop

focused on their display during silence, the laptop appears to constitute some kind attention magnet.

These results suggest that when more laptops are present, less attention is available for other tasks (coordination, writing down the results, etc.). However, these results should be considered with care, not only because they come from few participants but especially because the aggregation of the 6 groups in 3 different conditions hides important disparities inter and intra group that we address now. Figure 3 shows the same data for each group. The proportion of gaze toward one's own laptop is important (for those who have a laptop): between 45% and 79% (upper part of Fig. 3).

Figure 4a shows a strong variation in the number of gazes on the instructions sheet and on the whiteboard, which is higher for students without laptops. Gazes to

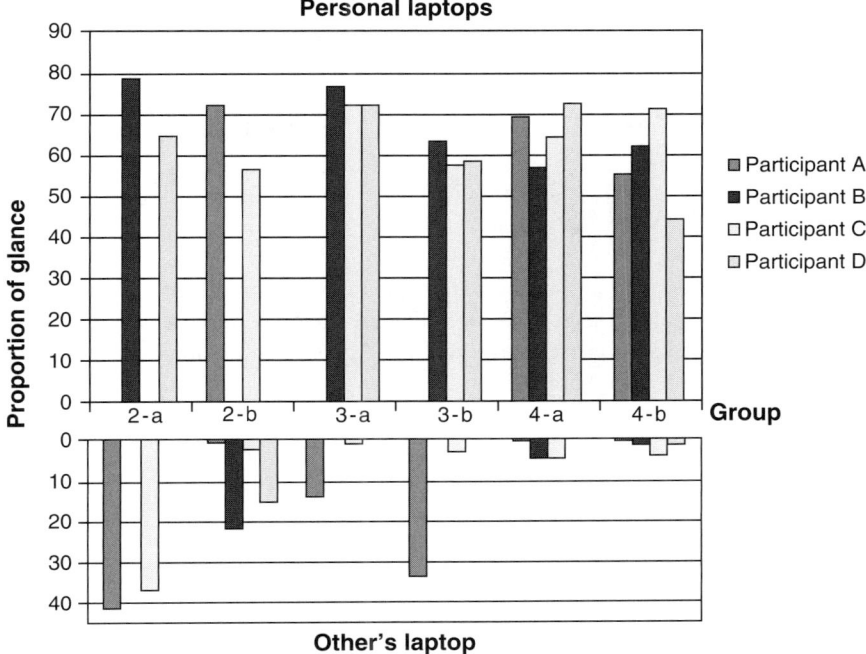

Fig. 3 Proportion of gaze towards their own and others' laptops for the different participants of the different groups

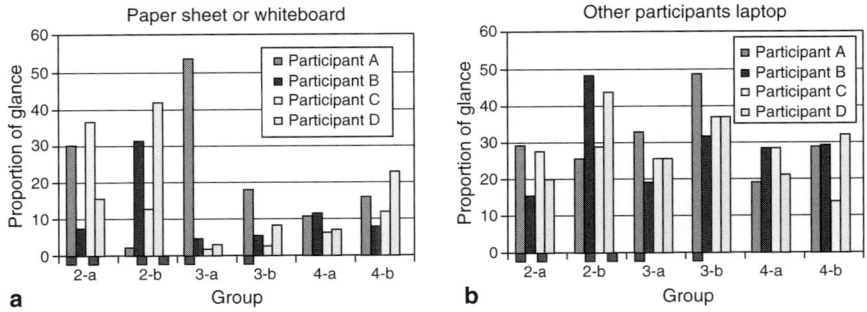

Fig. 4 Proportion of gaze toward the instruction sheet or the whiteboard (**a**, left) and toward the other participants (**b**, right) The red squares mark the participants without laptops

other participants reach 14–48% (Fig. 4b) with less difference between conditions, although the participants without laptops always have the highest scores of their group. These two results, looking at other participants or their laptops, confirm the attraction of laptops.

In summary, participants with a laptop spent twice as many gazes toward their laptops than towards other participants during verbal exchanges. Even the participants without personal laptops directed their gaze to the laptops of others participants. As the distribution of gazes is an emerging group phenomenon, it is difficult to provide more precise explanations which such quantitative measures. The qualitative analysis presented in the next section will shed some light on these processes.

6   Qualitative Analysis

The analysis of the video and of the transcripts reveal that collaboration processes depend on many factors, such as the strategy adopted, the individual knowledge, and natural leadership. We first present the analysis of coordination in group 4a and then compare it with what happened in the other groups.

6.1   A Case Study

Group 4-a (Fig. 5) clearly illustrates the effects of having four laptops.

Participants' gaze location is plotted and annotated in Fig. 6 in order to depict the collaboration phases and events. The upper line shows the moments of collective discussion (at least three participants looking at each other during verbal exchanges). The four lower bands represent the gaze location for each participant: the height of the bars indicates an increasing order of sociability of gaze location: own laptop, instruction sheet, whiteboard, another's laptop and another participant.

The shaded boxes in Fig. 6 show collective coordination episodes, i.e., when individual actions target the same sub-goal. The episodes between these boxes are composed of individual activities or local coordination episodes, which are indicated by smaller boxes with zebra stripes. We now analyze these episodes in detail.

Beginning. In the first coordination episode, the discussion concerns the strategy. Participant C starts by proposing a first possible destination. Despite the fact that

Fig. 5 Snapshot of group 4a video recording

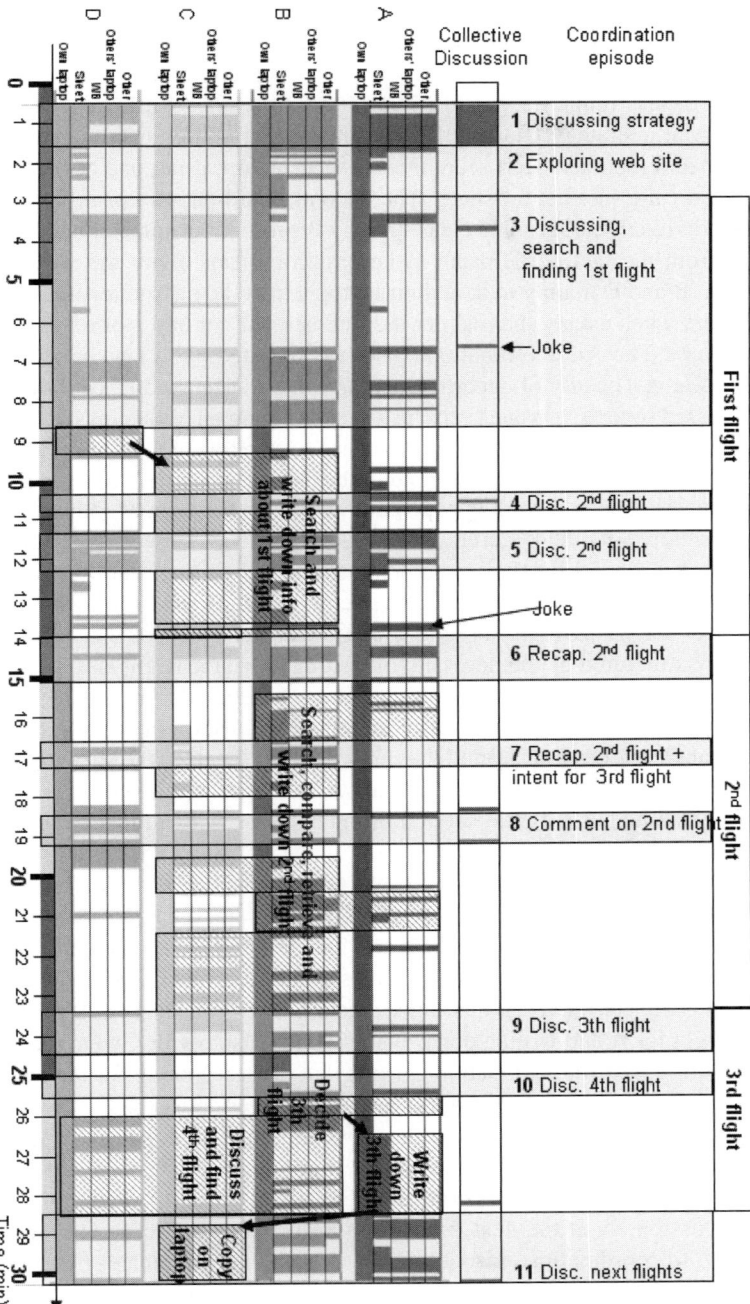

Fig. 6 Group discussion and participants' gaze location during the experiment

everyone participates to this discussion, all participants look at their own laptops at some point and at the instruction sheet or even put their hands on the keyboard without typing (A and D), showing they are willing and ready to start searching. They nonetheless remain engaged in the discussion. As soon as an agreement is reached about a strategy (starting from a place and finding far but cheap destinations), all team members start searching on their laptop, using one of the web sites suggested on the instruction sheet. The second coordination episode consists of parallel individual searches. No clear strategy is present but some coordination that emerges from the fact participants make oral comments about the websites they explore. A, B and D mainly look at their laptop and at the instruction sheet. B looks at the others when asking them about their choice but nobody looks at B in return.

First flight. The 3rd coordination episode is initiated by D who asks a question about the flight. The city of departure and arrival are discussed since they have not been discussed so far. Everyone keeps his visual attention on his laptop, but occasional short gazes are directed at others (not counted as they were too short relatively to the gazes on laptops). At the third minute, the choice of the date raises a short collective discussion about avoiding expensive periods in the year. Moments of silence during parallel individual search are frequent, such as between 4:30 and 5:30, sometimes interrupted by short comments about websites or findings. At 6:37, a joke is cracked which moves everyone's attention to the group for a while. At 8:32 B announces that he has found a flight, which is accepted by the others. The following minutes are structured by the necessity of writing down the result and by individual comments regarding to the results sheet. When D hears B's finding, he leaves his laptop, gets the results sheet and starts writing on it. After looking at it for 25 seconds (rectangle on D's line around the ninth minute), D gives the sheet to B (arrow on Fig. 5) because he does not know what should be written down. At that time, C announces that he has a digital version of the results sheet and that he can also fill in the results there.

Second flight. Finding the second flight takes more than 8 min (from 15:20 to 23:40) during which B has a central position. He does not only choose the flight but also compares the information with C's previous findings, writes down the information on the results sheet, transmits it to C and searches for missing information (arrival date, kilometers, etc.). During this time, A and C occasionally help B (searching a cheaper flight for A and writing down B's info on his laptop for C). On the contrary, D states during the 7th coordination episode that he is searching for the next flight, even though no clear arrival airport and date has been established.

Third flight. When B is done writing down the 2nd flight, he asks and receives the date and the airport abbreviation for the flight that is being searched (9th coordination episode). Everyone goes on searching silently for 30 s, after which C initiates a discussion about the next destination even though the current search is not yet over (10th coordination episode). Right after that, A announces he has found a price and date for the 3rd flight, while keeping his eyes on his laptop. After asking for information about the airport arrival, B gives his agreement but goes immediately back to his laptop, without showing any more interest or writing down the result on the results sheet. As a consequence, A takes this sheet and writes it down. At the same moment (25th–28th minute), while A, C and D discuss the next flight, B, who has been compiling all the information from the beginning, gets confused about locations and dates as he has not taken into account the flight just found by A. The A, C, D subgroup finally agrees on D's very expensive suggestion as they still have plenty of money to spend. The last minutes are devoted to the discussion about the next flights, without finding a precise date and airport combination and without writing down the 4th flight.

6.2 Identifying Roles

The distribution of visual attention during verbal exchanges shows how much participants keep their eyes on their laptop screen: from 56% for B to 72% for D. The instruction sheet also had a significant attraction on gaze: 12% for B and 11% for C (including looking at the list of websites and monitoring B's work). The disparities presented in Figs. 3 and 4 can be partly explained in terms of the roles played by each participant. General roles have been identified from the confrontation of the six experiments. These roles do not form a proper partition of the emerging group activity: some roles are not played in some teams, one role can be played by two persons or one person may also partially play some role (Table 1).

In the detailed analysis presented above, the roles were not cleanly distributed:

- A and D are mainly searchers, even if they participate in the discussion about strategy at the beginning and if A writes down the 3rd flight. Most of their activity is, however, carried out on their laptops.
- C is a searcher but also a scribe as he is maintaining a digital copy of the results sheet (with no final benefit for the team). All his activity is carried out on his laptop, except his participation in the collective discussions.

Table 1 General roles taken by the participants in the various experiments

Role	Responsibilities
Leader/Strategy	Encouraging participants to share goals and information.
	Defining heuristics for searching flights (long flights, hub airports).
	Eliciting the constraints and their application.
	Deciding between alternative flights.
	Making proposition/decision about task distribution.
Searcher	Finding flights that match the expressed constraints.
	Finding additional information (number of km, map).
Scribe/Keeping track	Keeping track of found flights on the whiteboard.
	Reporting results on the results sheet.
	Keeping track of the current search focus.

- B plays all roles. He chooses flights, sometimes alone, and triggers most of the collective discussion (leader). He finds two of the three selected flights (searcher) but also writes down the results on the sheet (scribe). He stops updating the sheet after the 2nd flight to go back to his laptop.

Because this distribution of roles is not consistent over time and since the team does not elaborate a strategy at the outset, it fails to respect some task constraints and manifests poor coordination. Participant C writes the results on his laptop, making B and D's writing useless. Participant B plays multiple roles and is hence both a strength and a limiting factor of the group's progress. When B stops writing down the results, he looses track of the different searches and has to rely on C, who is himself not aware of what is going on since he was busy copying results from the sheets.

While other factors certainly come into play, the analysis provides evidence that laptops are cognitive attractors (Lahlou 2000, Lahlou this volume),[1] in the sense that they catch participants' attention, even when they are engaged in a discussion and that this attraction appears, to the external observer, to limit the performance of this group. This attraction is found in many occasions during the experiment and is even more striking during the collective discussions.

- During the initial discussion, participants are keeping a part of their attention on the laptops and on the list of websites. After a tacit agreement on a minimalist strategy (starting from an airport and finding the furthest one), the collective discussion about the starting place ends after only 1 min and the participants start searching for a yet unspecified flight on the web.
- The second moment of collective discussion (at 3:40) lasts only a few seconds. Everyone is commenting about his search on his laptop. Opposite opinions are exchanged about the pertinence of choosing a holiday period. Everyone's gazes meet only when B strongly expresses his opinion ("have you ever searched a flight during holidays?"). After this moment, the discussion continues but with gaze focused on each laptop.
- The third moment of collective discussion is as short as the previous one. Searching is interrupted and gazes meet, but only during the joke.
- The fourth moment of collective discussion does not last longer and happens at 10:30 when A starts a discussion about the next destination but stops 10 s later when A leaves this discussion to go back to his laptop.
- The two short last moments of collective discussion are jokes.

Collective discussion happens when an individual has problems for searching the web, when a joke is cracked or when a point has to be shared (1st and 2nd moments). These moments however remain very short.

---

[1]A cognitive attractor is defined as a set of material and immaterial elements that potentially participates in a given activity and which are simultaneous present from participant's point of view. It is assumed that, when choosing an activity, a human actor will engage himself in the stronger perceived attractor, according to its pregnancy, the estimated cost and value of the anticipated activity.

7 Comparison between Experiments

7.1 Groups with Four Laptops

Group 4b shows a different organization in comparison to the previous group: A and D have the leadership as a subgroup (with more strength for D), while B and C are searching (Table 2). A collective discussion occurs at the beginning (length: 3′28) and, after the website exploration phase, D writes a list of destinations on the whiteboard (length: 3′25). Many non-collective discussions happen during the experiment (AD, AB, BC, CD). D uses the whiteboard to write down and to keep track of the found flights (18% of her gazes are on the whiteboard). She therefore spends less time on her laptop (44%, the lowest score for all groups). A also writes down the found flights, but to a lesser extent (10% on whiteboard only). C also does, but very occasionally.

Their strategy is completely based on the price, which does end up being a limiting factor. They therefore do not select the flights before having evaluated all the destinations. As a result, they not only start coordinating their dates very late (from 16:08, between A and D only) but they also start completing the result sheet even later (at around 25:00).

During the five last minutes, A and D are writing the list of completed flights on the whiteboard, not acknowledging the proposals and questions of B and C. C ends up doing nothing. Much information about the chosen flights is lost during the transcription on the whiteboard and is therefore not reported on the result sheet.

7.2 Groups with Three Laptops

Group 3a shows a very clean and efficient separation of tasks (Table 3). A coordinates, relays questions about constraints and eliciting them, arbitrates between possibilities and writes down the flights found by the two searchers. Among all participants in all groups, she has the highest proportion of gazes toward the whiteboard or the results sheet (53% in Fig. 4.a, which is distributed between respectively 8%

Table 2 Comparison of groups with four laptops. Red indicates a strong implication and orange a medium implication in a given role

Groups	4-a				4-b			
Performance	Low: Three flights with low respect of the constraints				Low: Four flights with low respect of the constraints and missing information.			
Participant	A	B	C	D	A	B	C	D
Leader								
Searcher	Flights	Flights	Flights	Flights	Flights	Flights	Flights	Flights
Scribe	Sheet	Sheet	Laptop		WB, sheet			WB, sheet

Table 3 Comparison of groups with three laptops. Participants without laptop are in bold. For any participant, red indicates a strong implication and orange a medium implication in a given role

Group	3-a				3-b			
	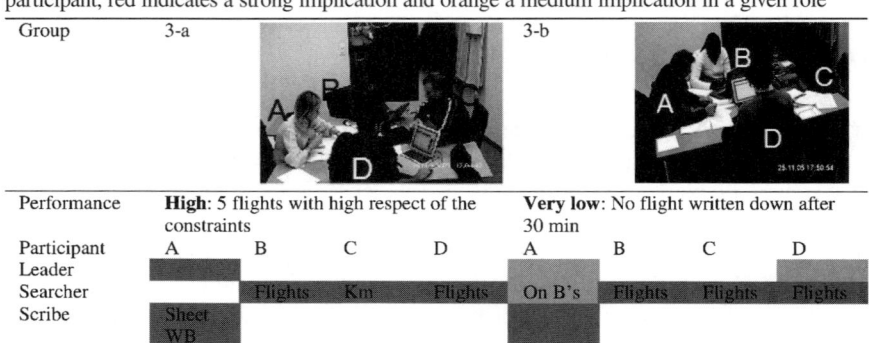							
Performance	**High**: 5 flights with high respect of the constraints				**Very low**: No flight written down after 30 min			
Participant	A	B	C	D	A	B	C	D
Leader								
Searcher		Flights	Km	Flights	On B's	Flights	Flights	Flights
Scribe	Sheet WB							

and 45%). B and D are exclusively searching for the flights, while C's role is to find the number of kilometres.

A starts writing the expected destinations and dates on the results sheet and completes them with the distance and flight information. However, since several anticipated flights are not possible without stops, she has to erase these lines. After 20 min, she starts writing the full itinerary on the whiteboard, which is easier to erase. A's central influence is confirmed by the analysis of coordination questions: On 17 questions about date or location, 10 are asked by the "searchers" and answered by A, 2 are asked by A when writing down the results, 2 are asked between searchers, while A is writing and the 3 remaining are simple requests for acknowledgment and are not answered. Only 2′21″ are spent in collective discussions. A did not initiate all the discussions, but as the results sheet capture less attention than laptops do, her availability fosters the teamwork. Finding the first flight takes a long time, but the coordination that is built between the searchers allows them to find five flights while respecting all constraints.

On the contrary, **group 3b** shows a strong leadership conflict. The group starts searching flights without defining a strategy. A, who has no laptop, asks B to participate in her search, while C and D are exchanging information in order to find complementary flights. The only collective exchanges are about websites. At 3′45″, a discussion starts about the coordination of flights. A conflict appears between A, who prefers to select many short flights to make sure that they are direct, and D who wants to choose the longest flights between hubs. The discussion lasts until 12:30, even though it is limited to A and D. As nothing is decided, everyone continues searching without coordination. D is spending a lot of time trying to figure out the price of a flight expressed in a foreign currency. At 17′28″, C goes to the bathroom and proposes that A uses his laptop. They switch places, A becoming C2 and C becoming A2 in our notation. When A2 comes back, there are 3 min of silence during which he is looking at B's laptop and then he initiates a new discussion. A list of countries is decided upon, as a junction of C2's and D's. For the remaining time, C2 is mainly searching the flights he has personally proposed. The subgroup ABD is coordinating its searches, A2 looking at both B and D's laptops. After 30 min, no flight is written down on the results sheet. This group, unlike others, was given 45 min. At the end of their experiment, three flights found by A2BD are written down but none of the flights found by C2 are integrated into the results.

7.3   Groups with Two Laptops

Group 2a shows an example of efficient specialization (Table 4). During the 11 first minutes, the subgroups AB and CD, with one laptop per subgroup, are concurrently searching flights to compare websites and destinations. They have moments of discussion to exchange information about their progress. During these episodes, A (without laptop) realizes the difficulty of coordinating direct flights between far destinations. At 11:30, he asks CD to search for kilometers, while he starts assisting B in searching flights.

Splitting the tasks allows centralizing constraints management. B searches without interruption, while A writes down the successive flights on the whiteboard and coordinates with CD (to tell them which distance has to be calculated). After 23 minutes, C and D finish finding distances for the selected flights. D starts checking the money spent and searches for the distances whenever a new flight is found. C transcribes the information from the whiteboard to the paper sheet. A shares his time between assisting B's searches, writing results on the whiteboard and commenting on them for C. As B is able to continuously search (reaching the highest ratio for all group: 79% of his gaze to his laptop), the group is able to find seven flights, respecting all constraints. A directs 29% of his gazes on whiteboard (26%) or on the sheets (3%), 42% on B's laptop and 29% on other participants.

Group 2b shows an example of clean but loose engagement. B and D have no laptops but they do not participate very much in the discussion nor do they propose destinations. After exploring websites for 3 min, A proposes a solution that allows the selection of 5 flights in one shot and shows his screen to the others. They are trying this solution, discussing the 5 successive destinations; but, at 9:40, this solution finally appears not to work. Later on, after comparing their findings for the first flight, C asks A to find the kilometres. C then searches the successive destinations proposed by the different participants. B is writing down the flights on the sheet and C is writing on the whiteboard both the kilometres and the money spent. The group finds eight flights but with a low respect of constraints.

Table 4 Comparison of groups with two laptops. Participants without laptop are in bold. For any participant, red indicates a strong implication and orange a medium implication in a given role

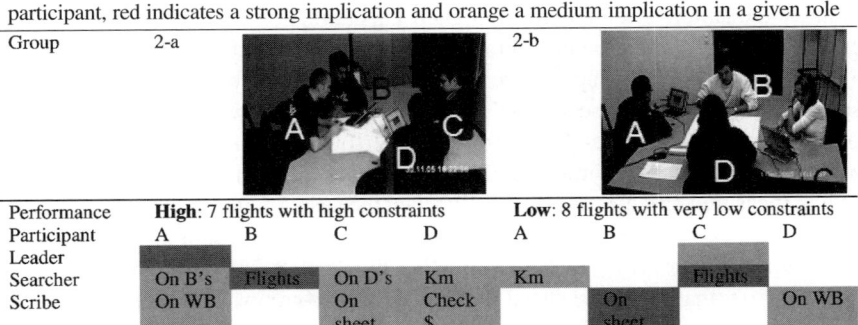

Group	2-a				2-b			
Performance	**High**: 7 flights with high constraints				**Low**: 8 flights with very low constraints			
Participant	A	B	C	D	A	B	C	D
Leader								
Searcher	On B's	Flights	On D's	Km	Km		Flights	
Scribe	On WB		On sheet	Check $		On sheet		On WB

8   Conclusions

Even if only few teams were analyzed, confronting quantitative and qualitative results provides interesting material about the influence of laptops.

8.1   Cognitive and Social Territories

The physical features of laptops and whiteboards influence how social processes create territories (cf. Sect. 3.2). Firstly, the whiteboard offers a large writable surface in the middle of the table. It can be used as a "group territory" dedicated to a shared external memory. Few groups actually did so. The impossibility of rotating this central whiteboard may explain this under-exploitation. It also appears that using the whiteboard as a shared memory required that someone takes the responsibility of maintaining its content:

- Participant A of group 3a used the whiteboard after a while because it was easier to update than the paper sheet. She was then able to keep track of the finished and ongoing searches. She used it to coordinate others participants, verbally referring and gesturing toward the information on the whiteboard.
- Participant A of group 2a also used the whiteboard, not only to record B's searches but also to transmit the information, with oral comments, to C and D who where copying, checking and completing the data.

Most of the groups did not develop a collective use of the whiteboard. It was mainly used for individual note taking by group 4b, 3b and 2b. In group 4b, A and D just developed a common use at the end. It was also used by group 3b to write down the compromise that calmed down the conflict. Group 4a almost never used the whiteboard; everyone was using either his laptop or the paper sheet.

On the contrary, laptops appear to strongly foster the creation of "individual territories". They were observed to act as cognitive attractors. They captured most of the visual attention. The proportion of utterance-related gazes directed to the personal laptop ranges from 44% to 79%, with an average of 65%. As laptop owners were mostly looking at their screen between verbal exchanges, the proportion of time spent looking at the laptop is actually much higher. This attraction can be explained by two factors. Cognitively, they require an important concentration and even a strong physical engagement. Socially, laptops were most likely to create boundaries than shared displays. They can hardly be shared. In group 2b, A was showing his laptop to everyone in order to get input and adhesion when performing a multi-flights search. The other participants that had little visibility and no possibility of action were, however, showing measured enthusiasm (especially when the search failed). Only strong verbal directions allowed a leader to share a laptop over a searcher's shoulder (A directing B in group 3b, A directing B and C directing D in group 2a). The screen creates a physical barrier that limits the visual field, especially in groups with four laptops. The layout of the table had an effect. For group 4b, it only allowed glancing on the screen of the participant on the size and, for group 4a, on the screen of the participant ahead. Moreover, laptops were observed to be used to disengage from the group activity (as presented by Sundholm et al. 2004). In group 3b, A and B were mainly keeping their attention on B's laptop during the conflict between C and D. In group 4b, after A and D started coordinating their flights together, B and C were staying busy browsing the web for items unrelated to the task.

Finally, the ability of whiteboard to enact "group territories" appears to be superseded by the propensity of the laptop to attract participant in a "personal territory" and to capture full or partial attention. This attraction was measured by the proportion of gaze during verbal exchange and appears to be independent of the number of laptops. Consequently, the more people who have a laptop, the less time is available for thinking about strategy and for sharing information with full attention.

8.2 Critical Thinking Performance and Learning

This task requires the participants to efficiently deal with several constraints. As the strongest one is time, rapid decisions about flights and centralization of information are necessary in order to rapidly find flights or to maintain parallel searches. The most efficient strategies were elaborated by participants who had no laptop and therefore some availability to observe what was going on around. They were therefore able to develop critical thinking that leaded to changes in the organization of the team. These verbalizations of knowledge and social interactions are also considered, in the field of collaborative learning, to be the processes that lead to learning. Aside from factual knowledge about international flights, the main learning that occurred from these experiments concerned the difficulty of working together and coordinating tasks under time pressure, as shown during the best performances:

In group 3a, A took a clear leadership position. Being the only member without laptop, her only activity was to keep track of the searches and to coordinate the others. Throughout the whole experiment, she expressed herself verbally about the constraints of the task and took decisions accordingly.

In group 2a, after 11 min of concurrent parallel searches, A strongly expressed his mind about the lack of efficiency and proposed a division of labour in which he was coordinating more specialized works.

In most teams that did not perform well, the participants with a laptop did the most immediate task – searching flights on websites – even if the found flights were not always useful. In team 4.a, everyone started searching without defining any strategy. The result was that no coordination occurred and most of the efforts were useless. In team 4.b, D took the dominant position, arbitrated the strategy (comparing prices) and coordinated the flights. Even though she had the lowest proportion of gazes at her laptop (44%), she was not able to see the flaw in her strategy until shortly before the end. Participants, captivated by their laptops, only communicated with partial and fugitive attention and were likely to leave a collective discussion at the first occasion, even when the discussion was about an important issue.

Having fewer laptops than team members does of course not guarantee team performance. Efficient coordination requires the elaboration of a strategy, to agree on task distribution and to have an efficient tracking and circulation of information. However, a high number of laptops appear to be a limiting factor. Everyone is tempted to overuse his laptop and has his attention at least partially captured. The danger seems to be that participants think that they are able to handle strategy while keeping an eye on their laptop. However, these experiments suggest that an attention only partially available greatly hampers critical thinking, which was identified as an important factor not only for performance but also for learning.

8.3   Limits and Recommendations

Understanding the benefits and drawbacks of laptops requires a global analysis of the team dynamics, described in terms of roles and coordination mechanisms. Our analysis confirms the relevance of analyzing participants' course of action (Theureau 2003) and of a distributed cognition perspective (Hutchins 1995), in which cognitive functions are distributed over the participants and their laptops but also other artefacts such as the paper sheets and the whiteboard. The drawback of our qualitative analysis is that we cannot prove the "generalisability" of our observations. Especially since our results are bound to a specific task which required a tight coordination and fast circulation of information more than deep conceptual negotiation. The effect of leadership could indeed be lower in tasks demanding creative thinking or divergent productions. Hence, our analysis does not experimentally establish statistically significant effects but reveals phenomena and parameters, which could be used as independent variables in controlled experiments.

This study nonetheless produces partial design recommendations. Even if the group dynamics can overcome the design of the table and more precisely the number of individual laptops, our study shows these factors do have implications on group interactions. The general layout of the table has an effect on collaboration. Regulating access to laptops might avoid hampering rich social interactions. A table dedicated to pedagogical situations could help in defining roles: Providing a place without personal display but with tools to monitor the group's activity would for instance foster the leader/coordinator role. For more experienced users, more liberty should be granted to set up the configuration that is the best suited to the collaboration context, including the number of personal displays. Movements between private and public spaces should not be a private functionality but the results of a gesture that act as a public request for taking control of the public space. These results led to the design of a specific artefact, the DockLamp, which can be found at http://craft.epfl.ch.

Acknowledgements   Thanks to Guillaume Raymondon and Michael Ruffin who worked on this tabletop projects as well as to Nicolas Nova and the EPFL students in CSCW who conducted the experiments. This project was funded by the EPFL Fund for Innovation in Training.

References

Argyle, M., & Cook, M. (1976). *Gaze and Mutual Gaze*. Cambridge: Cambridge University Press.
Argyle, M., & Graham, J. (1977). The Central Europe Experiment – Looking at Persons and Looking at Things. *Journal of Environmental Psychology and Nonverbal Behaviour*, 1, pp. 6–16.
Baker, M. J. (1999). Argumentation and Constructive Interaction. In G. Rijlaarsdam & E. Espéret (Series Eds.) & P. Coirier J. Andriessen (Vol. Eds.), *Studies in Writing: Vol. 5. Foundations of Argumentative Text Processing*, pp. 179–202. Amsterdam: University of Amsterdam Press.
Blaye, A. (1988). Confrontation socio-cognitive et résolution de problèmes. *Doctoral dissertation*, Centre de Recherche en Psychologie Cognitive, Université de Provence, France.
Bly, S. A. (1988). A Use of Drawing Surfaces in Different Collaborative Settings. In Proceedings of CSCW'88, pp. 250–256.
Buxton, W., Fitzmaurice, G. W., Balakrishnan, R., & Kurtenbach, G.(2000). Large Displays in Automotive Design. *IEEE Computer Graphics and Applications*, 20(4), pp. 68–75.
Clark, H. H. (1996). *Using Language*. Cambridge, England: Cambridge University Press.
Clark, H. H., & Wilkes-Gibbs, D. (1986). Referring as a Collaborative Process. *Cognition*, 22, pp. 1–39.
Dietz, P. H., & Leigh, D. L. (2001). DiamondTouch: A Multi-User Touch Technology. In ACM Symposium on User Interface Software and Technology (UIST), November 2001, pp. 219–226.
Dillenbourg, P., & Traum, D. (2006). Sharing Solutions: Persistence and Grounding in Multi-modal Collaborative Problem Solving. *Journal of the Learning Sciences*, 15(1), pp. 121–151.
Dillenbourg, P., Baker, M., Blaye, A., & O'Malley, C. (1996). The Evolution of Research on Collaborative Learning. In E. Spada, & P. Reiman (Eds.), *Learning in Humans and Machine: Towards an Interdisciplinary Learning Science*, pp. 189–221. Oxford: Elsevier.
Doise, M., Mugny, G., & Perret-Clermont, A.-N. (1975). Social Interactions and the Development of Cognitive Operations. *European Journal of Social Psychology*, 5, pp. 367–383.
Fussell, S. R., Setlock, L. D., Yang, J., Ou, J., Mauer, E. M., & Kramer, A. (2004). Gestures Over Video Streams to Support Remote Collaboration on Physical Tasks. *Human-Computer Interaction*, 19, pp. 273–309.
Gubman, J., Oehlberg, L., & Yen, C. (2004). The Mapnews Table: Group Collaboration at an Interactive Horizontal Interface. Available online at: http://ix.stanford.edu/downloads/iXCHI04.pdf
Gutwin, C. & Greenberg, S. (1999). The Effects of Workspace Awareness Support on the Usability of Real-Time Distributed Groupware. *ACM Transactions on Computer-Human Interaction*, 6(3), pp. 243–281.
Hutchins, E. (1995). *Cognition in the Wild*. Cambridge, MA: The MIT Press.
Isaacs, E., & Tang, J. (1993). What Video can and can't do for Collaboration: A Case Study. In Proceedings of Multimedia, pp. 199–205. Anaheim, CA: ACM Press.
Joiner, R., Scanlon, E., OShea, T., Smith, R. B., & Blake, C. (2002). Synchronous Collaboration Support for Adults Evidence from a Series of Experiments on Videomediated Collaboration: Does Eye Contact Matter? In G. Stahl (Ed.), *Computer Support for Collaborative Learning: Foundations for a CSCL Community*. Proceedings of CSCL' 2002, pp. 371–378. Boulder, CO., Hillsdale: Erlbaum.
Kendon, A. (1967). Some Functions of Gaze Direction in Social Interaction. *Acta Psychologica*, 32, pp. 1–25.
Lahlou, S. (2000). Attracteurs cognitifs et travail de bureau. *Intellectica*30, pp. 75–113.
Patten, J., Ishii, H., Hines, J., & Pangaro, G. (2001). A Wireless Object Tracking Platform for Tangible User Interfaces. In Proceedings of the ACM Conference on Human Factors in Computing Systems (CHI) 2001, pp. 253–260.
Prante, T., Streitz, N., & Tandler P. (2004). Roomware: Computers Disappear and Interaction Evolves. *IEEE Computer*, December, pp. 47–54.
Rekimoto, J., & Saitoh, M. (1999). Augmented Surfaces: A Spatially Continuous Workspace for Hybrid Computing Environments. In Procceedings of CHI'99, 1999.
Ryall, K., Morris, R. M., Everitt, K., Forlines, C., & Shen, C. (2006). Experiences with and Observations of Direct-Touch Tabletops. In Tabletop 2006, Adelaide, Australia.

Scott, S., Grant, K., Carpendale, S., Inkpen, K., Mandryk, R., & Winograd, T. (2002). Co-located Tabletop Collaboration: Technologies and Directions. Workshop at CSCW2002. In Extended Abstracts of the ACM Conference on Computer-Supported Cooperative Work (CSCW)'02, p. 21.

Scott, S. D., Grant, K. D., & Mandryk, R. L. (2003). System Guidelines for Co-located, Collaborative Work on a Tabletop Display. In Proceedings of ECSCW'03, European Conference on Computer-Supported Cooperative Work, September 2003, pp. 14–18. Helsinki, Finland.

Scott, S. D., Sheelagh, M., Carpendale, T., & Inkpen, K. M. (2004). Territoriality in Collaborative Tabletop Workspaces. In Proceedings of the 2004 ACM Conference on Computer Supported Cooperative Work Table of Contents, pp. 294–303. Chicago, Illinois, USA.

Shen, C., Everitt, K. M., & Ryall, K. (2003). UbiTable: Impromptu Face-to-Face Collaboration on Horizontal Interactive Surfaces. In Proceedings of UbiComp'03, pp. 281–288.

Shen, C., Lesh, N., Vernier, F., Forlines, C., & Frost, J. (2002). Sharing and Building Digital Group Histories. In Proceedings of the ACM Conference on Computer-Supported Cooperative Work (CSCW) 2002, pp. 324–333.

Shen, C., Vernier, F. D., Forlines, C., & Ringel, M. (2004). DiamondSpin: An Extensible Toolkit for Around-the-Table Interaction, In ACM Conference on Human Factors in Computing Systems (CHI), pp. 167–174.

Stewart, J., Bederson, B. B., & Druin, A. (1999). Single Display Groupware: A Model for Copresent Collaboration. In Proceedings of the ACM Conference on Human Factors in Computing Systems (CHI) 99, pp. 286–293.

Sundholm, H., Artman, H., & Ramberg, R. (2004). Backdoor Creativity: Collaborative Creativity in Technology Supported Teams. In COOP 2004, pp. 99–114.

Tang, J. C. (1991). Findings from Observational Studies of Collaborative Work. *International Journal of Man-Machine Studies*, 34, pp. 143–160.

Theureau, J. (2003). Course of Action Analysis & Course of Action Centered Design. In Erik Hollnagel (Ed.), *"Handbook of Cognitive Task Design."* Lawrence Erlbaum Associates.

Underkoffler, J., & Ishii, H. (1999). Urp: A Luminous-Tangible Workbench for Urban Planning and Design. In Proceedings of the ACM Conference on Human Factors in Computing Systems (CHI) 99, pp. 386–393.

Vertegaal, R. (1999). The GAZE Groupware System: Mediating Joint Attention in Multiparty Communication and Collaboration. In Proceedings of the SIGCHI Conference on Human Factors in Computing Systems: The CHI is the Limit (Pittsburgh, May 1999), CHI '99, pp. 294–301. New York: ACM Press

Vertegaal, R., & Ding, Y. (2002). Explaining Effects of Eye Gaze on Mediated Group Conversations: Amount or synchronization? In CSCW 2002, pp. 41–48.

Webb, N. M. (1991). Task Related Verbal Interaction and Mathematical Learning in Small Groups. *Research in Mathematics Education*, 22(5), pp. 366–389.

The Disappearing Computer: Consequences for Educational Technology?

H. Ulrich Hoppe

Keywords disappearing computer, interactive educational media, computer-integrated clasrooms, ubiquitous computing

1 Introduction: A Redefinition of Computers in Education?

Computers are present in the one or the other way in almost any school within the European Union and many other countries world-wide. Over the last couple of years, we have seen considerable progress in networking, both in terms of school Internet connections and in terms of intranet solutions. Also developing countries have implemented ambitious programmes to establish computers and Internet connections in their schools. A prominent example case is the Chilean nation-wide "Enlaces" programme (Hinostroza and Hepp 1999). The introduction of new information and communication technologies (ICT) in schools has been accompanied by the quest for pedagogical innovation, i.e., new learning methods and curriculum revision. Whereas the proliferation of computers in the schools is a visible reality, the practical answers to the pedagogical challenges are much less consistent and clear. It is evident that pedagogical innovation cannot be directly "synchronised" with technical innovation. Over the last decades, we have seen qualitative changes in ICT at a very rapid pace. In not more than 10 years, the paradigm of more or less isolated personal computers, which was introduced in the early 1980s as a successor of mainframes and timesharing systems, has been replaced by the networked computing paradigm. It is inconceivable that each paradigm shift in ICT could be reflected by a revision of our basic educational methods and goals. Now, there are signals from within the ICT community that future developments may no longer be centred around "the computer". So, we may face a situation in which educationalists still adhere to techno-centric paradigms that are already questioned by pioneers of the technology. We should take this as an indication that the strategy of pedagogy following technology is inadequate. The conception and design of learning environments (in a broad sense, including physical space, heterogeneous resources, roles and responsibilities) is primarily a pedagogical problem, and pedagogy is based on long lasting and historically grown principles. The rapidly changing technology is a secondary, instrumental parameter.

P. Dillenbourg et al. (eds.), *Interactive Artifacts and Furniture Supporting Collaborative Work and Learning*,
DOI: 10.1007/978-0-387-77234-9_4, © Springer Science + Business Media, LLC 2009

If we analyse and reflect the predicted and partly already observable new notion of the computer from an educational point of view, this will not be another adaptation of pedagogy to the development of ICT. Paradoxically, it is this new vision of ICT that downplays the role of the technology.

This view of ICT is most sharply crystallised in the notion of the "Disappearing Computer" (cf. TIME digital, Feb. 28, 2000), which has also been the theme of a European research initiative at the crossroads of computer science, social sciences and innovative design. A similar vision has been propagated by D. Norman in his book the "The Invisible Computer" (Norman 1998). The central claim associated with these notions is that interactive computing technology will no longer appear with a uniform product interface (standard screen, keyboard, a box and cables), somewhat screaming at the observer "Look, I am a computer!". New interfaces come with a variety of peripherals and different designs, and they will be embedded into spatial and physical "roomware" scenarios (cf. Streitz et al. 1999). Computing facilities may be amalgamated with the environment in the form of specific "smart objects" or "tangible bits" (Ishii and Ullmer 1997). Weiser and Brown (1997) claim that such forms of ubiquitous computing will lead to a new age of "calm technology" which is characterised by having multiple computerised services around us in an implicit and unobtrusive way. This technology will no longer define the focus of our attention. Even the current notion of a "user" would be misleading if this vision were completely materialised. The point would no longer be the human-computer relationship but the availability of certain services located in the physical (and virtual) environment.

This notion of the "disappearing computer" creates a new perspective on ICT, but there are also some problems and potential misunderstandings:

– Already today, we see multiple processors being invisibly embedded in many technical devices such as automobiles, dish washers and other equipment in workplaces and homes. This should not be confounded with invisible computing in the above sense. In these other applications, computers essentially serve as controllers and regulators of processes within a device or between technical devices. The innovation that we are interested in has to do with information processing in which "the human is in the loop", i.e., with *interactive and cooperative* applications. Here, "explicit computing" is still predominant.
– Irrespective of its new shape and varied embedment, a computer remains a universal information processor in the abstract sense of a Turing machine. The ideas of universal computing, formal computer languages and the various computational abstractions that have been created to bring the programming of computers and the reasoning about computing to its current stage are not at all obsolete. They are also important for education as essential contributions to the human intellectual and scientific development. These fundamental ideas have to be reflected in our curricula for mathematics, informatics and philosophy, but this does *not* imply that the educational use of new digital media and ICT should be centred around the old explicit and uniform view of the computer. Whereas the universality of computing is a given, the relative uniformity of real computers will most likely disappear.

– The notion of the "disappearing computer" does, of course, not imply that computers would become obsolete, would no longer be used or would be replaced by alternative information processing devices. The latter may be another possible vision of the future, but it is not inherent in our understanding of the disappearing or invisible computer. Yet, there is more in this vision than the idea of computers getting out of sight (though potentially multiplied) in a concrete sense: Also on a conceptual level, social and technological innovation will most likely find new targets or "forefront technologies" beyond computers and also beyond the Internet. This, again, does not mean that these will be replaced. We see this in other areas such as, e.g., energy transformation technologies. There is still "local" innovation (today, for example; in the area of fuel cells), but there are also old technologies with only small increments of innovation. There are no serious claims that energy transformation technologies will revolutionise our lives dramatically within a short period of time, as this is currently associated with computing and communication technologies. ICT as "calm technology" may imply that the changes are less dramatic than predicted. The new digital technologies can also be used to mimic classical technologies. This is the case with digital musical instruments, such as e-pianos, or with electronic paper. Of course there is a value added beyond the mimicry: you can use your e-piano directly conserve and replay your performance, you can convert into an editable representation using MIDI, you can feed it into a sequencing program etc. But basically, you can still rely on the old skills that you may have acquired with a non-digital medium.

In the sequel, I will try to explore some consequences of this new view of ICT under the "disappearing computer" heading for educational applications and particularly for our schools. A central question is in which ways computers may disappear in or from our classrooms.

2 Computer-Integrated Classrooms

An early approach of how to adapt ubiquitous computing technology to the classroom has been described in Hoppe et al. (1993). It featured a combination of new hardware devices, namely big interactive screens ("LiveBoards") that had recently become available (cf. Elrod et al. 1992), with a networked classroom environment in which typical patterns of information exchange in a classroom were supported by specific groupware functions. One of the basic ideas was the provision "electronic worksheets" which could be distributed and collected by the teacher and which could be used in synchronous cooperative mode between students or be shared through the LiveBoard. This type of scenario was called a "computer integrated classroom" (CiC), reflecting the central idea of using computer and communication technologies to support both interaction and information exchange in a face-to-face classroom. The approach was first demonstrated in 1993 by a fully functional prototype at the institute GMD-IPSI in Darmstadt. This was a proof of concept, yet the environment was installed in a laboratory and not in a real educational setting.

The CiC idea was put into practice in the European long term research project "Networked Interactive Media in Schools" (NIMIS, 1998–2000, cf. Hoppe et al. 2000). As defined in the European ESE ("Experimental School Environments") call for projects, NIMIS aimed at supporting early learning, here particularly the first years of primary school. The NIMIS hardware includes a big interactive screen with a height-adjustable touch-sensitive glass surface particularly designed for the specific target group and interactive pen-based LCDs tablets integrated with the children's tables. The computers are connected in a local network and located in a separate room next to the classroom. The children's interface consists of the tablets and earphones or loudspeakers which can be used alternatively. Figure 1 gives an impression of this classroom installation with integrated hardware components and a big interactive board. The installation at a Duisburg public primary school is still in everyday use. Similar classrooms have been installed in a Portuguese school near Lisbon and a rural school in England.

The NIMIS software includes a special application for initial reading and writing ("Today's Talking Typewriter", see Tewissen et al. 2000) using pen-based input and speech synthesis, as well as a full desktop environment which facilitates archiving and communication functions for early learners even before they are skilled in reading and writing. The implementation and visualisation of login procedures, the flow of information, and ownership of data was one of the major

Fig. 1 Scenes from the NIMIS classroom in Duisburg

challenges in designing a CiC for early learners. As a child orientated metaphor for handling and visualising data and different media, we introduced the metaphor of a "companion" as a virtual representative of a child's assistant. The companion is both a symbol of being logged in and a container for the data objects that the child has produced. Initially, the companion comes with a standard icon (here a frog) and a number. Later it is typically replaced by an image chosen by the child, e.g., an image of a favourite pet. Metaphorically speaking, the child logs in to the computer by *calling the companion*. The companion appears and shows the child's documents (results of previous learning episodes, multimedia messages from classmates etc.) in the form of small preview images, organised using tabulators (see Fig. 2). Data organisation for young children is supported by means of automatic arrangement and distribution in folders marked with icons. Later, children may create their own folders and use drag and drop operations to arrange their documents. Different from standard operating system conventions, two children can log in at the same time on one machine and work together at their desktop. Then two companions would be shown on the desktop at a time. When the child logs out, the companion disappears and *goes to sleep*. The companion also disappears in its original place, when a child logs in on a different machine: The child is automatically logged out in the former desktop, i.e., at a given point in time, a child's companion has only one defined location. This is also interesting for supervision and analysis since the log of a child's companion represents the trajectory of this child in the classroom.

The specific policy of login (presence) and ownership materialised in the companion also allows for supporting classroom processes. Figure 3 shows a typical action cycle and flow of information: Going to the scanner, the child "calls" his or her companion. The companion appears on the screen next to the scanner and shows the newly scanned image. Returning to the child's workplace he or she calls the companion again. The companion disappears on the scanner machine and appears at the workplace's interactive display, "carrying" the scanned image. The metaphor of letting a virtual companion carry and manage the child's data turned out to be a very natural way of promoting awareness of different concepts of data processing for the 6-year-old children. Parallel experience with a normal windows desktop in

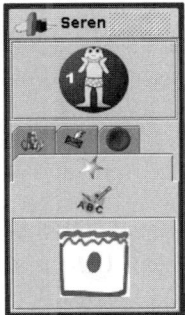

Fig. 2 A companion showing a child's data

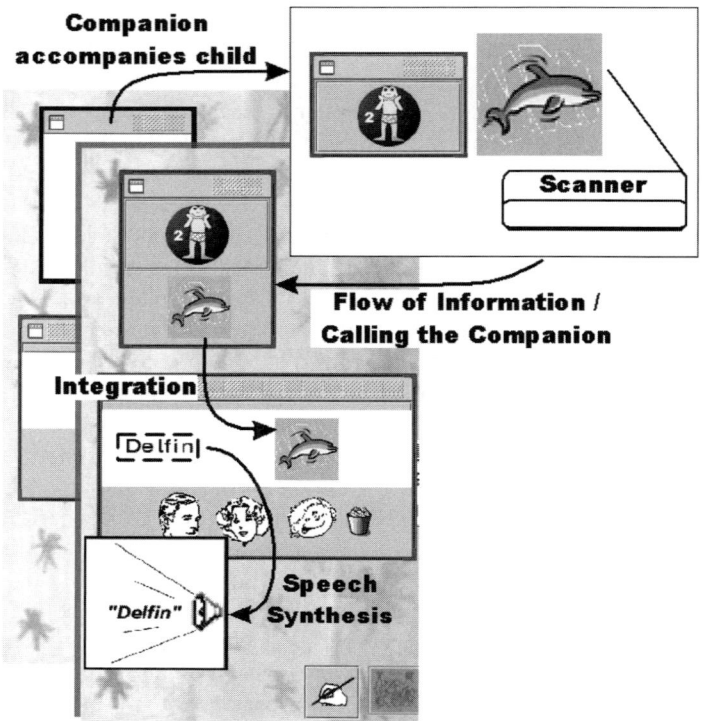

Fig. 3 Flow of information in a CiC activity

another classroom showed that pupils of the same age and even higher literacy levels were not able to handle their data in comparable way using standard tools.

To make sure that new media technology supports learning and does not negatively interfere with well suited pedagogical procedures, we studied existing interactions and curricular activities in the three NIMIS primary schools. Although the new technology was defined in such a way as to support grown pedagogical approaches, especially classroom procedures, we have also seen new roles evolving from these special environments for the teachers and the children. Originally, in the specific method for teaching reading/writing skills ("reading through writing"), the teacher had to provide individual feedback by reading out what a student had written by composing letters from a palette. Of course, with a single teacher, the number of students that could be "served" during a certain period was limited. In the NIMIS environment, this feedback function was provided through automatic speech synthesis. This allowed teachers to concentrate on children with special difficulties and needs. In general, the CiC creates a new role for the teachers to act as information manager. This implies that teachers have to learn about new ways of accessing information and about judging and handling qualitatively new kinds of information. The same is true for the children: Without explicitly mentioning the computer as a topic, the children get used to managing their own data and to working with different devices and in different group constellations.

3   Principles for Introducing Digital Media to the Classroom

Generalising from the NIMIS experience, we can formulate principles for introducing networked interactive media (rather than "computers") in the classroom:

3.1   *Unification of Media and Learning Activities on a Digital Platform*

Educational media of the future will be unified on a digital platform. Negroponte's vision of "Being Digital" (Negroponte 1995) is particularly fruitful for educational scenarios since integrated digital media facilitate a free flow, re-use and recombination of the materials and products of learning in a classroom. New types of collaborative activities arise from these scenarios. However, the objects of learning are not only digital: Easy transitions between the physical and the digital world are facilitated and become a subject of learning processes.

3.2   *Supporting the Classroom as a Whole Through an Integrated Networked Infrastructure*

Connecting learners in the NIMIS sense goes beyond providing internet access in a computerised classroom. Intranet facilities are seen as prior to internet access, not only for early learning. Integration, i.e., connectivity and inter-operability, fosters the communal aspect of the classroom and collaborative learning by giving flexible access to classroom resources for teachers and students and by facilitating a high degree group awareness.

3.3   *Design for Reflection*

In the NIMIS perspective, two types of reflection in learning environments are considered: (1) As an implicit result of the educational design of learning environments, learners have access to previous results and learning episodes as objects in the environment (e.g. through the visualisation of problem solving trajectories or through the provision of object repositories with versioning). This kind of reflection is an interactive process on the part of the human participants, such as learners, tutors or teachers. (2) Additionally, certain types of analysis and interpretation on the part of the machine are also possible. The basis is a general architecture which includes history transcripts and plug-in facilities for intelligent monitoring and diagnosis (Mühlenbrock et al. 1997). However, we do not intend to build systems in which the learning process is under control of the machine as it was intended for "intelligent tutoring systems". Monitoring and analysis will provide local and partial feedback to learners or it can serve as decision aid for tutors or teachers.

3.4   Priority of Pedagogy over Technology

Despite certain differences in educational tradition and culture between member states of the EU and even between single schools, European pedagogy for early learning is on average child centred and orientated towards active and constructive learning. Learning activities in primary school classrooms are typically distributed, the teacher being a manager of these multi-threaded activities. Certain technological scenarios might lead to more centralised control or to higher shares of individualised learning as opposed to partner work. Such potential changes originating from the inherent logic of the technology without a clear pedagogical justification should not be accepted. The design of educational scenarios should in first place be based on pedagogical premises and objectives.

3.5   Consequences for Teachers' Roles and Competence

We believe that tomorrow's teachers will have to fulfil the role of classroom information managers. Already, today particularly primary school teachers act as managers of rich distributed classroom activities and of a variety of resources. With the help of advanced technologies, certain routine tasks such as the detection and correction of individual errors may be partially left to a computerised support system. This will enable teachers to concentrate even more on aspects of knowledge management and on supporting special needs. Given the ease of use of the new technology, there is no need for spending more efforts than today on system-specific ICT training for teachers. However, classroom information management will become a new prominent issue in teacher training and in teachers' professionalism. It will involve aspects of knowledge processing and representation, the design of learning materials and group scenarios for collaborative learning and new technology supported methods for reflection and analysis of classroom experience.

4   Patterns of Disappearance

The concrete examples and suggestions put forward so far can be seen as arguments for new and more intensive forms computer use in classroom. So, is the "disappearing computer" argument not more than a provocative rhetoric? Certainly, it is intended to be also rhetorical in that it questions an existing hidden agenda of ICT in education (e.g. the hope that bringing computers and Internet to schools will somewhat magically improve the quality of learning). Yet, certain concrete aspects of disappearance that have been attributed to new forms of computing technology in general are also reflected in specific ways in pedagogical scenarios:

4.1 "Computers in Disguise" (Mimicry)

In the NIMIS classroom, the pupils' workplaces do not have too much in common with a standard PC. It was interesting to see that initially, parents in first place, but also the children expected the NIMIS classroom to be a "computer room", but when we asked the children after a while if they were really working on a computer we found considerable doubt and few direct affirmative answers. Indeed, the NIMIS workplaces with the tablets mimic the traditional school desks with slates. Pen based interaction was not known to the kids as a form of operating a computer before. In this sense, the NIMIS classroom successfully demonstrates a form of mimicry. As for other forms of computer mimicry, the example of digital musical instruments had already been mentioned. These are obviously also pedagogically relevant. Chess computers are one of the few commercial examples of computerised interactive devices with interface mimicry in the form of physical objects, namely the chess pieces. Similar forms of interface mimicry have also been tried out in educational contexts (cf., e.g., Kusunoki et al. 1999, Eden 2002).

The educational use of pen based pocket computers or PDAs (cf. Roschelle and Pea 2002, Pinkwart et al. 2003) is a new phenomenon of its own, not a form of mimicry. PDAs come with the claim to be miniature versions of universal computing devices, although the form is an issue for graphics based applications. The classification under the "mimicry" criterion would be more likely attributed to mobile phones with multimedia interfaces than to PDAs, but the educational relevance of these is still limited.

4.2 Hidden Computers and Conceptual Disappearance

In the NIMIS classroom, the pupils do not see and do not directly interact with "the computer". This makes a conceptual difference since it is plausible to assume that non standard interfaces do not evoke fixed ideas about using a computer (which are nowadays even present in very young learners). From a technical point of view, we can conceive the "hidden computer architecture" as a network of servers and services connected to very differently embedded and shaped interfaces, including task-specific interactive objects and pen based interfaces.

Pen based interfaces such as tablets, e-book readers or big interactive displays mimic paper and pencil or chalk and chalkboard, they support the "paper metaphor" also without being electronic paper in the narrower sense of the word (cf. Ditlea 2001).

We found that particularly older students and adults show a certain resistance to using "fuzzy and imprecise" free hand input for annotations and sketches if they are aware that there is computer behind. Conversely, if we could achieve a good acceptance of free hand interfaces for certain tasks (e.g., design and creative planning), this would indicate that the users' conceptual understanding or their mental models of the situation were no longer focused on the computer. In this case, the computer would not have disappeared physically, yet, in a sense, mentally. We can assume this is true for any kind of successful interface mimicry.

4.3   Computers Outside Classrooms

Very interesting debates are centred around the question where to place computers in schools. Should computers in higher numbers (one computer for one or two students) be concentrated in "computer rooms"? If put into classrooms, how many computers make sense, how should they be arranged and located? Here, our experience confirms that the general form of classroom organisation makes a big difference for the use of computers in classrooms: In primary schools with distributed and multi-threaded activities, it is no problem to put one or two computers in a corner and to use them as one potential learning station in the classroom "learning parcours". In secondary schools which, at least in Germany, rely on a more homogeneous teacher centred and all-students-in-a-line learning style, it is much more difficult to make use of a small number of computers. In this case, alternative locations (if not the "computer rooms") could be the school library (if there is still one, it should certainly have computers and Internet connection) or rooms for "digital group work" in phases of distributed project orientated learning. This, of course, requires changes in the prevailing teaching and learning styles and in the organisation of the learning process.

5   Focusing on the Expressive Function of Interactive Educational Media

The basic notion and understanding of "media" tends to mirror the actual usage of media technologies in the respective application areas. In education, commercially oriented approaches to "e-learning" would see the basic functions of media as containers of information (or "content") plus mechanisms of distribution. Certain gaming applications may focus on a combination of interactive and immersive features of media as virtual environments. In our approaches of integrating interactive media with classroom environments we have focused on forms of learning and teaching based on intellectual production. This brought us to setting the focus on the expressive and communicative function of media as opposed to their container function in "content delivery".

For a foundation of this understanding of media we refer to Dewey (1934). Dewey's notion of media focuses on the function of media as means of intellectual and artistic expression (and not on the function of representing content!). This concept of expressive media subsumes notations such as those used in mathematics, music and language as well as modern "digital media". A media-theoretical re-interpretation and adaptation of Dewey's concept of media has recently been presented by Vogel (2001) as a starting point for developing a definition of rationality which is not grounded on a prior notion language as, e.g., in linguistic pragmatics. The alternative opened by Dewey and adopted by Vogel takes action, particularly expressive and communicative action as a starting point. Vogel's interpretation of Dewey is condensed into five criteria:

M is a medium **if** (by definition)

(1) *M is used intentionally*;
(2) *M is used for expressive (and/or communicative) purposes*;
(3) *M is a genuine constituent of the acts or products generated*;
(4) The specific use of M is (a) established in the framework of a performative practice (culture), or (b) *constituted by social rules*;
(5) *M allows for producing expressive acts or artefacts which can be publicly performed or exhibited and which constitute an integrated experiential episode for certain observers.*

Evidently, (5) is especially related to the use of media in arts. Leaving this apart, (1)–(4) give an adequate and useful characterisation of media also in a broader, more general sense. Compliant with this definition it is evident that, e.g., voice, writing systems, formal notations, but also the stone which is carved by a sculptor are all media. The third criterion expresses the claim that the medium in which something is construed or expressed is closely related to its content, not in the extreme sense of McLuhan's statement "the medium is the message" (McLuhan 1964). Rather, the medium leaves its "trace" on the content being expressed (Krämer 1998) such as a speakers voice, beyond the illocutionary aspects of intonation, lends a specific flavour to what is said.

Each medium has its specific representational potential and specific representational characteristics. The above criteria do not make very explicit assumptions about such representational qualities. For our purposes, we do postulate certain representational qualities in order to qualify something as a medium (of educational interest). An important aspect is the one of flexibly structuring what is being expressed or represented. e.g., the representational flexibility of notation systems (ranging from alphabets to programming languages) stems from what could be called "symbolic compositionality": obeying certain syntactic constraints of the medium itself, a wide, often infinite, variety of expressions with different meanings can be generated. This is not only true for formalised representation systems such as mathematical notations or programming languages, a similar kind of compositional or combinatorial flexibility can be found in painting and musical performance (as distinguished from musical composition which already uses a formalised notation). Based on this consideration of representational qualities, we suggest to replace the fifth criterion by the following:

(5) *M affords representational flexibility through compositional or combinatorial structuring of expressions.*

We claim that interactive digital media constitute *new forms* of intellectual and artistic expression in the very sense of Dewey's principles (including the above modification). Accordingly, bringing this potential to education is not a choice of means but it is an end in itself in that it constitutes an add-on to the learner's intellectual development. So, it is a challenge for education to help students in appropriating these new means expression. The appropriation process has several facets, including

- a gradual improvement of mastery in using certain media to express and communicate ideas;
- the development of intellectual and artistic creativity, which is reified in products externalised and substantiated in the medium;
- active involvement in a learning community, in our field of application particularly the classroom community;
- the adoption of different roles in collaborative learning scenarios, such as "initiator/proposer", "listener" or "critic".

To foster these activities in the classroom, teachers have to take a leading role, i.e., they should be pioneer users of the interactive tools.

6   Interactive Media in Educational Settings

In the framework of the European SEED project (IST-2000-25214, 2001-2004), the Collide research group has explored new forms of using digital media in the classroom in a participatory approach with a group of associated teachers. This endeavour was based on the premise of accepting the given curriculum. i.e., it was not about introducing new computer orientated content, but about maintaining, possibly enriching, each teacher's grown teaching style and preferences. Together with the teachers, we wanted to achieve a *richer and more integrated form of using interactive digital media in the classroom.*

Based on the general focus on the expressive and communicative function of media, we have tried to involve teachers and students processes of actively appropriating interactive media as standard elements of everyday classroom activities. The starting point taken by the SEED project was to enable and actively involve teachers in this process of appropriation. The following lines of development were pursued in this project:

- The provision of flexible authoring tool kits to allow teachers to create their own interactive learning materials or micro worlds. These tool kits are made up of educational software components as building blocks.
- The provision of "collaborative mind tools" (Hoppe 2004) as a *synthesis of interactive and collaborative learning environments.* Here, computer support for collaborative learning is not limited to computer-mediated communication, but includes creating and processing computational objects.

Fig. 4 Modelling tools for stochastic

– The provision of *cooperation tools for communities of educators and learners*, including portal technologies and content management systems.

Figure 4 illustrates the use of a modelling tools with pen based input devices in a probability course in 9th grade (Kuhn et al. 2004). The particular support for the modelling and analysing stochastic is provided as one of several visual languages in the collaborative modelling environment (*"Cool Modes"*, cf. Pinkwart et al. 2001). The focus of using *Cool Modes* is on model building (here: the setting up of a probability experiment), simulation and sharing of results. A typical example, a model of the famous "birthday experiment" (how likely is it to have at least two identical birthday dates in a group of N people?), is shown in Fig. 5.

Figure 5 could be the result of a teacher's presentation with hand written annotations explaining the different elements of the model. In general, a *Cool Modes* workspace can contain different formal or semi-formal representations together with hand written input as a conceptual extension of a paper notebook. This resembles (and indeed takes up) Alan Kay's *Dynabook* idea (Kay and Goldberg 1977).

The modelling environment also supports the sharing of workspaces between computers and the creation of shared objects to accumulate data from different working groups. These tools are used to orchestrate a specific scenario of group including experimentation in a small group, aggregation of results in shared

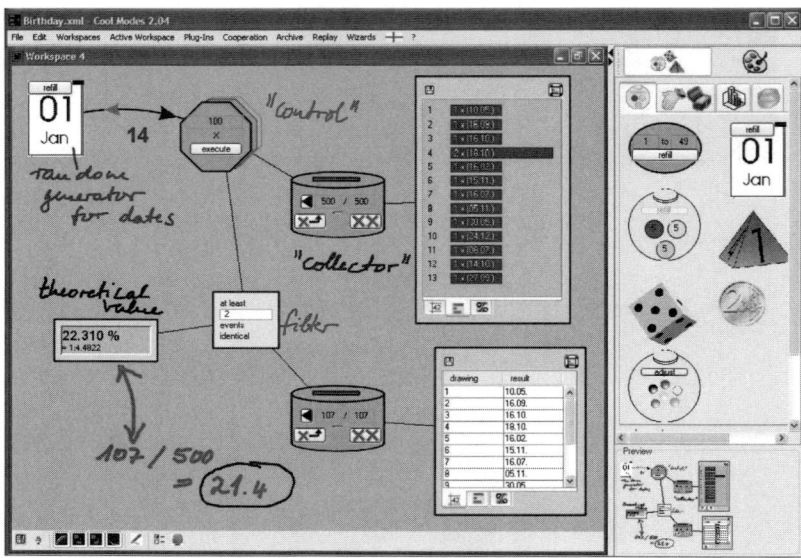

Fig. 5 The "birthday experiment" in Cool Modes

container objects as well the final discussion of results on an interactive whiteboard handled by the teacher.

In our general vision of classroom applications, we see multi-functional and multi-representational tools such as Cool Modes as digital, active extensions of the chalkboard and paper and pencil. The tools should ideally be used in networked ubiquitous and potentially mobile computing environments to support modelling, interactive presentation and group discussion in a variety of educational scenarios, including traditional lectures (presentation) as well as tutorials and collaborative work in small groups.

Figure 6 is taken from a biology course in 12th grade on system dynamics (comprising themes such as exponential and logistic population growth, consumption of natural resources, interacting populations such predator-prey models). In the concrete situation, the teacher works with a big interactive display using the *NoteIt* free hand annotation tool. A scanned-in image of the development of coffee production in Brazil has been loaded into a *NoteIt* page. These data exhibit a periodic pattern but also an increase over time. The teacher wanted to construct a linear approximation of this overall increase. Since *NoteIt* does not provide parameterised geometrical shapes but only free hand input, he took a ruler designed for the chalkboard to draw a straight line on the electronic board. The result was perfectly adequate, but the teacher articulated afterwards that he felt uneasy using the physical device as an add-on to the digital representation. He thought the computer tool should provide a line drawing operation and found that his "fuzzy" way of achieving the goal was inferior to a "clean" computer operation.

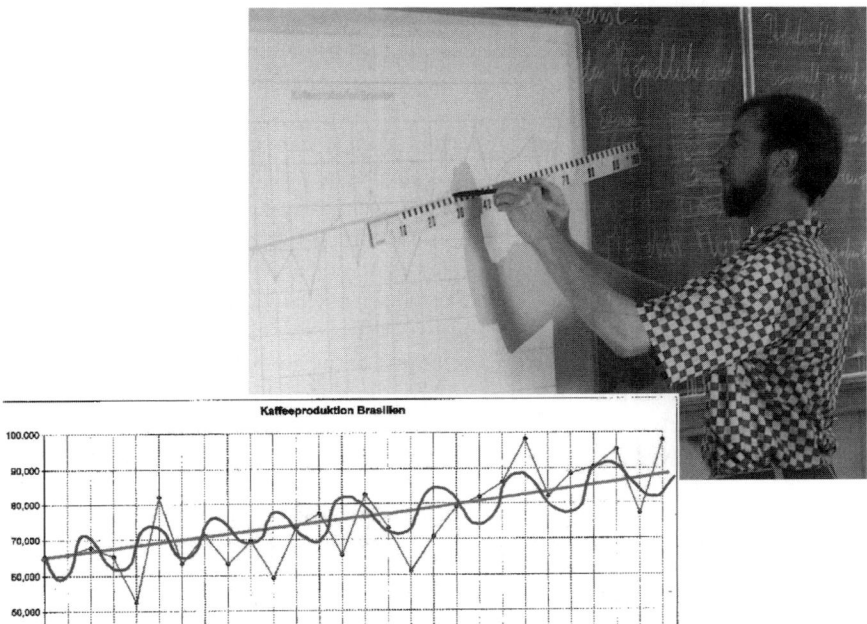

Fig. 6 Ad hoc use of an analogue device over a digital whiteboard

This example is very much in line with the general observation stated in the "patterns of disappearance" section above. Yet, what is really bad about this blend of the digital and the physical-analogue? The result is on a digital level and thus maintains the full potential of being electronically archived, re-used, distributed, multiplied and post-processed. As for the input process, a line-drawing operation would not necessarily have been better than this "brute force" method: The analogue device is clearly visible to the audience, and, as for the adjustment of the straight line, it offers more degrees of freedom than a computerised line drawing operation which usually requires fixing one point first or just allows for parallel movement of a given line. Even though the teacher was not satisfied with his solution, the idea to take the ruler was ingenious! In all our previous experience, we had not seen this specific combination of digital and physical tools. In an unbiased view, this example shows that the "digital mimicry" works and is spontaneously accepted, though questioned intellectually.

7 Conclusion

The NIMIS and SEED experiences demonstrate that a new understanding of interactive digital media beyond explicit computing can indeed lead to innovative ways of using ICT in various teaching/learning settings. New dimensions are opened beyond individual usage by supporting group interactions, beyond information delivery (so typical for web based scenarios) in terms of expressive and creative use of the media and beyond the traditional expectations regarding computers by crossing the physical-digital barrier.

Currently, this view faces new opportunities and new challenges regarding the incorporation of mobile and wireless technologies as well as Web2.0 types of community support based on social software. Both tendencies support the conceptual disappearance of the computers in their conventional form. In the integrative view advocated here, mobile devices and possible "smart objects" will be one more element to enrich learning environments, but we would not expect a single type of new device to constitute a new mode of learning (such as "mobile learning"). Rather, we expect to see more "functional differentiation" between different types of devices in integrated settings (cf. Bollen et al. 2006). On a social and organisational level, community software will allow for sharing learning activities and exchanging learning results between classrooms and local learning groups.

Acknowledgements I want to express my gratitude and appreciation for the teachers who have creatively adopted our somewhat strange suggestions for transgressing the well known and accepted educational usage of computers. The outcome was not predictable but we feel encouraged by the results. Thanks also to all members of the COLLIDE research group for making this experience possible. The work reported here has been supported by the European Commission under the contracts ESPRIT 29301 (NIMIS) and IST-2000-25214 (SEED).

References

Bollen, L., Juarez, G., Westermann, M., Hoppe, H.U. (2006). PDAs as input devices in brainstorming and creative discussions. In Hsi, S., Kinshuk, Chan, T.-W., Sampson, D.G. (eds.). Proceedings of *WMUTE 2006* (4th International Workshop on Wireless, Mobile and Ubiquitous Technologies in Education) (pp. 137–141). Los Alamitos (USA): IEEE Press.

Dewey, J. (1934). *Art as Experience*. Reprinted 1980. New York: Perigee Books.

Ditlea, S. (2001) The Electronic Paper Chase. *Scientific American*, November 2001.

Eden, H. (2002). Getting in on the (inter)action: Exploring affordances for collaborative learning in the context of informed participation. In G. Stahl (ed.). Proceedings of *CSCL 2002* (Conf. on Computer Support for Collaborative Learning) (pp. 399–407). Hillsdale (USA): Erlbaum.

Elrod, S., Bruce, R., Gold, R, Goldberg, D., Halasz, F., Janssen, W., Lee, D., McCall, K., Pedersen, E., Pier, K., Tang, J., Welch, B. (1992). LiveBoard: a large interactive display supporting group meetings, presentations, and remote collaboration. In Proceedings of *CHI '92* (ACM Conference on Computer-Human Interaction) (pp. 599–607). New York: ACM Press.

Hinostroza, E., & Hepp, P. (1999). Use of the web in the Chilean educational system. *Journal of Computer Assisted Learning* 15/1, 91–94.

Hoppe, H.U. (2004). Collaborative mind tools. In Tokoro, M. & Steels, L. (eds.). *The Future of Learning* (pp. 222–235). Amsterdam: IOS Press.

Hoppe, H.U., Baloian, N., Zhao, J. (1993). Computer support for teacher-centered classroom interaction. In Proceedings of *ICCE '93* (International Conference on Computers in Education) (pp. 211–217). Taipei (Taiwan)..

Hoppe, H.U., Lingnau, A., Machado, I., Paiva, A., Prada, R., Tewissen, F. (2000). Supporting collaborative activities in computer-integrated classrooms – the NIMIS approach. In Proceedings of *CRIWG 2000* (International Workshop on Groupware) (pp. 94–101). Los Alamitos (USA): IEEE Press.

Ishii, H., & Ullmer, B. (1997). Tangible bits: Towards seamless interfaces between people, bits and atoms. In Proceedings of *CHI '97* (ACM Conference on Computer-Human Interaction) (pp. 234–241). New York: ACM Press.

Kay, A., & Goldberg, A. (1977). Personal Dynamic Media. *IEEE Computer* 10, March 1977, 31–41.

Krämer, S. (1998). Das Medium als Spur und Apparat (The medium as trace and apparatus). In Krämer, S. (ed.), *Medien-Computer-Realität* (pp. 73–94). Frankfurt/Main (Germany): Suhrkamp.

Kuhn, M., Hoppe, H.U., Lingnau, A., Fendrich, M. (2004). Evaluation of exploratory approaches in learning probability based on computational modelling and simulation. In Isaias, P., Kinshuk, Sampson, D.G. (eds.). Proceedings of *CELDA 2004* (IADIS Conference of Cognition and Exploratory Learning in Digital Age) (pp. 83–90). Lisbon (Portugal), November 2004.

Kusunoki, F., Sugimoto, M., Hashizume, H. (1999). A system for supporting group learning that enhances interactions. In Proceedings of *CSCL 1999* (Conference on Computer Support for Collaborative Learning) (pp. 323–327). Stanford (USA), December 1999.

McLuhan, M. (1964). *Understanding Media – The Extensions of Man*. Reprinted 1994. Cambridge (USA): MIT Press.

Muhlenbrock, M., Tewissen, F., Hoppe, H.U. (1997). A framework system for intelligent support in open distributed learning environments. In du Boulay, B. & Mizoguchi, R. (Eds.), Artificial Intelligence in Education – Knowledge Media in Learning Systems (Proceedings of AI-ED '97, Kobe, Japan, August 1997) (pp. 183–190). Amsterdsm-Tokyo: IOS/Omsha.

Negroponte, N. (1995). *Being Digital*. New York: Vintage Books.

Norman, D. A. (1998). *The Invisible Computer*. Cambridge (USA): MIT Press.

Pinkwart, N., Hoppe, H.U., Gaßner, K. (2001). Integration of domain-specific elements into visual language based collaborative environments. In Borges, M.R.S., Haake, J.M., & Hoppe, H.U. (eds.). Proceedings of *CRIWG 2001* (International Workshop on Groupware) (pp. 142–147). Los Alamitos (USA): IEEE Press.

Pinkwart, N., Hoppe, H.U., Milrad, M., Perez, J. (2003). Educational scenarios for cooperative use of Personal Digital Assistants. *Journal of Computer Assisted Learning* 19/2 (Special issue on "Wireless and mobile technologies in education"). 383–391.

Roschelle, J., & Pea, R. (2002). A walk on the WILD side: How wireless handhelds may change CSCL. In Stahl, G. (ed.). Proceedings of *CSCL 2002* (Conference on Computer Support for Collaborative Learning) (pp. 51–60). Boulder (USA), January 2002.

Streitz, N.A., Geißler, J., Holmer, T., Konomi, S., Müller-Tomfelde, C., Reischl, W., Rexroth, P., Seitz, P., Steinmetz, R. (1999). i-LAND: An interactive landscape for creativitiy and innovation. In Proceedings of *CHI '99* (ACM Conference on Computer-Human Interaction) (pp. 120–127). New York: ACM Press.

Tewissen, F., Lingnau, A., Hoppe, H.U. (2000). "Today's alking Typewriter" – Supporting early literacy in a classroom environment. In Gauthier, G., Frasson, C., VanLehn, K. (eds.). *Intelligent Tutoring Systems* (Proceedings of ITS 2000) (pp. 252–261). Berlin: Springer.

Vogel, M. (2001). *Medien der Vernunft – Eine Theorie des Geistes und der Rationalität auf der Grundlage einer Theorie der Medien*. (Media of Reason – A Theory of Mind and Rationality based on a Theory of Media.) Frankfurt a. M. (Germany): Suhrkamp.

Weiser, M., & Brown, J.S. (1997). The coming age of calm technology. In Denning, P.J. & Metcalfe, R.M. (eds.). *Beyond Calculation – The Next Fifty Years of Computing* (pp. 75–85). New York (USA): Copernicus (Springer).

Supporting Collaboration with Augmented Environments

Design and Dissemination Issues

Saadi Lahlou

Design of augmented furniture should address interaction with and between people, as devices that simply satisfy technical requirements are not enough. Often, good practice does not emerge spontaneously, especially during activities which require some extra individual effort to bring collective benefits and the artefacts themselves should then be the catalysts for good practice.

Our design approach is to provide affordances which support collaborative activity and foster good practices in individual and collaborative work, by making good practice *easier* than poor practice. Our design process is based on observing actual interaction in the workplace, and gradually develops, with users, new solutions to problems encountered in actual use.

Our studies of real work meetings show that participants often lose awareness of common goals, are easily sidetracked by technical failures, need many common large display surfaces (whiteboards etc.), prefer seeing distant participants than simply hearing them, and that many meeting outcomes may be lost when, as is often the case, no proper recording of decisions is done.

We describe here how we implemented affordances for augmented collaboration in meeting rooms. This includes shared interactive boards, video-conferencing systems (embedded in walls or on mobile trolleys). We are not using "augmented furniture" per se. Rather, we integrate off-the-shelf components to make the meeting room as a whole an augmented system, enabling interaction with the information infrastructure and distant locations. This integration will be described in some detail.

We also provide details about our practice of interaction design and techniques for dissemination of augmented environments inside large corporations.

Keywords augmented environments, videoconferencing, affordances, cognitive attractors, activity theory, meetings, dissemination, observation techniques, subcam, offsat

P. Dillenbourg et al. (eds.), *Interactive Artifacts and Furniture Supporting Collaborative Work and Learning*,
DOI: 10.1007/978-0-387-77234-9_5, © Springer Science+Business Media, LLC 2009

1   Introduction

Augmented Environments (AE) where embedded Information and Communication Technologies (ICT) enhance classic objects and furniture may provide support for complex activities by responding to users according to their needs, and displaying relevant affordances (Gibson 1967, 1982) for action. Ideally, the environment should play the role of an intelligent and cooperative partner, offering proper resources in a timely manner. But AE design is still in its infancy. Current AE does not yet provide comfortable user experiences. Designing AE means designing both at a technical level and at the level of practice, which, in many cases, is social practice such as meetings. This co-evolutionary design process (or co-adaptation: MacKay 2000) has yet to be mastered; it is a chicken-and-egg problem. One of the issues is reaching a usability threshold for technical devices, in order to start working with users on the aspects of the interaction design.

While AE are still in the preliminary stages of development, rooms supporting meetings at a distance are one of the few areas where there is now a good deal of experience.

In this chapter, we present a design method for augmented office environments that we developed in the usability lab of a large non-IT industry (Electricité de France). Our objective was to enhance individual comfort and global efficiency of office workers (over 60,000 in France). We take into account that users are focussed on their job and use, as a whole, a variety of multi-vendor equipment. This is why we based the research technique on *human activity* analysis, rather than on human-computer interaction with specific devices. Of special interest to us were the acceptance and diffusion phases since dissemination, operation, maintenance and evolution are internal costs for us on the organisation side, while they remain externalities for most system designers (Lahlou 2007). There is a trade-off between the cost of interface design and the learning costs on the user side.

We consider here the whole meeting room in its physical, digital, and organisational dimensions as an Augmented Environment. Our approach is to assemble Commercial Off The Shelf (COTS) components as much as possible, and to add specific devices or code only when absolutely necessary. Therefore, this chapter does not describe a specific new artefact with embedded technology, but rather a setting which empowers a meeting room to afford new functions such as easy connection to remote sites, construction and access to group memory and goals, and interaction formats that can be customised according to specific activity needs. For example, the displays are large screens embedded in the walls, but to interact with them, we provide long range wireless mouse and keyboards which can be used at the meeting tables, and remote controls for embedded lighting, blinds and video-conferencing equipment. Supporting fluid interaction is a matter of offering new functionalities, but also of solving many "small" issues to make the global system user-friendly.

Up to now, standard meeting rooms have barely solved such trivial aspects as where to plug in the speaker's technical devices, displaying the presentation on some adapted media shared by all participants, enabling attention and response with good multimodal quality (e.g. quickly showing electronic material brought from the audience), creating and storing minutes, or simply providing the proper arrangement of tables for videoconferencing; not to mention the fact that tables should be set up differently in a creative or a decision-making meeting (Abric 1999). In many cases, standard meeting rooms hardly even support local meetings in a decent way.[1] This may appear surprising, as meetings are an important aspect of work, and distant meetings are getting more frequent. As distant meetings still often produce poor user-experience, practice – and hence good practice – is increasing slowly.

The technical state of the art in ICT is sufficient to offer almost any kind of service to users: from simple document management to automatic customisation of the work environment according to user's preferences and present state or goals. But, in fact, we are far from providing such services in a fluid and relevant way. There is a big gap between what could be done and what is actually made. The bottleneck is not technical; it is at the user-experience level. Even when a room is "technically" able to provide the required services, operating it often requires a technician "wizard" because the *users do not know how to use it*. Of course, users could learn. But when would they? They don't even care to read the user manuals of software which they use everyday in a "satisficing" (Simon 1945) but non-optimal way; and this, even when users *are* convinced that learning proper procedures and shortcuts would spare them precious time. Now this is natural: the user's goal is not to learn the best way to use the system, but to perform an activity and reach her own goals. Learning how to use the system is, therefore, a waste of time in the user's perspective.

But the quality of interaction is the product of both the technical system and user participation. What part the users are ready to play in this interaction must be negotiated with them. The design challenge is then to find a design path to co-produce new environments with users.

Section 2 presents some preliminary findings, which led us to our present approach. Section 3 provides a general framework which highlights the various points of the system on which the interaction designer should focus. It quickly presents the cognitive attractors model. Section 4 describes how we design augmented meeting rooms for videoconferencing, and the present state of our system. Section 5 is about the technique we use to disseminate socio-technical practices within the company.

---

[1] Our experience also shows that non-IT characteristics of the room are crucial, namely, flexibility, accessibility, lighting, acoustics. A good augmented meeting room is before anything else a good meeting room *per se*. This obvious fact is often forgotten and too many meeting rooms are located in blind spaces e.g. in basements.

2   Don't Try to Change the People, Simply Change the Affordances

How can we practice participative design for real users, who care for their own businesses but not about our systems? Users are under such pressure that they will discard new systems if they fail to *satisfice* at first use. They tend to revert to their old routines, which may be inefficient but are indeed reliable. How can we design artefacts that will produce good emergent practice at the *collective* level?

These issues are well known by designers. A now common practice is to progress by trial and error, through testing successive versions with users, starting with a prototype based on some functional analysis. Most of the time, there are only a few design loops – except in a few sectors like aerospace or nuclear industry, where safety comes before cost. The actual criterion for the final state of the product may, in the end, be the amount of excess tolerated in project delay or budget, rather than optimal user experience. User costs are an externality[2] for the designer, but project costs are not. Another issue is that artefacts must reach a minimum of usability before being given to the user for testing and starting the participative design process. This means that the systems have already undergone extensive development by designers, and are thus often difficult to change because of money, time, and emotions invested. Techniques like the Wizard of Oz (Salber and Coutaz 1993), virtual reality and video mock-ups address this issue, but only up to a certain point. Discussing possible uses with future users is often not enough to forecast emerging social effects.

In the socio-technical domain, the devil is often in the details. The non-technical part of the design is usually the one which causes problems. Nevertheless, these techniques for quick prototyping and user participation are a huge improvement over classic engineering methods and we use them to develop AE.

2.1   New Affordances Modify Behaviour

It was in the course of collaborative design for office environments that we accidentally discovered a new design strategy.

A few years ago, we were testing some artefacts for document management in offices equipped with new "double-deck" desks (Figs. 1 and 2).

We observed the long term (over months) evolution of paper stacks and piles arrangement on volunteer's table desktops with time-lapse cameras attached to the ceiling of their office ("offsats": Lahlou 1998).

The camera stayed fixed in the same position for 1 month before changing (baseline) and 8 months after, enabling us to monitor changes in behaviour by

---

[2] An externality is an effect from one activity which has consequences for another activity but is not reflected in market prices. Externalities can be either positive, when an external benefit is generated, or negative, when an external cost is generated from a market transaction. An externality occurs when a decision causes costs or benefits to stakeholders other than the person making the decision. (Wikipedia).

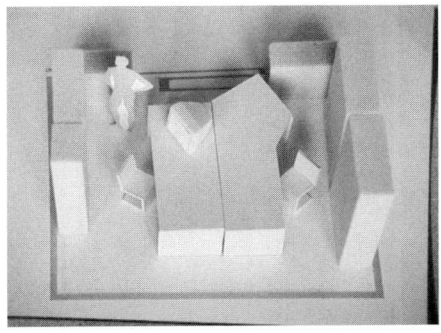

Fig. 1 and 2 Settings in the same office before and after a change of furniture

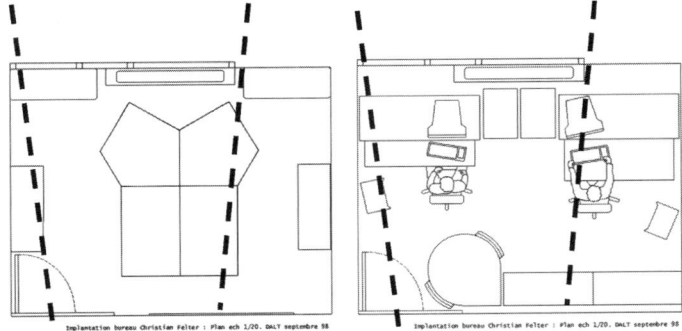

Fig. 3 and 4 Same office plans before/after. Filmed zone is between dotted lines

office users. Figures 3 and 4 show the limits of the field monitored by the offsat, which provided views such as those shown in Figs. 5 and 6. Successive images were automatically compared with software which produced maps of the office. In these maps, zones where movements take place appear as in grey (see Figs. 7 and 8). Users were satisfied with the artefact tested, a "rangepile", which enables vertical storage of piles of paper in order to recover activity space on the desktops. As a side effect of changing the furniture in offices, we discovered not only did the pattern of piles, change in the offices, but so did human activity. The new desks (which had a smaller footprint) combined with the LCD display had produced a dramatic change.

Figures 5 and 6 are pictures taken from the same office, monitored by offsat from November 1998 to May 1999. Two people, C1 and C2, occupy the office. The picture in Fig. 5 shows the office "before" the transformation, which took place in December 1999, and the picture in Fig. 6 shows the office "after" the transformation. The offsat, situated above C1, covers about 80% of the office, and stayed fixed during the entire experiment. C1 can be well seen in Fig. 5.

Figures 7 and 8 are obtained by automated analysis of movements (pixel comparison of successive pictures from the offsat). Areas where activity takes place are

Fig. 5 and 6 Settings in the same office before and after a change, as seen with the offsat

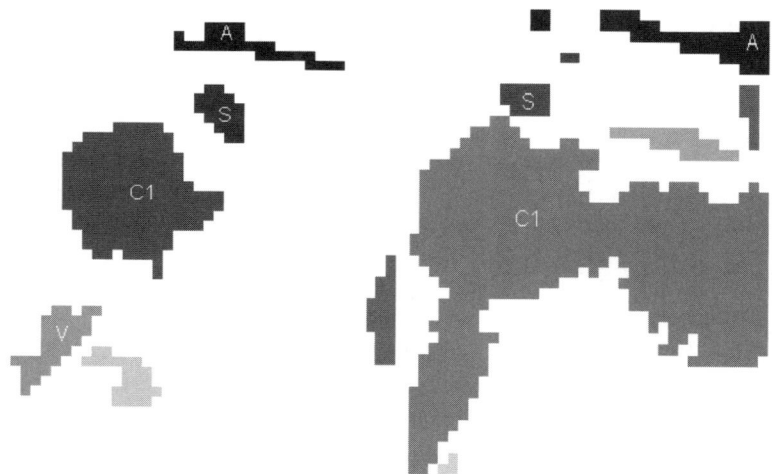

Fig. 7 and 8 Movement zones in the same office before and after change

plotted in grey. Figure 7 results from the analysis of 27,000 pictures (3 weeks of real time) in November 1998 (old environment). Figure 8 results from the analysis of a series of 27,000 pictures in February 1999 (new environment). These figures can be superimposed on Figs. 5 and 6. For example, area S corresponds to the computer screen (that is a movement area). The "before/after" comparison shows a change in the shape of the areas of activity.

Observation of the speeded up films shows that the increase of activity zone around C1 position corresponds to collaborative sessions of two or three individuals, facing the screen, while work in previous period was more solitary. Zone C1 (which in the "before" situation was so static, one could even see the limits of the mouse pad on the right) changes and fuses with zone V (visitors). Visitors now do not simply stand on the door-step as they used to do in baseline setting, but sit in for discussion in front of screen. Pictures in Figs. 5 and 6 are typical of the situations observed. Zone A is an artefact (curtains moving in front of window).

So users, who used to work alone in the baseline setting, started to have frequent collaborative sessions with colleagues from neighbouring offices after the change of furniture. During a presentation of these results, the managers of this group expressed surprise: they had tried for years to obtain this result (collaboration) but never succeeded. Interestingly, this behaviour had occurred spontaneously after our office refurbishing, simply because the new setting offered good affordances for collaboration: a large enough space for two or three seats facing a good display. This affordance was not planned by us, but it produced effects anyway. The new behaviour, documented 2 months after the installation of the new setting, remained stable.

2.2   Addressing the Activity by Adapting the Context

This result is rather trivial: put a bench in the street and suddenly people will start to sit there. The fact that changing instruments will change practices and vice-versa has been known and documented for a long time (Bödker 1996, Engeström 1990, 1993, Engeström and Middleton 1996).

The fact that merely providing new affordances could spontaneously produce new behaviours, in a smoother and more effective manner than managerial pressure, was an insight for us. This strategy became the basis for our building of social change: "don't try to change people, simply change the context". This strategy has some advantages: context is persistent, and can "talk" to the users any time they will use it, which a teacher cannot. Also, there are fewer power and social issues in interacting with context; therefore it provokes less resistance among users.

But some questions remain: how should we specify the affordances? How can we make users prefer the context that we provide them with, and make them interpret it in the "right" way? How can we construct and disseminate the non-physical guidelines for the activity? The following section provides a framework with which to tackle these issues.

3   Guiding Micro-Decisions Along the Activity Path: Cognitive Attractors

3.1   A Pinball Model of the Office Worker

We collected several hundred hours of the natural activity of (volunteer) office workers, using a "subjective" miniature video camera fixed at eye-level worn by the workers ("subcam": Lahlou 1998, 2006). This first-person set of data shows that users, unlike what is predicted by classic psychological theories, often *do not do what they intended*, even when they could have. Days of office workers rather look like the path of a ball in a pinball machine. Subjects continuously get sidetracked into unplanned activities. They are captured by interrupting colleagues (telephone...), by the context (fixing the copier...), by activities planned by others (meetings ...), or by themselves through sidetracking routines (answering email, storing documents, clearing "small" or "urgent" tasks off their desk). Any disruption in a planned task (e.g. not finding immediately the right contact address for someone) may result in opening a new activity path. In the course of this new path, the original activity track may be lost.

As a result, people often do not manage to do what they had planned for themselves in their day. In one of our unpublished surveys (on 501 office workers: Lahlou & Fischler, 1999), 62% of subjects declared that they partially or totally agree with the item "I lose an incredible time attending to details", 61% with "I am continually interrupted in my work", 62% with "I cannot manage to do what I had planned for the day", and 50% with "I sometimes come home exhausted but wondering what I've spent my day doing".

This sidetracking to complete micro-decisions along an activity path happens in a somewhat automatic way. It may also occur against the subject's own will.

3.2 Cognitive Attractors

At an individual level, cognitive attractor theory (Lahlou 2000) describes how subjects are led into a specific activity path by a combination of patterns in the context ("data") and the corresponding subject's embodied knowledge and skills ("lata"[3]) which, in conjunction with each other, produce an automatic interpretation of the context, e.g. I see a colleague and engage into salutation; I receive an e-mail and I open it.

Interpretation should be understood here both in the sense of understanding (meaning), and of playing (like a musician would interpret a piece). Cognitive attractor theory predicts that if a critical mass of data and connected lata are present, the drive for the corresponding *activity* spontaneously emerges.

What is amazing is that the process of interpretation emerges beyond the subject's will: "it just happens", just like gestalt *imposes* a pattern on perception when a sufficient portion of the pattern is present (Fig. 9). Once seen, this pattern cannot be ignored.

Attractors are a different notion from stimuli. For example, they may need to be disambiguated, they do not exist independently of the observer's frame of mind, they may be ignored and have no systematic impact on the subject's behaviour. Any given setting may contain many different attractors for the subject. The issue is *which* attractor will be seized by the subject. It is a matter of competition between attractors.

A classic example is the coffee discussion. A couple of colleagues chatting next to the coffee-machine are an attractor for a "coffee discussion". Such an attractor is so strong that some colleague who comes by during a pause in his activity (say, report

---

[3]In Latin, "data" means "what is given", and "lata", "what one carries along".

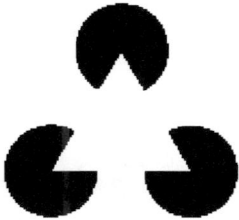

Fig. 9 This set of elements is "naturally" interpreted as a single triangular pattern

writing), with the sole intention of taking a coffee and going back to his office, has few chances to escape it and will probably stay and chat for a few minutes, although a debrief will show that this was *not* his intention in the first place. This subject escaped from his initial intent (here: writing a report) and got "caught" in the coffee discussion.

These behaviours are not systematic or compulsory, but obviously some situations *attract* us into performing a specific type of activity, which indeed produces some kind of benefits. Salutations, putting things into order, checking incoming information are of this kind. Social prompts are almost impossible to avoid answering; e.g. interruptions or jokes call for a response. A close-up look at users' video tapes suggests that a substantial part of our everyday activity is composed by following the paths of these stereotyped attractors.

This does not mean that subjects do not display original and creative behaviours, they do indeed. Most of the time, though, creation is a new assembly of existing routine segments, just as a new text can be composed by assembling pre-existing words, expressions or sentences.

3.3   Data in the Environment and Lata in the Mind

Attractors are a combination of data (located in the environment) and lata (located in the observer). The combination of both may form patterns which trigger activity. Therefore, presence of the relevant data in the environment will change the probability of occurrence of a given activity. By affording a specific activity path, they will foster it over another possible activity. By evoking the associated lata, they may induce motivation for an activity. Space is too scarce here for a full description of the cognitive attractor theory and its psychological basis, which are described in more detail in Lahlou (2000, 2007). Let us simply note that subjects are continuously confronted with a large numbers of attractors in their context. An attractor acts like a script which "feeds forward" the action.

The system of determination of behaviour can, therefore, be sketched as follows (Fig. 10). Configurations of data in the context, and lata in the mind, may evoke an attractor. This attractor will feed forward the subject on the associated activity path, where the subject will perform behaviours coupled with the environment.

As long as the activity is fluid, with continuous coupling with the environment and adequate system response, chances are that the subject will continue on the

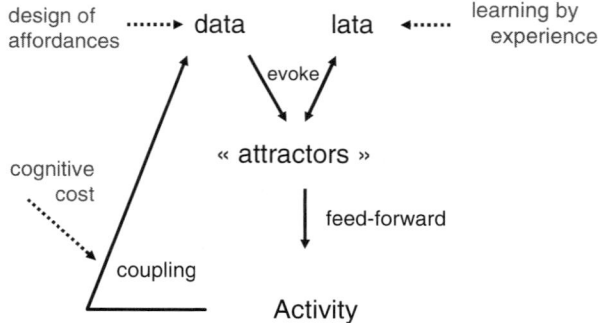

Fig. 10 A simplified model of attractor and their design entries

same path. But if some obstacle or failure occurs, there may be a reconsideration of "what to do" and some locally stronger attractor may take over. For example, in the course of some activity, Robert needs to send an e-mail to someone. He opens his mailbox to do so and sees a newly arrived message from his big boss. There is a high probability that he will open the message, and get sidetracked.

3.4 Tuning Attractors

Cognitive attractor theory focuses on situational patterns which trigger specific user behaviour. The strength of attractors is a combination of three factors, two are positive: "pregnance" (attraction of attention), value (attraction of desire); and one is negative: cost to be completed (attraction of effort). For example: a strong noise or a blinking light, will attract attention in an almost inescapable way; an activity intended to reach a very desired goal or to avoid a very undesired state will call for strong priority; a quick and easy action (e.g. reading a short e-mail) may take precedence over more "important" but longer or more difficult actions.

Of course, a routine practice in a well known environment will have a low cost and hence a stronger attraction force. At some stage, it becomes automatic in a given situation, and is executed beyond consciousness. In this process, conscious "actions" become what Russian activity theory calls "operations" (Rubinstein 1940, Leontiev 1978, Nosulenko & Rabardel 2007).

As designers (see Fig.10), we can address these factors by acting upon the environment ("data") when we provide affordances or pregnance. We can also address the embodied skills and representations with which the subject interprets the environment (lata) by creating or disseminating new interpretations of the situation or raising motivation (e.g. by training people so some actions become easier to perform; by changing values etc.). We can finally address the level of *coupling* the subject with the system, by changing the costs of accessing a specific resource or engaging in a specific action in a given situation (e.g. helping synchronisation of available resources, or creating password or cost barriers). In doing so, the designer may confront the user with situations in which one branch among all possible activity paths appears more natural and easy, therefore fostering good practice.

Basically, our approach is not to design artefacts or devices, but to understand activity and functions, and then embed, in the environment, a set of affordances to keep the subjects on "best practices" paths. From this perspective, the environment is considered as a whole, and the strength of attraction comes simultaneously from several factors (e.g. technical artefacts plus technical skills plus social rules).

Ideally, the best-practice-activity path should be designed in such a way that, at every step, it has a lower cognitive cost than other paths, as subjects naturally follow the easiest slope. This includes the first adoption phase. Of course, we hardly ever succeed completely. But if a good practice activity path is kept at low cognitive cost, e.g. by erasing the high cost steps, spreading good practice is easier and social control may become a strong enough safeguard to keep the good practice dominant. Specific to our approach is doing this at social level, and considering environments as a whole. As already mentioned, this is a chicken and egg problem.

4 Experimental Reality Design of Augmented Meeting-Rooms

Adopting such an approach means working in co-operation with subjects, and requires substantial amount of testing. We provide subjects with a new version of their environment and observe where they encounter difficulties. We solve these with new design, and then retest. This is good way to get motivated user feed-back. Subjects in real conditions are merciless with the system, which puts a positive pressure on designers. On the other hand, in such conditions, subjects become more creative in their efforts to transcend the system's shortcomings. They thereby provide interesting suggestions to designers, and also sometimes enthusiastic feed-back when the system is efficient; both of which help designers cope with frustration and pressure, and push the system forward.

Another reason why we chose to work with real subjects is: we believe that end-users should have some control over the design of the systems they use everyday.

4.1 Experimental Reality

The "experimental reality" procedure, by which we enrol both users and designers in a continuously monitored designed process, has been described elsewhere (Lahlou et al. 2002). The general idea is to obtain the enrolment of a population of subjects in a long term protocol where they test successive versions of the system being developed, in the course of their normal activity, under intensive observation. As this is demanding for users, designers must ensure the contract with users is fair, and that they get actual benefits from their participation.

In practice, we managed to have a real "advanced" work environment installed under continuous observation. The system is a prototype for testing, but is kept operational from the user's perspective. This meant a considerable back-office installation with technicians and developers to keep it running, in a transparent manner for the users. Experimental reality needs a special project structure where engineers, designers, social scientists, and ergonomists work together in the same team to solve design issues on the fly as they emerge in actual use.

For augmented meeting rooms, we provided a comfortable meeting room (Figs. 11 and 12) which could be reserved for free, in an industrial facility housing more than 2,000 office workers (engineers, scientists, administrative personnel). This meeting room had much better video-conferencing equipment than the other meeting rooms, and large interactive screens.

The room is freely accessible, but there is one condition: users are allowed to use it only if they accept that their meetings be recorded for analysis. They know the analysis is used to design better rooms, and are asked to sign an "informed" consent form. We use this room to test successive versions of attractors.

Proper room settings vary with meeting type and number of participants. The design of our rooms aims at lowering the cost of installing the right setting for any given meeting. Tables are foldable and on wheels, and chairs are stackable. After use, the conference room is "reinitialised" (Fig. 11) by folding and stacking up the furniture. This is easy and actually takes less than 3 min. So, when participants come into the room, they are naturally guided into setting up the furniture according to number of people and the kind of meeting they are having (creativity, presentation, decision, problem-solving, locally or in videoconference...). Furniture disposition templates are provided to inspire users. In one of our spaces, some templates are drawn with red tape on the floor.

Figures 13 and 14 shows how the room changed over time as we took into account user experience. Note how the interactive screen became larger for better display of multiplex videoconferencing.

Fig. 11 and 12 The RAO augmented meeting-room at EDF R&D Clamart facility, in the Laboratory of Design for Cognition

Fig. 13 and 14 Evolutions of the RAO room in 2000 (left) and 2002 (right). Screen size has almost doubled

For document sharing, we connect this room with a media-space accessible from anywhere on the internet, "Gridboard" (Lahlou, 2007b). Turning on the screens, videoconferencing, connecting a local PC to the large displays, opening a shared screen with distant sites etc. can be set up simply by putting an RFID tag with the proper label on a board. This ensures that users will not mess up with the system controls, and that the system is very simple to use. To call another site in videoconferencing they simply have to choose the tag with the name of this site and lay it on the board, and the system does all the operations in less than 3 s.

It is better to have some follow-up with the groups, so they can see the impact of their design suggestions and become more motivated. We recorded 120 weekly meetings of a same project group, including over 100 in this experimental room (Figs.13 and 14). To apply this kind of follow-up strategy, it is easier to involve an insider of the group in the experimental set-up, this helps in clearing up privacy issues.

Heterogeneity of participants is a constant problem in collaboration systems. This heterogeneity will remain, because each participant is caught in the rhythm and specifications of her own organisation, e.g. for version updates or security policy. It would be naïve to design a system without taking into account this constraint of inter-operability and coordination with the "out there" systems of potential users.

This is one of the reasons of our strategy of integrating COTS components instead of designing in-house specific code and artefacts. Collaboration systems should therefore be tested with participants from different backgrounds. In our case we used our meeting support system in the monthly meetings of the RUFAE group, which federates a dozen of the leading laboratories running AE worldwide (www. rufae.net). Over 20 international meetings of this group have been monitored for analysis. These analyses led us to modify the tools in order to inter-operate with a wide range of different installations (e.g. behind various firewalls, with PC and Macintosh, different languages etc.). For example, even when most participants use a Microsoft Windows office suite, the versions and the language are different so users may get lost in the menus or be unable to read the pop-ups. And of course, versions change all the time. For the sake of inter-cultural usability, we had to level down the functionality of the system. Participants have different levels of technical proficiency and capacity to customise their systems (not everyone has administrator status on their systems). To cope with this constraint, the system must be able to self-configurate in a transparent manner, according to the local resources of each participant.

4.2 Design Strategy

We monitor actual use of the room during meetings and focus on defects or side-tracks in the activity path.

For example, observation of meetings reveals numerous "cognitive loops" where participants get sidetracked. During one meeting (recorded in a classic meeting room), as participants are following the agenda and discuss a sub-entry of an agenda items (preparing a congress/selecting workshop topics), the speaker apologises because his (vinyl) slides are badly printed. He says he had a problem with the colour printer. As another participant declares he has the same problem, a discussion takes place (during 8 min) where participants propose various hypotheses to solve the issue. Then, as they lost track of what they were doing, they return to the agenda, but at root level (congress general goals) instead of resuming at correct sub-entry level (workshops). After they talked for 2 min, one of the participants (the chair) gets an urgent phone call on her mobile, but stays in the room (it's a long conference table, she is stuck on the end far from room door). For 1 min, all participants stop discussing, while she talks. Then they resume, this time at the correct agenda sub-entry (workshop).

To fight these frequent sidetrack loops, we enhance the pregnance of the meeting agenda, by displaying it continuously on a large screen. This displayed agenda plays the role of a major attractor. Its large size and position attract attention and re-capture participants when they are distracted. As this display is synchronously shared by all (local and remote) participants, it helps in focussing everybody on the same object of attention. The agenda is directly annotated by the meeting secretary with the comments and decisions; it gradually becomes the meeting minutes. This helps both the animator keeping meeting on track at low cost, and ensuring the meeting minutes are indeed taken and approved "live" by participants by the end of the meeting. Our observations show that writing the meeting minutes afterwards causes delay, misinterpretation, and dissatisfaction among other participants. It also provokes re-discussion of the issues in the next meeting, especially if there are new participants.

This shows how, when providing new possibilities, we manage to lower the cognitive cost of "good" alternatives, and physically embed good practices in the environment. Experience shows that when large displays are available, participants tend to use them. Shared displays reduce misunderstandings, and trigger creation of common representations.

This large display is shared live on the media-space by distant participants, who can see it on their PC screen at native resolution (e.g. 1,280 × 1,024, which is better than current videoconference screen resolution). This enables them to see the presentations live, read the texts, and also, as they can follow the progression on the agenda without entering the meeting, to connect in audio or video and participate for one item only. Too often, meetings are delayed because the presence of a specific high ranking participant is needed for one agenda item. These executive participants usually have packed agendas, where it is difficult to fit in a meeting with some travel. We tested with the delay to obtain a time slot for a 30 min meeting on site vs. on a distant site with 1 h travel with actual agendas of managers. The mean difference in delay was from 1 week to almost 2 weeks.

Providing the affordance for distant participation limited to a single item of the agenda, in good conditions (this also means the capacity to get some discreet comments from one's colleague before entering the meeting) enables the meeting to take place sooner. As a consequence, the problem discussed may be easier to solve, especially if there are deadlines. Another condition is that distant participants have easy access to a proper setting for participation and that bandwidth, connection, security and OS issues are solved. All these issues are gradually addressed, detail by detail, as users report problems or discomfort, until the interaction is "sufficiently" calm and fluid.

It is a never-ending process, but after a while the system is stabilised enough to be considered a deployable version. We usually maintain a "current" (deployed) version and an "advanced" version under progressive design with a sub-set of "friendly users". This proves useful, since technology continuously changes. Having a "mother room" where new technology is continuously evaluated enables keeping all rooms in the company up to date.

4.3   Zeroing Adoption Costs

For meetings, one cannot expect to train all participants beforehand. We must then check that there is no initial cost barrier in the learning curve for novice users, and adapt the system accordingly. The system must have the following specifications on the client side: *zero training necessary, zero installation procedure, zero impact on client devices configuration, zero cost, zero maintenance, high security*. Unless these requirements are met, when a new participant tries to connect on the fly in a meeting, something will usually get in the way. These requirements may seem high, and were impossible to reach a few years ago, but the situation now is much better because of the dissemination of internet access, standard protocols (especially web-services) and user abilities.

A good cognitive design will rely on what users already know, provide obvious affordances, and systems which respond accordingly to implicit expectations. This is easier to do when subjects already share a common socket of competences. All the designer has to do then is to program interaction using these implicit skills.

Let us illustrate this with the case of our live shared desktop for distant collaboration ("Gridboard"). From the user's side, it has the attractor of "being together in front of the same machine and sharing the mouse and the keyboard with the usual interface". Instead of being physically in front of the machine, participants all see it live on their local own screen, and are in audio contact by audio conference or videoconference.

Technically, we provide the user a URL where the user, with his browser, opens a window which *is* that shared screen, and *is* a Microsoft Windows desktop. The screen behaves exactly as users expect, because *it is actually* a (virtual machine) Microsoft Windows desktop, containing the standard Microsoft Office suite, and other classic software (Lotus Notes, SAP, etc.) used in the company (Figs. 15 and 16). All users simultaneously access the same machine, they share the mouse and keyboard (using their own, and resolving conflicts by voice channel, phone conference or videoconference: "Don't use the mouse, I'm writing!").

This interface is "simple" because every user *already* knows how to use such a desktop (Macintosh users can also share it, but it is still a Windows interface for them). Experience shows that incoming first-time users use the system fluently within seconds, simply because this is in fact not a "new" environment to them.

As usual, simplicity on the user's side is paid for by some complexity at programming level. It took us about 2 years to strip down the initial interfaces we had made until we reached something really simple. The file exchange issues and the access rights managements were not trivial, and there user feedback was precious.

Figure 16 shows actual use of the media-space. On this screenshot, three colleagues (F. Jegou and J. Liberman in Brussels, T. Winograd in Stanford) discuss a document (presentation of the European Privacy Design Guidelines for Disappearing Computers). The screenshot is taken from Jegou's PC in Brussels. The videoconference image is in the upper left window; the document is a Microsoft PowerPoint slide displayed "full screen" by Jegou on the media-space (larger window), which all participants can see and modify on the fly. Using this media-space enabled discussing these Guidelines (Lahlou and Jegou 2003, Lahlou 2008) in-depth with a group of experts worldwide, quickly and at a low cost. This kind of positive experience is an incentive for users to advertise the system to their colleagues.

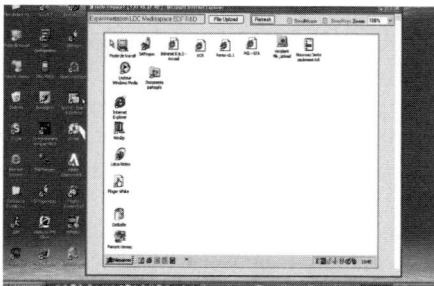 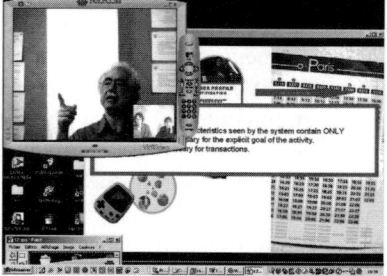

Fig. 15 and 16 The Gridboard media-space in 2003. Screenshot at opening (left) and in use (right)

As the screenshot shows, there are still screen real-estate issues if the system is used with only one screen. The ComBoxes and portable media-spaces systems which we now deploy inside the company always use twin screens, one for presentation and minutes, and the other for videoconferencing.

5 Disseminating Practice: Trickle Down and Social Anchoring

Working with real users is necessary because emergent effects are not always foreseeable, and also because social effects sometimes do not appear right away. In one of our previous attempts to design virtual meeting rooms, we came up with a very efficient system called KCR for meeting participation and management. KCR was accessible with any browser, provided shared video of the meeting room, data on presence, on-the-fly shared meeting minutes; all in one single window. Planning a meeting with the planning system interfaced with the rooms planning and the company LDAP enables, in less than a minute, in a few clicks, to check room availability on three sites, plan meetings, insert agenda and upload meeting documents, and automatically e-mail the participants a link to the meeting.

We were proud of this system, which was quickly adopted and praised by project managers. But it encountered strong resistance from some groups distributed over three sites who held monthly meetings, although they had been among the most insistent to get the product. These users said the system was not useable because of bad ergonomics, which obviously was not the case for other groups.

Closer examination of meeting video recordings showed that, in the course of our design, we had forgotten to take into account several findings, even though we had documented them in the beginning. Our system was focussed on optimizing the processing of the meeting agenda, tracing decisions, minimizing sidetrack loops. But clearing the agenda is only one of the goals of participants. People come to meetings for other reasons too, such as the obligation to represent one's unit, showing one is intelligent and push one's career, making sure no decisions are taken that could have unpleasant consequences for one's unit, touching base with distant colleagues, solving issues informally with other participants during pauses or after meeting, etc. Let us call these "informal goals".

As a matter of fact, unpublished surveys from our lab on the same population, by Nosulenko and Samoylenko, showed that when arriving at a meeting, and although they all had received the agenda, 30% of participants did not know the agenda at all, only 11% could list all points of agenda, and 6% listed points which were not in the agenda. 31% arrived at the meeting without clear goals, 51% had goals that matched meeting agenda items, and (this is the most interesting point) 18% declared goals which did not match agenda items.

In every group, as described by Russian activity theory, there is some discrepancy between individual goals and common goals. Our KCR system had forgotten to account for informal and individual goals. As a result, we had to change the system, and come up with a "meeting boarding" procedure which afforded informal contacts by putting more emphasis on systems which enabled informal distant contact with light, individual, videoconferencing, and developing specific distant social meetings at ritual times in the coffee areas ("i-coffe").

Cognitive attractors are constructed through habit, and inserted in a complex fabric of socio-social practice. For example, in road traffic control there are roads, but also traffic lights, signals, rules. Mediating structures (Hutchins 1995) transfer representations and enable users to behave accordingly (e.g. speedometers enable drivers to compare their pace with speed limits). We do not address isolated users, but populations. Many behaviours (in our case: meetings) cannot be performed alone, and need to rely on a cooperative behaviour. This is why users will change only if "others" change also. Successful dissemination means also that there are shared social rules, and that users can expect other users to know the rules. Therefore we must ensure that these social representations (Moscovici 1961) (shared knowledge of what is the object, including its social user manual) get disseminated.

5.1 Social Anchoring

One technique we use for dissemination is based on individuals, the "trickle down" theory (Veblen 1899). We enrol high status workers, typically directors of large units, as test subjects. When they appreciate a device, they spontaneously use it in public occasions; this fosters social demand, and gives the new system a positive aura. This is a way of adding "social strength" to the attractors we design.

Another technique we use is "social anchoring". Observation of adoption (Leppämaki and Lahlou 2004) showed that under some conditions, subjects may durably adopt a technological solution proposed by one legitimate member of the group. When what we have designed is considered ready for diffusion, we spot situations where our solution would provide immediate benefit to a group of motivated users. This is quite easy for distant meeting solutions or mobility solutions in general. Then, we manage to train one of the group members to use the solution. We offer these users the possibility to use our solution in one of the spotted situations. In such an occasion, the trained group member will naturally propose testing the solution. As this solution is proposed by an in-group member, there is little resistance. If the solution indeed provides benefits, most members of the group are converted, and, after a few more uses, become themselves "trained users" who will disseminate the practice in other groups. It is very important that the solutions are experienced by novice users in an in-group context. This way, they get exposure to the social practices that go with the system, and get more deeply involved in it. This type of group effect in adoption of novelty has been documented since the seminal works of Lewin (1952), and is still efficient today. Normative practice is an attractor, like a river bed collecting water. Once it is started, it will reinforce its attraction force. But the adoption phase is crucial, and this is why there should be as little learning cost as possible.

6   Conclusion: A Design Process Uneasy to Plan

Although this design approach based on cognitive attractors certainly does not solve all issues, it seemed, in the cases where we applied it, to shorten development time and produce positive results.

How far this approach can be generalised is still an empirical issue which we are presently exploring. One of the questions is whether the design team should necessarily be internal. Another is how far one should segment populations to create different social practices, since, as shown by Grudin (2004) the same software may be used in different ways e.g. by executives and managers.

Among the limitations of the approach, one should note that it requires support from multidisciplinary teams, including both technical developers and social scientists. Another is that this approach makes explicit the dissemination costs which are usually externalised by developers: few organisations are willing to explicitly pay these costs. Another difficulty is that, for a user company, this kind of design may be perceived as "not in the core business". This is not true, of course, since in many organisations most of the work is now done in offices, and global efficiency depends crucially upon the quality of the back-office procedures. Simply buying standard hardware and software is not enough; procedures and attractors should be designed to fit in the local culture and practice, which may differ widely between organisations. Still, in present corporate cultures, it is legitimate to invest efforts in optimizing the assembly chain production processes, but not the office production processes.

Another issue, noted by a reviewer, is that our "design for cognition" strategy does not leave much space for innovation: we decided to use Windows because everybody knows it, but this reinforces the present state of things.

Finally, a main difficulty is that emergent effects, and hence the whole design process, follow a timeline which is difficult to forecast precisely. So this approach of "continuous design" does not fit well in organisations where project management or workflows impose a strict schedule with fixed deliverables. Even if, in the end, this development process proves to be faster and to yield better results, the fact that the development path is not step-by-step predictable from the time of the project launch may prevent it from receiving funding, unless it is strongly supported by a visionary sponsor.

Still, one should also note that, although our first attempts (2000–2002) were supported partly on such a visionary basis, the return on investment since was evaluated positively enough to continue the process "because it works", and because it has produced a series of solutions now appreciated by users within the organisation.

References

Abric, J.-C. (1999). *Psychologie de la communication*. Paris: Armand Colin.

Bödker, S. (1996). Applying Activity Theory to Video Analysis: How to Make Sense of Video Data in Human-Computer Interaction. In: B. A. Nardi (ed.), *Context and Consciousness: Activity Theory and Human-Computer Interaction*. Cambridge: The MIT Press, pp. 147–174.

Engeström, Y. (1990). *Learning, Working and Imaging: Twelve Studies in Activity Theory*. Helsinki: Orienta-Konsultit.

Engeström, Y. (1993). *Interactive Expertise*. Helsinki: University of Helsinki.

Engeström, Y., Middleton, D. (eds.). (1996). *Cognition and Communication at Work*. Cambridge: Cambridge University Press.

Gibson, J. J. (1967). Notes on Affordances. In: E. Reed, R. Jones (eds.), *Reasons for Realism. Selected Essays of James J. Gibson*. London: Lawrence Erlbaum Associates, 1982, pp. 401–418.

Grudin, J. (2004). Managerial Use and Emerging Norms: Effects of Activity Patterns on Software Design and Deployment. *Proceedings of the 37th Hawaii International Conference on System Sciences – 2004*.

Hutchins, E. (1995). *Cognition in the Wild*. Cambridge, MA: MIT Press.

Lahlou, S. (1998). Observing Cognitive Work in Offices. In: N. Streitz, J. Siegel, V. Hartkopf, S. Konomi. (eds.), *Cooperative Buildings. Integrating Information, Organizations and Architecture*. Heidelberg: Springer, Lecture Notes in Computer Science, 1670, pp. 150–163.

Lahlou, S. (2000). Attracteurs cognitifs et travail de bureau. *Intellectica*, Vol 1, No 30, pp. 75–113.

Lahlou, S., Nosulenko, V., Samoylenko, E. (2002). Un cadre méthodologique pour le design des environnements augmentés. *Social Science Information*, Vol 41, No 4, pp. 471–530.

Lahlou, S. (2006). L'activité du point de vue de l'acteur et la question de l'inter-subjectivité: huit années d'expériences avec des caméras miniaturisées fixées au front des acteurs (subcam). *Communications*, Nov. 2006, No 80, pp. 209–234.

Lahlou, S. (2007). Human Activity Modeling for Systems Design: A Trans-disciplinary and Empirical Approach. In: D. Harris (ed.), *Engineering Psychology and Cognitive Ergonomics*, HCII 2007, Lectures Notes in Artificial Intelligence, 4562. Berlin- Heidelberg: Springer-Verlag, pp. 512–521.

Lahlou, S., Jegou, F. (2003). *European Disappearing Computer Privacy Design Guidelines V1 [EDC-PG 2003]*. Ambient Agoras IST-DC report D15.4. LDC, EDF., Oct. 2003. 8p. (www. rufae.net/privacy)

Lahlou, S. (2008) Identity, Social Status, Privacy and Face-Keeping in Digital Society. *Social Science Information*, vol. 47, n°3, pp. 227–252.

Leontiev, A. N. (1978). *Activity, Consciousness, and Personality*. Englewood Cliffs, NJ: Prentice-Hall.

Leppämaki, S., Lahlou, S. (2004). *Approaching New Technologies: Representation, Anchoring, Action and Influence*. 7th International Conference on Social Representations. Guadalajara, Mexico, 10–14 Sept. 2004. Clamart: EDF R&D,. p. 19.

Lewin, K. (1952). Group Decision and Social Change. In: G. E. Swanson, T. M. Newcomb, E. L. Hartley (eds.), *Readings in Social Psychology*, New York: Holt, 1952.

Mackay, W. (2000). "Responding to cognitive overload: Co-adaptation between users and technology". *Intellectica*, Vol 1, No 30, pp. 177–193.

Moscovici, S. (1961). *La psychanalyse son image et son public*. Paris: P.U.F., 1976.

Nosulenko, V., Rabardel, P. (eds.). (2007). *Rubinstein aujourd'hui. Nouvelles figures de l'activité humaine*. Toulouse – Paris: Octarès – Maison des Sciences de l'Homme.

Rubinstein, S. L. (1940). *Osnovy Obshchei Psikhologii* (Foundations of General Psychology). Uchpedgiz, Moscow, U.S.S.R., pp. 595.

Salber, D., Coutaz, J. (1993). A Wizard of Oz Platform for the Study of Multimodal Systems. *INTERCHI'93 Adjunct Proceedings*, Amsterdam, May 1993, pp. 95–96.

Simon, H. A. (1945). *Administrative Behavior*. N.Y. Free Press, 1976.

Veblen, T. (1899). *The Theory of the Leisure Class*. New York: Modern Library, 1934.

Rethinking the Podium

A Rich Media Control Station for Next Generation Conference Rooms

Maribeth Back, Surapong Lertsithichai, Patrick Chiu, John Boreczky, Jonathan Foote, Don Kimber, Qiong Liu, and Takashi Matsumoto

As the use of rich media in mobile devices and smart environments becomes more sophisticated, so must the design of the everyday objects used as controllers and interfaces. Many new interfaces simply tack electronic systems onto existing forms. However, an original *physical* design for a smart artefact, that integrates new systems as part of the form of the device, can enhance the end-use experience. The Convertible Podium is an experiment in the design of a smart artefact with complex integrated systems for the use of rich media in meeting rooms. It combines the highly designed look and feel of a modern lectern with systems that allow it to serve as a central control station for rich media manipulation. The interface emphasizes tangibility and ease of use in controlling multiple screens, multiple media sources (including mobile devices) and multiple distribution channels, and in managing both data and personal representation in remote telepresence.

Keywords Interactive furniture, smart podium, smart rooms, collaborative artifacts, teleconferencing

1 Introduction

Next generation meeting rooms are designed to anticipate the onslaught of new rich media presentation and ideation systems. Even today, high-end room systems feature a multiplicity of display screens, smart whiteboards, robotic cameras, and smart remote conferencing systems, all intended to support heterogeneous data and document types. Exploiting the capabilities of such a room, however, can be a daunting task. Faced with three or more screens, all but a few presenters opt for simply replicating the same image on all of them.

At the same time, creating engaging meeting experiences can improve communication, facilitate information exchange, and increase knowledge retention. The incorporation of media-rich engagement strategies in meetings creates a need to provide the presenter with appropriate tools for managing these media.

The Convertible Podium is a central control station for rich media manipulation. Designed as an experiment in intelligent meeting support and capture, it is a way

P. Dillenbourg et al. (eds.), *Interactive Artifacts and Furniture Supporting Collaborative Work and Learning*,
DOI: 10.1007/978-0-387-77234-9_6, © Springer Science + Business Media, LLC 2009

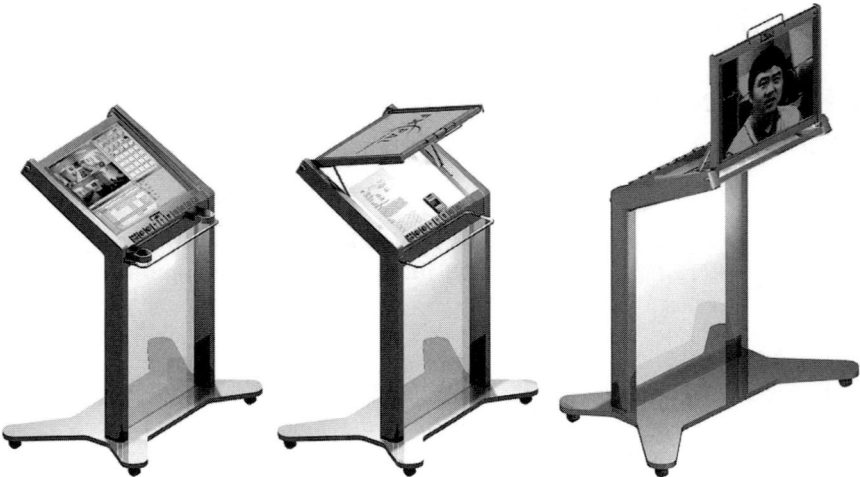

Fig. 1 Design sketch: a convertible podium converting from a media-screen podium (a), to a capturing device (b), to an upright mode that can be used for an avatar representation of a remote presenter, an interactive whiteboard, or an information board (c)

station for directing digital information, allowing presenters to integrate rich media experiences into a meeting. It is also an experiment in integrating physical design and form with rich media functionality (Fig. 1).

The Convertible Podium is a lightweight, mobile design that switches modalities and functionalities by converting its form. It converts from an interactive rich media presentation podium to other functions useful in a conference room environment, including image-capturing devices, an avatar representation for a remote presenter, an interactive whiteboard, and an information board. An important design imperative is that all devices are integrated into the frame structure of the podium. Some devices are assigned multiple functionalities, depending on what interaction mode is active. However, only one mode of interaction is possible at each physical conversion. Similar to multi-purpose furniture or "Roomware" (Streitz et al. 1998) the Convertible Podium combines its affordances as a regular podium with the capabilities of other presentation devices while maintaining its primary form and usefulness as a podium.

The Podium provides a focal point for the attention of the meeting and directs information in different directions —both locally and remotely. It allows one person to manage multiple documents and streams of information directed to or from the conference room, or to multiple displays within the room. The Podium also controls the physical room environment: lights, sound, and projector controls. One person can easily and rapidly convert the system between its active modes.

Interacting with the Convertible Podium can be done in three physical configurations (Fig. 1). In the interactive podium mode, a local presenter uses this podium to make presentations using multiple screens in a random-access fashion, using the familiar drag-and-drop technique to project anything, in any order, from a pool of slides or other media. Of course it is also possible to present media in the more familiar linear fashion, just as one presents PowerPoint slides on a single screen. Or, a presenter can switch between these modes, choosing random access to slides at times, and using pre-scripted linear segments at other times (Liu et al. 2004).

When the Podium's hood is lifted halfway, it goes into "Capture" mode, allowing the capture of documents and images via scanner and camera. A scanner which lies under the LCD monitor is exposed and is used via the "second screen": a small-form networked computer (OQO 2005). The presenter can also use the exposed document cameras for live demos or for showing off objects during a presentation.

In the third mode, "Avatar/Telepresence", the Podium's hood is fully upright. In this mode, it can be connected to a remote avatar for teleconferencing, or converted to an interactive whiteboard or an information board for supporting different presentation activities in the room. As an avatar appearing on the upright LCD screen, a remote presenter can access the Podium from a remote desktop, a laptop, or another Convertible Podium. The multiple room displays and the room speakers can output live video and audio from the remote presenter.

For example, during a discussion, the display can be used as an interactive whiteboard to capture annotations and notes contributed by participants in the room. If the Podium is not actively in use, it can also be placed in front of a room and used as an information board to display a room calendar, or other kinds of asynchronous messages, similar to a bulletin board.

2 Context: Rethinking the Conference Room

The Convertible Podium project is informed by contextual inquiry into the implications of rich media for the kinds of work conducted in meeting rooms and lecture halls. It is designed to integrate with continuing research in multimedia, education, collaborative work and knowledge sharing systems. As new technologies like e-paper (electronic paper) make displays more ubiquitous, the challenge becomes the management of rich media content across a number of screens. Added into the mix are meeting participants and the devices they carry with them: laptops, cell phones, PDAs (Fig. 2).

Opening up a meeting room's media systems to support distributed collaboration raises yet another set of presentation and display issues. We are interested in analyzing and supporting not only the room systems, but also the process of work that happens there. For example:

- How should the room support presenters and participants during a variety of situations, including formal and casual meetings, discussions, and presentations?
- What capture technologies and media database functions are appropriate, and how do they support ongoing collaborations?
- How can both presenters and meeting participants interact with multiple-screen, multimedia, remote presentations?
- What are the implications of new technologies like e-paper as well as current technologies like RFID, cell phones, PDAs, and other multi-function devices (Fig. 3)?

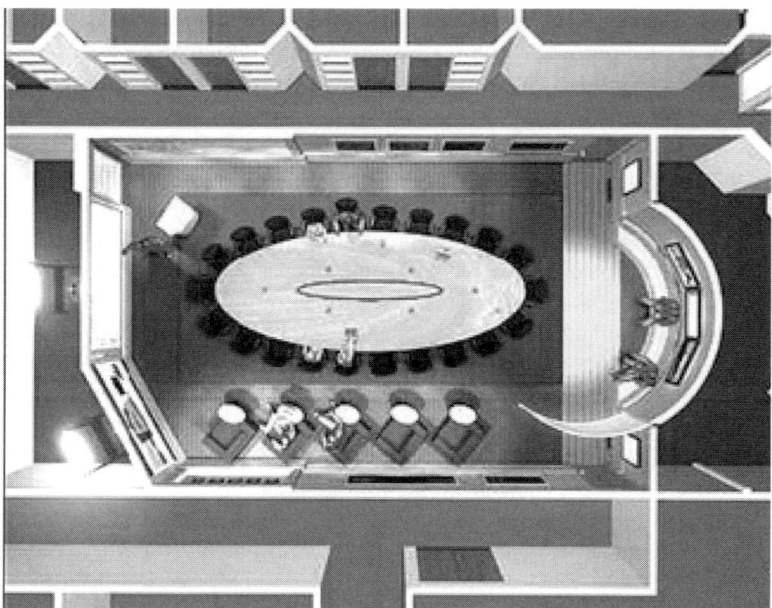

Fig. 2 A top-down view of a design for a rich media conference room, showing a variety of options for multiple wall-mounted displays, varied seating to encourage informal as well as formal meetings, and embedded interfaces as well as connectivity for mobile devices

Fig. 3 A design view of a rich media meeting room: integrating multiple modalities (audio and visual), wall-sized screens, encouraging formal and informal interchange, and creating channels for shared input from meeting participants via portable devices

2.1   Function Follows Form: Interactive Furniture
for Meeting Rooms

The Podium's deliberately sleek aluminium form references tools or equipment as well as furniture. As such, it encourages hands-on participation and control. Our approach to the design of the Convertible Podium has its roots in Mark Weiser's (1991) ubiquitous computing and Hiroshi Ishii's tangible media (Ishii and Ullmer 1997). Weiser's (1991) vision of widely distributed, networked devices permeating our living and working spaces has begun to be realized with the advent of cell phones, PDAs, and smart environments. At the same time, Ishii's research into the affordances of tangible controls for complex software systems has driven the work of many research designers. Tangible devices and ubiquitous computing are a natural match; Fishkin (2004) has created a taxonomy detailing research in this area. A number of researchers have combined these two ideas in the context of devices for reading, writing, and document management which map well to frequently occurring meeting tasks (Back et al. 2001, Nelson et al. 1999, Schilit et al. 1999) (Fig. 4).

Researchers at labs such as the MIT Media Lab and the Aware Home project at Georgia Tech (among others) have built smart networked objects, including interactive furniture, for home, personal and business environments (Kidd et al. 1999, Omojola et al. 2000). A major criterion in this podium design is a form factor that is both elegant and functional. We also wanted to create an article of smart furniture with physical dynamics – that changed its physical shape as well as digital content. This is a "transformer" metaphor, where current functionality is mapped to the physical state of the object: function follows form.

2.2   Related Work

Early versions of the electronic conference room focused on television and telecommunications technologies to support remote collaboration or distance learning, or to capture an electronic record of meetings. Today's media technologies for the meeting room are generally digitally integrated and often serve a variety of ends: multimedia presentation, meeting capture, note taking, informal design sessions, discussion group support, and Web use, as well as traditional live lectures. A huge amount of research has been undertaken in this area (Abowd et al. 1998, Johanson et al. 2002, MacIntyre et al. 2001,Moran et al. 1997,Chiu et al. 1999), along with work done at our lab (Chiu et al. 2003, Foote et al. 2004,Liao et al. 2003, Zhang et al. 2004). In the Podium project, we make an effort to fold much of this technology into the Podium itself, streamlining both the communication methods and the control systems for them. Many current podiums are ad hoc repositories for such centralization, with bits of technology added on; we are designing this centrality deliberately.

Fig. 4 The Convertible Podium's first operational prototype is CNC-machined from aluminium and acrylic panels and incorporates an onboard computer, WiFi, RFID, and custom sensing and control electronics. A counterbalance system is installed within the aluminium strut along the left side of the Podium's faceplate, to enable easy manipulation of the 37-lb hood

Commercial podiums on the market are mostly podium enclosures designed to accommodate a variety of equipment that is used to facilitate different presentation needs in a classroom or lecture hall. A typical podium designed for a multimedia room is equipped with devices ranging from large devices such as a PC, a display, or a document camera to small add-on devices such as light visors, microphones, or an A/V switching device. Each stand-alone device has a specific function and requires a dedicated space for installation. Packaging all these devices into a single podium requires a bulky and heavy enclosure with several tethered (and often, many untethered) cables, creating a tangle and making it difficult to move the podium from one room to another, or even to a different spot in the same room.

Since this combination of the convertible design and functionalities is unique, there is no other podium available that incorporates these features or is similar in implementation. However, there are a few systems that are similar in part.

Teleportec (2003) has a product called the Teleportec lectern which is a podium with a reflective screen similar to a teleprompter's set up. It uses a monitor that lies flat at the podium base to display video of a remote presenter and a large 30" × 40" transparent projection surface angled at 45° facing the front of the podium to reflect the display on the base. Using reverse chroma key, the background is removed and the presenter appears visible behind the podium. However the Teleportec lectern has no user interactivity and cannot be used by a remote presenter. It is a fixed set up that requires a backdrop wall to hide a videoconferencing camera behind the podium and in some cases a canopy to avoid direct light on the glass surface. The image of the remote presenter on the reflective screen may not be fully visible at extreme corner viewing angles. Because of its fixed setup, it is not portable and cannot be easily moved from one room to another.

Smart Technologies Inc. (2003) has a product called Sympodium which comes in four variations; an interactive lectern, a tabletop lectern, and two integration modules. The Sympodium interactive lectern is equipped with a touch sensitive LCD display that allows users to annotate over documents and control applications from a connected internal PC, laptop, or document camera. The desktop image is displayed through an external projector or large presentation screen allowing audiences to view annotations from the presenter's display. Sympodium has only three video source inputs which can be manually switched by the user. It cannot integrate more input and output devices and cannot control presentation devices or environmental settings.

ETH – Zürich has produced a prototype interactive podium called the "Speakers Corner" (Kunz and Kennel 2003) designed to facilitate local and remote teaching. This system is a customized podium enclosure equipped with a touch screen LCD display, a document camera, a dual-processor PC, a fold away keyboard, and an integrated connecter with USB, video, and network connections. It provides a multimedia platform for a presenter to show his/her slide presentation while making real time annotations on the slides. However, each input device implemented here is a stand alone device, designed for a specific application. They are placed in separated parts of the podium and cannot be used for multiple applications.

3   Rich Media and Active Meeting Participation

Rich media is usually understood to mean a combination of static and dynamic images and text, including video and multimedia documents available locally or via the internet. As displays become larger and more ubiquitous, the uses and designs of rich media will also change. How can we comfortably control, for example, three parallel video streams, along with presentation slides and a live remote presenter? What kind of content maps well into such a rich environment? How do local participants interact with the information they see projected around them, and how do remote participants interact with the same information? Based on the ethnographic research underlying the design, the cluster of information applications in the Podium can enable these common tasks and interactions:

- Participant interactions with leader and with each other via online text, in-room backchat, and sending text or images from mobile devices like cells and PDAs
- In-sequence presentations, especially a quick series of them (six or seven people each presenting a five-to-seven minute talk, for example)
- Drawing onscreen (live whiteboard, capture to web instantly)
- Multiple side-by-side comparison views – not just two-way as with most slide projector setups

- Guest lecturers via remote viewing – avatar mode plus rich media presentations
- Printing and paperwork including JIT (just-in-time) printing
- Document camera for demos or quick capture for images from workgroup sessions

4   Operation: Functionality Follows Form

One person easily accesses and controls complex functionality through simple physical manipulation. As the counter-weighted hood swings open, the Podium can switch modes and applications, from presentation, to capture, to remote conferencing or networked whiteboard. More detail on the functionality within each mode is detailed below.

4.1   Mode 1: Rich Media Presentation

The Podium uses ePic, a rich media presentation application developed to handle multiple screens as its primary presentation mode for showing slides, web, video, or other media. Live annotation is available via touch screen (using finger or pen). Any image can be transferred to any screen with a flick of the finger across the touch screen; alternatively a sequence of slides and other media can be pre-programmed to execute across any number of screens, in any order. Audio speakers are also individually assignable for audio output.

Because the monitor screen shows not only control systems but also the content of the screens themselves, a presenter does not need to turn away from the audience to the screen, in order to read the contents of the slide. This, though simple, is one of the biggest affordances of the Podium: allowing a presenter to face the audience, rather than continually turning away to refer to the slide (Fig. 5).

4.2   Mode 2: Image and Data Capture

As the hood of the Podium hinges into the half-way open position, the Capture Mode becomes available. Digital images and real-time video demos are captured via onboard scanner and a document camera (Fig. 6). A visor light provides needed light levels for the camera. Image capture is controlled via a small secondary computer (originally we planned to use a PDA, but we have decided instead to use a small-form-factor Windows XP computer, made by OQO 2005). Images can be directed to room screens, to nearby or remote printers, or filed in a meeting media database.

As the LCD screen flips upwards, a document or object placing area is revealed beneath the screen, along with a thin scanner. Beneath the screen is a light visor to highlight the area. A high-resolution digital camera is centred at the top edge of the screen. In this mode, the camera is used as a document camera to take snapshots of a document or to stream video of an object demo.

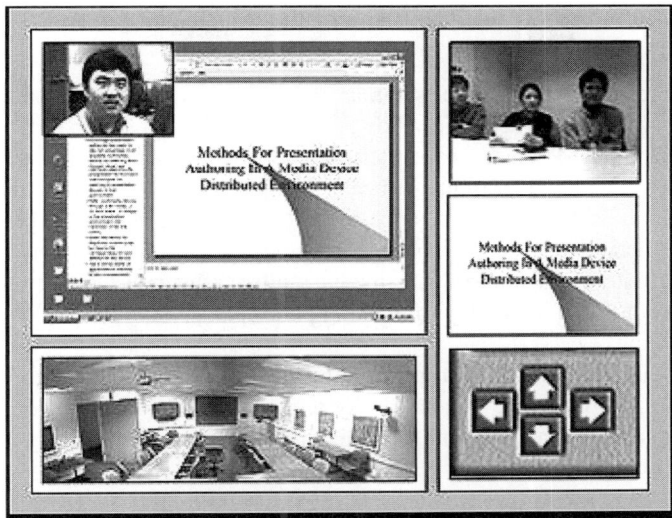

Fig. 5 An early example of a user interface: ePic multi-screen remote presentation

Scanner for on-the-spot document capture
Document camera with visor lighting
Small screen computer for capture systems
JIT (just in time) printing

Fig. 6 Design sketch: during capture mode, the high-resolution digital camera becomes a document camera for capturing documents or physical objects

4.3   Modes 3 and 4: Avatar/Interactive Whiteboard

Avatar/telepresence mode supports human-scale video avatars for teleconferencing. In an effort to enliven the static talking-head video image often associated with teleconferencing, the Podium's Avatar/telepresence mode features a life-sized, centre-screen image of a remote presenter's face. The image appears on the Podium's LCD screen when it is fully upright, appearing there at approximately human head height. The facial image can also appear on one of the room screens if desired. Remote presenters can control rich media multi-screen presentations from their remote locations, and interact with meeting participants via high-quality video and audio streaming.

If no avatar is needed, the upright position can be used for networked interactive whiteboard and interactive annotation systems, to enable local or long-distance group work such as planning, brainstorming and discussion.

4.4   Post-Laptop Design

Though the Podium is designed as a post-laptop device, it allows the connection of many kinds of external devices including laptops, PDAs, cell phones, and portable USB/FireWire drives. Through the use of a network application using RFID cards (Hilbert and Trevor 2004) one's personal files can be securely uploaded from any networked computer on the LAN.

5   Physical Design and Technology

The Convertible Podium is designed as a human-scale mobile control centre. Intended to avoid tangles of cabling, its mobile design allows the front of the room to be a flexible space. It is easily wheeled aside to allow different room configurations according to group needs.

- **Aluminium and acrylic** are the basic building materials, plus built-in custom electronics: tangible control strip, LCD monitor/touchscreen, LEDS for mode indication and a visor light for the document cameras.
- **An acrylic panel** (a 24' × 38.6" vertical support bent to a 24" × 20" lectern surface that is 31.6° from horizontal) is outlined and supported by **one-piece aluminum/alodine-finish side supports.** The body of the podium consists of an acrylic panel shaped like a slightly angled upside down letter "L". The panel can be sidelit with LEDs (coloured according to mode). Along both sides of the panel are two aluminium frames that are the main structure of the podium and hold the entire body together. These side supports are also used as conduits for internal wiring and cables as well as a holder for wireless network antenna.

Fig. 7 The control strip features large, user-friendly physical buttons and knobs that map to software and environment controls. The control modules are modular and can be custom-designed for use with specific installations. In this case, software controls appear on the right; room controls (lights, sound volume) are on the left

- The desktop surface area is a **touchscreen LCD display** measuring 24" diagonally. At the bottom edge of the display between the two side frames is a tray that holds the control electronics. The control unit is a strip holding physical controls such as dials, switches, and sliders that are used as physical controls mapped to certain functions or commands in the application currently in use. Beneath the controller tray is space for external connection jacks: USB, audio, and FireWire.
- The **wheeled base** (also aluminium/alodine) is a modified x-shape with an **underslung tray** that holds the **electronics** (laptop computer, AC power, A/D control card, USB hub and various USB remotes, network connections.)
- **Modal functionality** is cued from position of the **swing-open hood**: Presentation, Capture, Telepresence/Avatar or Interactive Whiteboard (Fig. 7).

5.1   Custom Electronics and Software

The Podium consolidates environmental and multimedia controls at a single access point. A custom analogue/digital hardware module, combined with the touch screen, controls many common meeting room tasks: screen/projector settings, room lighting, audio volume, presentation and annotation software, and remote teleconferencing. Modular design allows controls to be configurable in software, and if required, custom modules can be CNC-machined to meet changing needs (Fig. 8).

For all the applications – teleconferencing and remote presentation, meeting capture, media control, and document sharing – we use the same protocol to communicate with a suite of applications developed in our lab.

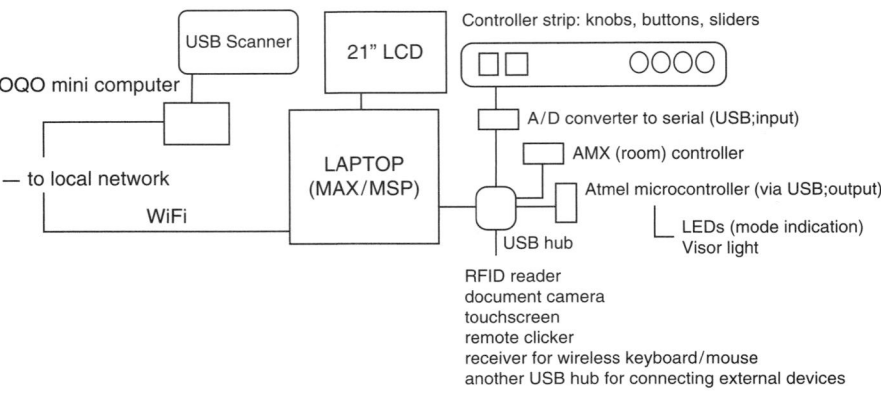

Fig. 8 Inside the Podium: system sketch

Fig. 9 The CNC drill and the right arm strut on the CNC mill bed

One application was developed for authoring and presenting on multiple screens and speakers, both locally and remotely (Zhao and Liu 2004). Another, AnySpot/PIP (Personal Interaction Points), allows a person to simply swipe an RFID card across a reader to automatically open a directory listing all her Powerpoint files on her own machine (as long as it's on the same local area network). When RFID chips become more common in cell phones (as the FeliCa RFID chip already is in Japan), that means that a presenter could use a simple swipe of her cell phone as an identifier to open the Podium's systems and upload a presentation automatically.

5.2 CNC-Machined Parts, Custom Modules

Computer-controlled machining was a primary element in the build process, chosen to provide modular adaptability to a particular client's needs (for example, an etched logo on the front of the control strip, or an extended set of controls for a more complex lighting setup). Most major Podium parts were computer milled (CNC, or computer numerical control, is a standard machining procedure) from aluminium, allowing a slim-line curved design with enough hollow space for the electronics and cabling. The relatively large number of onboard devices meant lots of room was needed for cabling – not only for the signal cables, but for power as well (Fig. 9).

6 Next Steps

Though much of the rich media authoring and control software that supports it has been under development for years, we have just completed the first operational physical prototype of the Convertible Podium. Before moving on to the next stage of design we will perform several usage studies, on each mode's software and how well it integrates with the physical aspects of the device. Results from these studies will inform the next iterations of the design and may result in modifications to the first prototype as well.

Acknowledgements The authors gratefully acknowledge the help and influence of our colleagues at the FX Palo Alto Laboratory. We would also like to thank the PARC (Palo Alto Research Center) machine shop for their help in the construction of the Convertible Podium.

References

N. Streitz, J. Geisler, T. Holmer (1998), Roomware for cooperative buildings: Integrated design of architectural spaces and information spaces. *Proceedings of CoBuild'98*, Springer-Verlag LNCS 1370, pp. 4–21.

Q. Liu, F. Zhao, J. Doherty, D. Kimber (2004), An EPIC enhanced meeting environment. *Proceedings of ACM Multimedia'04 (Video Demo)*, pp. 940–941.

OQO (2005), Handheld windows XP computer. http://www.oqo.com

M. Weiser (1991), The computer for the twenty-first century. *Scientific American*, 265(3): 94–104.

H. Ishii, B. Ullmer (1997), Tangible bits: Towards seamless interfaces between people, bits and atoms. *Proceedings of CHI'97*, ACM Press, pp. 234–241.

K. P. Fishkin (2004), A taxonomy for and analysis of tangible interfaces. *Journal of Personal and Ubiquitous Computing*, 8(5): 347–358.

M. Back, M. Chow, R. Gold, M. Gorbet, S. Harrison, D. Macdonald, S. Minneman (2001), Designing interactive reading experiences for a museum exhibition. *IEEE Computer Magazine*, 34 (1): 1–8.

L. Nelson, S. Ichimura, E. Pedersen, L. Adams (1999), Palette: A paper interface for giving presentations. *Proceedings of CHI'99*, ACM Press, pp. 354–361.

W. Schilit, M. N. Price, G. Golovchinsky, K. Tanaka, C. C. Marshall (1999), As we may read: The reading appliance revolution. *IEEEComputer*, 32(1): 65–73.

C. Kidd, R. Orr, G. Abowd, C. Atkeson, I. Essa, B. MacIntyre, E. Mynatt, T. Starner, W. Newstetter (1999),The Aware Home: A living laboratory for ubiquitous computing research. *Proceedings of CoBuild'99*, Springer-Verlag LNCS 1670, pp. 191–198.

O. Omojola, E. R. Post, M. D. Hancher, Y. Maguire, R. Pappu, B. Schoner, P. R. Russo, R. Fletcher, N. Gershenfeld (2000), An installation of interactive furniture. *IBM Systems Journal*, 39(3–4) 861–879.

G. Abowd, C. Atkeson, J. Brotherton, T. Enqvist, P. Gulley, J. LeMon (1998), Investigating the capture, integration and access problem of ubiquitous computing in an educational setting. *Proceedings of CHI'98*, ACM Press, pp. 440–447.

B. Johanson, A. Fox, T. Winograd (2002), The Interactive workspaces project: Experiences with ubiquitous computing rooms. *IEEE Pervasive Computing*, 1(2): 67–75.

B. MacIntyre, E. Mynatt, S. Voida, K. M. Hansen, J. Tullio, G. M. Corso (2001), Support for multitasking and background awareness using interactive peripheral displays. *Proceedings of UIST'01*, ACM Press, pp. 41–50.

T. Moran, L. Palen, S. Harrison, P. Chiu, D. Kimber, S. Minneman, W. van Melle, P. Zellweger (1997), "I'll get that off the audio": A case study of salvaging multimedia meeting records. *Proceedings of CHI'97*, ACM Press, pp. 202–209.

P. Chiu, A. Kapuskar, S. Reitmeier, L. Wilcox (1999), Meeting capture in a media enriched conference room. *Proceedings of CoBuild'99*, Springer-Verlag LNCS 1670, pp. 79–88.

P. Chiu, Q. Liu, J. Boreczky, J. Foote, T. Fuse, D. Kimber, S. Lertsithichai, S. C. Liao (2003), Manipulating and annotating slides in a multi-display environment. *Proceedings of INTERACT'03*, pp. 583–590.

J. Foote, Q. Liu, D. Kimber, P. Chiu, F. Zhao (2004), Reach-through-the-screen: A new metaphor for remote collaboration. *Proceedings of PCM'04 (Pacific Rim Conference on Multimedia)*, Springer-Verlag LNCS 3333, pp. 73–80.

C. Liao, Q. Liu, D. Kimber, P. Chiu, J. Foote, L. Wilcox (2003), Shared interactive video for teleconferencing. *Proceedings of ACM Multimedia'03*, ACM Press, pp. 546–554.

H. Zhang, Q. Liu, S. Lertsithichai., C. Liao, D. Kimber (2004), A presentation authoring tool for media devices distributed environments. *Proceedings of ICME'04*, pp. 1755–1758.

Teleportec (2003), Teleportec Lectern System. http://www.teleportec.com

Smart Technologies Inc. (2003), Sympodium, 2003. http://www.smarttech.com/products/sympodium/index.asp

A. Kunz, T. Kennel, Speakerscorner. ETH – Zürich. http://www.icvr.ethz.ch/ConfiguratorJM/thesis/finished/Funktional_121830986273051/aufgabe_bucher_2003.pdf (last accessed on 20th Oct 2008)

D. Hilbert, J. Trevor (2004), Personalizing shared ubiquitous devices. *Interactions Magazine*, 11(2): 34–43.

F. Zhao, Q. Liu (2004), A web based multi-display presentation system. Proceedings of ACM Multimedia 2004 (Demo), pp. 176–177.

Collaborative Tabletop Research and Evaluation

Interfaces and Interactions for Direct-Touch Horizontal Surfaces

Chia Shen, Kathy Ryall, Clifton Forlines, Alan Esenther, Frédéric D. Vernier, Katherine Everitt, Mike Wu, Daniel Wigdor, Meredith Ringel Morris, Mark Hancock, and Edward Tse

Tables provide a large and natural interface for supporting direct manipulation of visual content, for human-to-human interactions and for collaboration, coordination, and parallel problem solving. However, the direct-touch table metaphor also presents considerable challenges, including the need for input methods that transcend traditional mouse- and keyboard-based designs.

Keywords Interactive furniture, Meeting support, Teleconferencing, Multi-screen presentation, Rich media, Smart environments, CSCW, Ubiquitous computing

1 Introduction

The term *display* suggests a device used solely to output visual information, untouched for fear of occluding or dirtying the screen. In contrast, a *surface* is free of this burden – it is part of the physical environment and invites touch. By superimposing input and visual output spaces onto surfaces, we can merge both ideas, creating touchable, interactive surfaces. Such surfaces have numerous uses; one exciting example is a horizontal, interactive, computationally-augmented tabletop.

Compared with traditional displays, interactive tables provide three potential benefits. First, because the table is both the display and direct input device, it can accept natural hand gestures and other intuitive manipulations as input. Such inputs can improve the fluidity and reduce the cognitive load of user/content interactions. Second, by leveraging people's tendency to gather around a table for face-to-face interactions, a horizontal tabletop surface provides opportunities for building and enhancing co-located collaborative environments. Third, large tabletop surfaces

P. Dillenbourg et al. (eds.), *Interactive Artifacts and Furniture Supporting Collaborative Work and Learning*,
DOI: 10.1007/978-0-387-77234-9_7, © Springer Science+Business Media, LLC 2009

have a spacious work area that can positively influence working styles and group dynamics. Users can also employ the surfaces' large visual field as an external physical memory (thereby extending their working memory capacity); it can further serve as an external cognitive medium for new forms of visual representation and direct manipulation.

Over the past few years, we have sought to exploit direct-touch surfaces' advantages and affordances. To this end, we have designed, implemented, and studied a variety of tabletop user interfaces, interaction techniques, and usage scenarios. We have also empirically evaluated our work and obtained preliminary findings on these approaches.

In this chapter, we explore tabletops' advantages by examining the interaction techniques we have developed. In addition to presenting six basic challenges we have encountered in our studies, we discuss the experiences gained and lessons learned.

2 Usability Challenges

Direct-touch tabletops are a new interaction form factor, and designers and researchers have not yet come to agreement on the appropriate user interfaces and interaction techniques to enable their widespread use. Existing research surveys include Scott and colleagues (2003), who summarize tabletop systems and design approaches and Kruger and colleagues (2004), who cover orientation approaches on a traditional meeting table.

Tables are commonly found in homes, offices, command-and-control centres, cafés, design centres, showrooms, waiting areas, and entertainment centres. As such, they provide a convenient physical setting for people to examine documents, layout and navigate maps, sketch design ideas, and carry out activities that are best performed in face-to-face collaboration. In contrast, digital documents are still commonly used only on desktop/laptop computers, vertical plasma or projected displays, and handheld devices. Making such documents available on direct-touch interactive tabletop surfaces involves several design and usability challenges, including tabletop content orientation, occlusion and reach, gestural interaction, legacy application support, group interaction, and walk-up/walk-away use issues.

2.1 Tabletop Content Orientation

In contrast to computer monitors or projected displays, people seated around digital tabletops do not share a common perspective on information. That is, information presented right-side up to one participant might be upside down for another. Content orientation has implications for group social dynamics (Kruger et al. 2004), readability (Wigdor and Balakrishnan 2005), and performance (Forlines et al. 2005). Because content-orientation solutions let researchers evaluate other tabletop applications and interaction techniques, it is an extensively studied issue.

Fig. 1 Content orientation in the DiamondSpin Tabletop Toolkit. Users meet around a multi-touch, multi-user interactive digital table (left). A bird's eye view of a DiamondSpin application (right), which constrains documents to face the tabletop's outside edge

We developed the DiamondSpin Tabletop Toolkit (Shen et al. 2004), which included a set of interaction techniques designed to address content orientation on a horizontal display. Figure 1 shows one popular layout technique in which the toolkit constrains documents to always face the tabletop's outside edge (the edge closest to the document). A user can move documents with a single-finger touch, and documents automatically turn to face that user. A separate corner widget allows users to override this automatic orientation and arbitrarily reorient a document. DiamondSpin also provides two other document orientation options: a lazy-Susan tabletop background that lets users rotate all documents together and a magnetizer that reorients all the documents to face the same direction.

There are many possible document orientation and movement schemes. We classified and compared five different rotation and translation techniques for objects displayed on a direct-touch digital tabletop display (Hancock et al. 2006). We then analyzed the techniques' suitability for interactive tabletops given their respective input and output degrees of freedom, as well as their consistency, completeness, GUI integration for conventional window-based documents, and support for coordination and communication. Our comparative usability analysis results indicate that the Polar Coordinate-based orientation and translation schemes offered in the DiamondSpin Toolkit are especially effective for usage scenarios which need consistency and GUI integration.

2.2   Occlusion and Reach

When users interact with displayed information through direct touch, they often visually obscure the information immediately below their hand, arm, or stylus. Furthermore, the tabletop's large workspace makes many display regions either uncomfortable to work in or completely unreachable. To contend with these issues, we developed three techniques: Context-Rooted Rotatable Draggables (CoR^{2}Ds)

(Shen et al. 2005), ExpressiveTouch puppetry (Wu et al. 2006), and occlusion-aware visual feedback.

2.2.1   Context-Rooted Rotatable Draggables

We designed CoR²D interactive popups for multi-user direct-touch tabletop environments. As Fig. 2 shows, translucent, coloured swaths visually root CoR²Ds to objects. Users can employ CoR²Ds to issue commands or display information. Users can freely move, rotate, and reorient CoR²Ds on a tabletop display surface using their fingers or hands; pointing devices (such as mice); or marking devices (such as a stylus or light pen).

CoR²Ds address five key interaction issues in tabletop systems: occlusion, reach, establishing context on a cluttered display, readability, and concurrent, coordinated multi-user interaction. Also, multiple people can use a single CoR²D or a pair of CoR²Ds to cooperatively complete a task (as in Fig. 2a). For example, one person

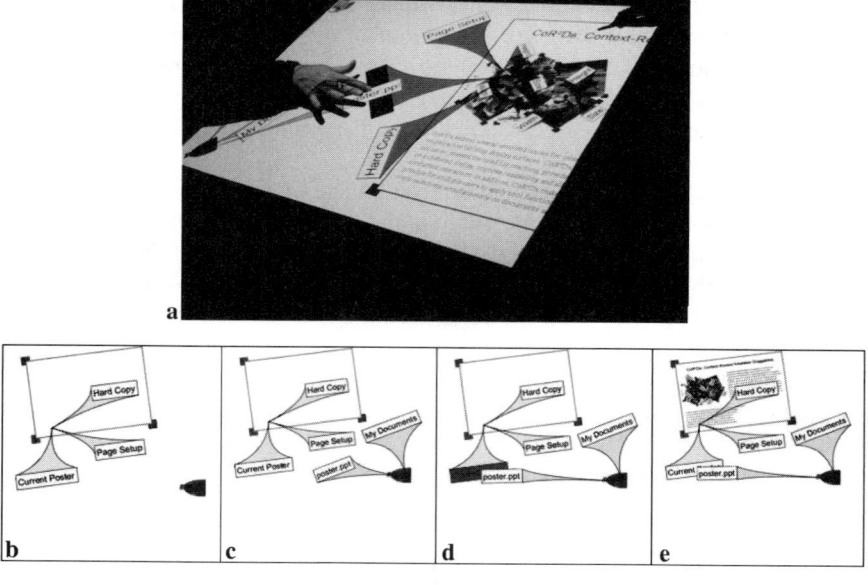

Fig. 2 Concurrent interaction on a large tabletop. (a) Two users employ CoR²Ds in a poster design scenario on an interactive tabletop. (b) A user double taps inside an empty poster document on the tabletop to launch its associated CoR²Ds. (c) A user double taps the USB reader icon, launching its associated CoR²Ds. (d) and (e) Users stretch and overlap "Current poster" and "Poster.ppt" from two separate CoR²Ds, completing the task of copying the Power Point file from the USB reader into the poster document on the table. This operation can be carried out bimanually by one user or by two separate users

can drag a CoR²D to a different part of the display surface while another user operates on it, thus facilitating multi-user operations. CoR²Ds let operators and operands function across a visual distance, eliminating on-object occlusion. Figures 2b through 2e illustrate the step-by-step operations of two CoR²Ds in a cooperative task in which a poster file is copied and opened from a USB device to an on-the-table poster document. This also lets users operate objects at a distance without losing the visual cue of the objects' menus or tools, which might be across the display and partially hidden among display clutter.

2.2.2 Puppetry

A tenet of interactive tabletops is that they are direct-touch: actions occur beneath the users' fingers. While consistent application of this principle is important, there are instances where doing so imposes undue limitations on user actions. Our ExpressiveTouch puppetry technique attempts to bridge this divide: users can conduct operations – such as copy and paste – on a distant document. This can be important when target objects are obscured from view, are too far from the user for comfortable manipulation, or when the operation is intended to have a larger area of influence than the user can specify with a gesture. To perform a copy-and-paste operation, for example, a user needs to specify two general parameters: the portion of the source object to copy and the destination in which to paste. In a puppetry implementation of this, the user selects the source object by touching it with multiple fingers, specifying a bounding region. Then, while still touching the table, the user slides her hands away from the document: the position of the hand now specifies the destination of the copy, as expected, but it also continues to adjust the selection box's location and size. As Fig. 3 (left) shows, four visual lines provide feedback to indicate the relationships between the hand and display regions. This is a visually tethered, indirect distant operation that solves the occlusion problem

Fig. 3 Bimanual, multi-tool gestural interaction. The tool decouples control and display spaces (left). Two users simultaneously perform copy-and-paste operations on the same image object (right)

on direct-touch surfaces. Our technique lets users comfortably control documents from various locations. The technique also mitigates physical interference, letting multiple people simultaneously use the same document from different sides of a table (see Fig. 3, right).

2.2.3   Occlusion-Aware Visual Feedback

When users' fingers are larger than a target object – say, a menu item or a button – it is difficult for them to touch that object in order to select it. Compounding this is the issue of occlusion; traditional windows, icons, menus, and pointing device (WIMP) systems generally offer in-place visual feedback on an action's target pixel. On a direct-touch interface, this feedback will always be occluded by the user's hand, thus removing much-needed feedback on target selection accuracy. Thus, traditional visual feedback – such as highlighting or drop shadows – is not always effective in direct-touch tabletop interactions.

To address this, we developed occlusion-aware visual feedback. Our solution provides both in-place and visible feedback on a direct-touch interface. Figure 4 shows an example: when the user successfully selects the target, it enlarges. This change in visual state clearly indicates activation and offers in-place feedback without occlusion.

2.3   *Gestural Interaction*

In a graphical user interface, users must manage a plethora of tools and interaction methods, typically using only a keyboard and mouse as input devices. Direct-touch surfaces that permit fluid, bimanual input could provide a more natural mapping

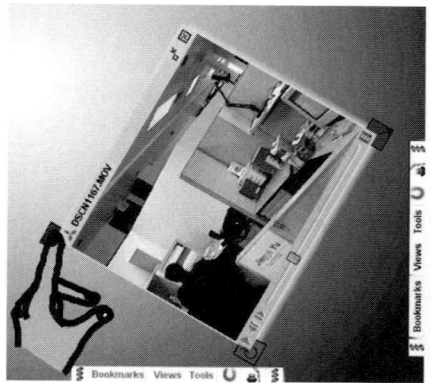
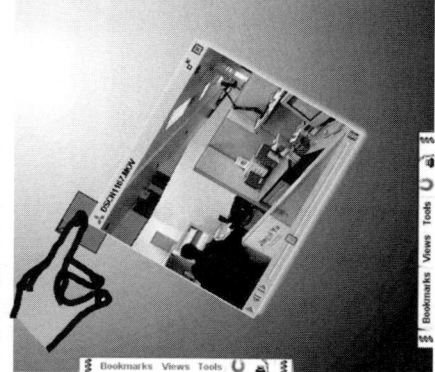

Fig. 4 Occlusion-aware visual feedback. A user's finger lands on a DiamondSpin object's "resize" widget, occluding part of it (left). The widget's size temporarily enlarges and grows transparent, to provide visual feedback and indicate its ephemeral nature, respectively (right)

between input and commands. For this to happen, we must first address several major questions:

- How should gestures map to various system functions?
- Should gestures map to the most common tasks or the most complex?
- Does each command require its own gesture – and, if so, how many gestures can we reasonably expect users to learn?
- How can hand gestures coexist with familiar point-based, mouse-like interaction?

Designers must develop gestures that address their applications' specific needs. However, guidelines for introducing new gestural commands into an application can help designers avoid overly complicated systems. Here, we offer guidelines for gesture reuse within tabletop applications that begin to address some of these research questions.

2.3.1   Registration and Gesture Reuse

In our solutions, each gesture operation begins with gesture registration, which sets the context for all subsequent interactions (Wu et al. 2006). A gesture registration action can be a posture of the hand, a simple touch, a dwelling of the hand in place, or a specific number of finger taps. Registration occurs when the system recognizes a distinctive gesture registration action on the table.

By separating the registration and action phases, registration lets users reuse gestures for different system operations. The same hand movements can thus produce different results, depending on which gesture action the user employs in the registration phase. For example, our desktop publishing application uses gesture registration to change stylus action modes. In normal operation, the stylus moves documents around the table and behaves like a mouse. However, if the user places two fingers on a document – as if to hold it in place – the stylus behaves like a pen, letting the user mark up and annotate the document. Through gesture registration, users can map the same stylus movements to multiple system commands. Gesture registration combined with gesture reuse is a powerful idea that lets designers define a variety of gestures using a small set of building blocks.

2.3.2   Modal Spaces and Gesture Reuse

Our Modal Spaces solution (Everitt et al. 2005) enhances conventional modal interfaces to permit reuse of gestures for different commands. It also clearly indicates the system's mode and lets users seamlessly change modes.

Modal Spaces divides the table into multiple workspaces, called *modal regions*. The system recognizes commands based on the target object, the user's gestural input, and the table's input region. As Fig. 5 shows, location mediates user input, and documents respond differently to the same gestures depending on where users execute them. In one modal region, for example, a touch might open a popup menu; in another, it might launch a stroke operation.

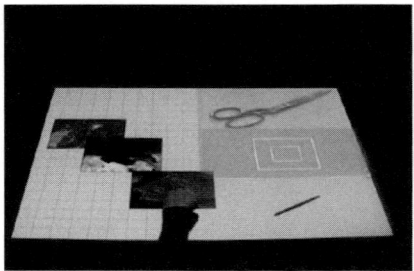 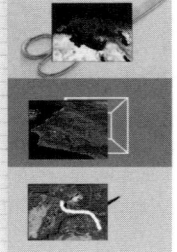 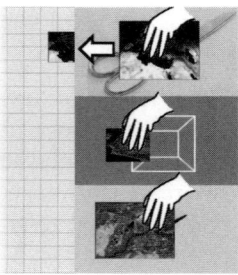

Fig. 5 Modal spaces for an image editing application. The touch-sensitive tabletop surface has four modal spaces: cutting, resize, annotation, and layout (left). A before-and-after look at the effects of three annotations: bounding box cut, shrinking, and clearing (right)

2.4   Legacy Application Support

As the tabletop interfaces field matures, developers will likely design more applications from scratch to take full advantage of multi-user horizontal workspace characteristics. Still, legacy applications are widely deployed and many are indispensable for real-world tasks. A digital tabletop environment must therefore address issues related to using pre-existing applications on a horizontal work surface. We have developed solutions here in two areas: one enables mouse emulation on touch surfaces; the other enables bimanual gestures for mouse-based applications.

2.4.1   Mouse Support for Touch-Based Interactions

To support existing mouse-based applications, we need a finger-touch mechanism that emulates a computer mouse. This entails several issues. Most tabletop systems detect finger position only when it is in contact with the table. With such a device, how does a user indicate mouse dragging versus mouse hovering (moving the mouse without pressing any buttons)? How does the user right-click? We also face a finger-resolution issue. A fingertip has a relatively large area, so how does the user specify a particular pixel, especially when his or her fingertip is obscuring the mouse cursor? Finally, traditional desktop applications assume (and support) only a single mouse. What happens if multiple users touch at the same time?

   Early work attempted to mitigate the effects of visual occlusion and limited pointing accuracy by introducing a fixed offset between touch location and cursor position. This approach breaks the direct-touch input paradigm. In contrast, our solution detects multiple concurrent touches from the same user (Esenther and Ryall 2006), allowing the user's hand posture to define the offset more logically. When a user touches the table with one finger, the left mouse button is activated to simulate dragging. When a user touches with two fingers at once, the mouse cursor jumps to the centre point between the touches; no mouse button is activated. Once already in contact with

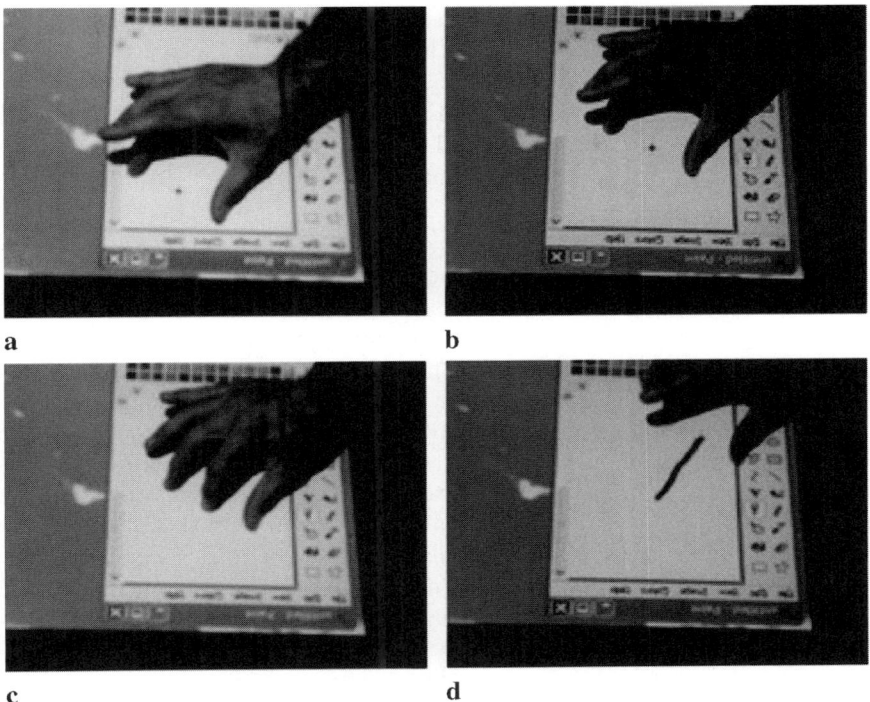

a   b

c   d

Fig. 6 Using precision-hover mode to transition between moving the mouse and drawing. (a) The user makes contact with the display; (b) the mouse remains centred between the user's thumb and middle finger as he moves his fingers and drags the mouse; (c) the user taps briefly with the index finger to toggle the left mouse button's state, engaging the drawing function; (d) the cursor remains between his two fingers, but by moving his thumb and middle finger, the user engages the left mouse button and the interface draws a line

the table, moving either or both fingers moves the mouse. As Fig. 6 shows, this precision-hover mode gives users an unobstructed view of the precise mouse cursor location between their fingers. This two-fingered control provides precision unobtainable with single-finger input. Similar to using a mouse with tool tips and image rollovers, our method allows users move the mouse without activating mouse buttons. While in precision-hover mode, tapping with a third finger in between the first two will toggle the left mouse button up or down. Users can thus fluidly switch between dragging and moving, without inadvertently moving the mouse cursor.

This technique is natural and intuitive if users employ the thumb and middle finger of one hand for the first two touches, and use the index finger to toggle the left mouse button. They press the right mouse button by placing one finger down at the desired location and then quickly tapping anywhere else with a second finger. Users can then either drag with the right mouse button held down, or – to generate a right click – let go with the first finger, too. We can use variations of this basic technique to support other mouse buttons. We can, for example, support multiple users by letting the first toucher win: the system ignores subsequent touches by other users until the first toucher stops touching the table. To allow the users to send mouse events to the edges and corners of the display, the projector can be set such that the margins of the tabletop have no display shown on them. This facilitates centring the mouse pointer between two fingers, even when one of those fingers is positioned off of the display area. Our initial user experiences with these touch-based mouse-emulation schemes have shown encouraging user acceptance and fast learnability.

2.4.2   Gestural Interactions for Mouse-Based Applications

Meaningful gestures on a tabletop can improve group awareness in ways that simple mouse emulation cannot achieve. For example, using a whole hand to pan a map might be more intuitive than selecting a pan mode and then panning with a single finger.

To allow multi-user gestural interaction with desktop applications, we map between gestures that a gesture engine recognizes and the keyboard and mouse events that legacy applications expect (Tse et al. 2006). Using the Microsoft Send Input API, we can map a single gestural act to a series of keyboard and mouse events to provide a more natural mapping between tabletop gestures and legacy input. Turn-taking protocols let us manage system responses when multiple people gesture simultaneously. As a result, legacy applications appear to directly "understand" freehand gestures from multiple people, despite the lack of any actual support for gestural or multi-user input within the software.

2.5   Group Interaction Techniques

Co-located, multi-user activities present many new challenges for UI designers. This is particularly problematic for applications and interface elements intended and designed for only a single user. Among the problems are: how can multiple users access conventional, single-user menu bars and toolbars? How can multiple users simultaneously explore detailed image or geospatial data without interfering with the global context view?

2.5.1   Conventional Menu Bar Access

Menu bars and tools are frequently used UI widgets. In a group setting, support for both shared use and personal use need to be facilitated. In DiamondSpin, we provide four types of menu bar usage patterns:

Draggable for sharing. With a single finger movement, a user can slide a group menu bar along the tabletop's edge to any parking position. Multiple users can thus share a single menu bar, passing it among themselves.

Lockable for private use. On a multi-touch, multi-user direct-touch tabletop, it is easy for one user to select items from another user's menu bar. Consequently, we built into the menu bar a touch-to-lock user-controlled option that lets users selectively prevent all other co-located users from operating their personal menu bars.

Replicated for convenience. Users can replicate their private menu bars and give copies to other collaborators at the table. Figure. 1b shows a usage scenario in which the user's replicated menu bar appears on both the top and bottom edges of the tabletop. This is a convenient usage pattern, but it requires social protocols to mitigate conflicting menu operations among co-located users.

Subset for restricted access. Finally, rather than duplicating an entire menu bar, users can replicate and distribute a menu bar subset to other users. Making limited menu bar actions available could be useful in situations with one power user, as in a teacher-student setting. The teacher's menu bar might have full functionality, for example, while the students' menu bars contain a smaller set of options.

2.5.2   Group Exploration of Geospatial Data

High-resolution satellite photographs, maps, and blueprints are often presented from a bird's eye view so that intelligence analysts, architects, and city planners can gather around rolled-out paper documents. Such experts are accustomed to viewing documents from a variety of perspectives as they work face-to-face around a table. In contrast, groups that work with high-resolution digital files on a tabletop display are hindered by the surfaces' inability to display a document's full resolution.

Tiling displays or projectors offer a promising solution, but they are currently prohibitively expensive. The single-user solution of zooming in and panning around the document is inappropriate in groups, as members might want to see a detailed view of different document regions at the same time. Furthermore, people often get lost in a data set when using pan-zoom interfaces, which sacrifice larger context when they zoom in for detailed views.

Our DTLens (Forlines et al. 2005a) is a multi-user tabletop tool that lets groups explore high-resolution spatial data without the panning and zooming drawbacks. As Fig. 7 shows, DTLens gives each group member an independent, zoom-in-context fisheye lens that they manipulate through multi-hand gestures performed directly on the document. Any group member can thus reach onto the table, grab a document region, and stretch the area to reveal more detail. By allowing simultaneous exploration of document details, DTLens lets group members move naturally from collaborative to independent activities as they work face to face around the tabletop display. DTLens also gives users a consistent interaction set for lens operations, thus minimizing tool switching during spatial data exploratin.

2.6   Walk-up and Walk-away Usage Issues

With traditional tables – in airports, cafés, and conference rooms, for example – people often spontaneously approach a table and collaborate with people who are already seated. In such scenarios, people generally bring their own material and

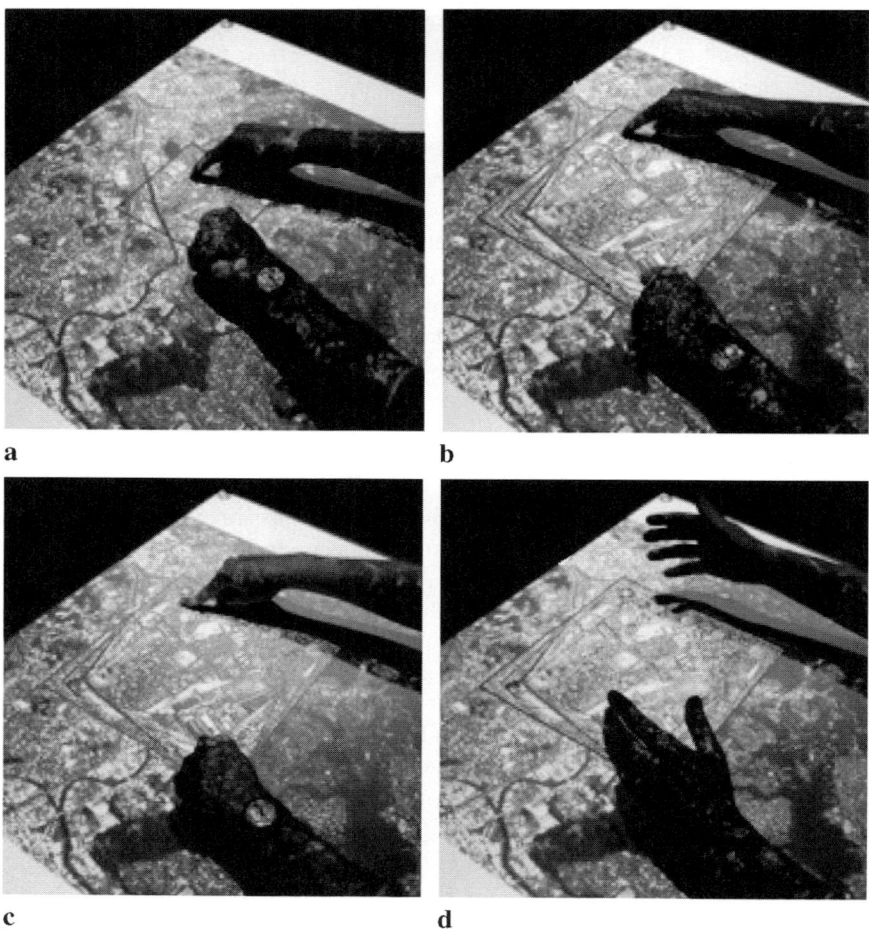

Fig. 7 Exploring a satellite image using DTLens on a multi-touch tabletop. (a) Using both hands, the user launches the DTLens tool and (b) stretches open the view. (c) The user presses down with his hands to tack the lens in place, which (d) frees his hands for other work

documents. Therefore, if we are to develop walk-up, kiosk-like digital tabletops, we must consider appropriate user interfaces. Although researchers have actively explored how to share personal data on public vertical displays, a key difference between shared use of a tabletop and that of a vertical display is that when people sit around a table, a particular table region is in their immediate physical proximity. Moreover, such regions are not visually equivalent for all users on all sides of a table. These physical and perceptual properties make these individual areas ideal choices for private work spaces (Scott et al. 2004). To this end, we developed a user interface design solution called UbiTable (Shen et al. 2003).

Fig. 8 Walk-up options for work sharing. Walk-up usage of a conventional table (left); walk-up usage of UbiTable, which offers users a private region for laptop displays, and personal or public regions on the tabletop (centre); the UbiTable interface (right). Green and pink borders indicate personal areas, blue portals are for data movement to and from private regions (laptops or other personal devices), and the central gray area is for document sharing

As Fig. 8 shows, UbiTable lets users dynamically connect personal laptops, cameras, and USB devices to an interactive tabletop so they can fluidly share, manipulate, exchange, and mark up data. At the same time, each user maintains explicit control over their documents' accessibility. We divided the UbiTable tabletop into two regions – personal and public – that have distinct access control properties, as well as different document interactions. Personal region documents are visible to all users, but can only be manipulated and moved by the document owner. Public region documents are accessible to all users, but only the owner can move it into a personal region. This gives the owner explicit control over how the document is distributed to other meeting participants. Documents that are displayed on the tabletop use coloured borders to provide feedback information for owners and users. Green and pink borders, for example, indicate personal document regions, while gray borders indicate public document regions. In addition to the public and personal areas, UbiTable designates personal devices, such as laptops, as private regions for users' data. It therefore offers three information-sharing levels: public, personal, and private.

3 Evaluations, Experiences, and Reflections

We have learned many lessons and gained many insights in the course of developing, using, and testing our solutions. Our experiences fall into three general categories that we have observed across numerous application prototypes and evaluation sessions: orientation side effects, input precision, and non-speech audio feedback for group interaction.

3.1 Orientation Side Effects

Providing interface-level support for flexible document orientation and positioning on a large tabletop has emerged as an important foundation for our work. The

DiamondSpin toolkit has supported many research prototypes and applications. In one project (Forlines et al. 2005), we evaluated and analyzed various orientation techniques' performance and differences. Our findings suggest that a more objectively precise technique does not necessarily translate into high qualitative ratings from users. Indeed, each technique seems to have a different feel for users related to interaction fluidity, how a technique behaves under the user's touch, and the technique's perceived naturalness.

We also observed two noticeable operational side effects of rotating tabletop documents that are independent of the rotation and translation methods. First, while users want the ability to reorient documents to suit tabletop collaboration, some orientations can severely affect a document's resize range. This problem occurs when a document is rotated out of alignment with a rectangular or square tabletop's canonical edges, as seen in three out of the five documents in Fig. 1b. Second, text readability can degrade when a document is rotated at an angle with respect to the canonical Cartesian x and y axes, due to aliased rendering for rotated text.

To solve these usability problems, we built a Table-for-N feature in the current version of DiamondSpin. When a user rotates a document, Table-for-N automatically snaps the document's bottom edge to align parallel with one of the tabletop's N edges. This function is convenient when several tabletop users are working independently on documents or images.

3.2   Input Precision

Although many touch-interactive surfaces provide high input resolution at single-pixel or finer precision, we have observed (along with other researchers) that pixel-accurate interaction is difficult with direct-touch interaction. This imprecision particularly manifests in terms of jitter – a shift in touched or selected pixels between input frames. Jitter is a problem in at least two cases.

First, some operations require repeated interactions, as when users must double or triple tap on the tabletop (with a single finger, multiple fingers, or the whole hand). However, such consecutive taps do not necessarily land on the exact same pixel region on the tabletop display. To solve this, we have built in a larger activation region for retouch. That is, when an interaction requires a user to repeatedly tap on the tabletop, the exact pixel area touched on the second or third landing has a built-in tolerance. For single-finger double or triple taps, for example, we find a tolerance of 10 pixels, or roughly 1/3 of an inch, works quite well.

Other researchers in touch-interaction precision have proposed to solve this problem through indirect (offset) or relative pointing. However, in our view, it is important to maintain direct full-handed touch and the bimanual interaction paradigm on a horizontal tabletop surface as much as possible.

Second, jitter is an issue when the operation's effect occurs when the user lifts his or her hand. During our user study for bimanual gesture design (Wu et al. 2006), for example, we noticed that some participants were troubled by their accuracy in selecting an image region during copy-and-paste (see Fig. 3). Often, as participants lifted their hands to complete the paste operation, the pasted image was slightly shifted in one or both dimensions.

To stabilize imprecise interaction jitter, we improved our gesture termination algorithm: it now looks back a few time frames from the instance that a user lifts his or her hand off the table. Specifically, our algorithm looks for a time window in which the user's hand has maintained a stable selection posture for a few frames of time. We take this selection box as the user's intended region for copy-and-paste. This improvement has offered fairly satisfactory performance.

3.3 Non-speech Audio Feedback

In a multi-user, interactive tabletop setting, the table serves as both a shared display and a shared input device. Because the display is visual, designers often focus on presenting information to users through the visual channel. Although visual feedback is the primary communication modality in this environment, we believe auditory feedback can also serve an important role. However, what that role is and how it might enhance users' experiences and assist in application building is not yet clear. In particular, simultaneous actions by multiple users can both increase efficiency and create interference.

In an initial UbiTable user study, we found that users were confused when the tool offered auditory feedback to indicate operational errors. Because an identical system beep sounded for both users, the common reaction was: "Who was that sound for?" In collaborative settings, users often work in parallel on individual tasks and might want to be aware of their peers' actions. Users might, for example, wish to know when another user accesses or manipulates screen objects outside their visual attention. Auditory feedback can be useful in these circumstances. While using redundant auditory feedback can increase group awareness in some cases, it can also hinder individual users' performance. Alternatively, sounds that are useful for an individual might overload the larger group's auditory channels. It is essential to consider this trade-off when designing co-located, collaborative applications.

Our study included two experiments using non-speech audio in an interactive multi-touch, multi-user tabletop surface (Hancock et al. 2005). In our first experiment, we investigated two categories of reactive auditory feedback: affirmative sounds that confirm user actions and negative sounds that indicate errors. Our results show that affirmative auditory feedback might improve a user's awareness of group activity at the expense of awareness of the user's own activity. Negative auditory feedback might also improve group awareness, but simultaneously increase the perception of errors for both the group and the individual.

In our second experiment, we compared two methods of associating sounds to individuals in a co-located environment. Specifically, we compared localized sound, where each user has his or her own speaker, to coded sound, where users share a speaker, but the sound's waveform is varied so a different sound is played for each user. Results of this experiment reinforce the first experiment's finding: a tension exists between group awareness and individual focus. User feedback suggests that users can more easily identify who caused a localized or coded sound, and that either option lets them more easily focus on their individual work. In general, these two experiments show that, depending on its presentation, it is possible to use auditory feedback in co-located collaborative applications to support either individual work or group awareness, but not both simultaneously.

4 Conclusion

Interactive, direct-touch digital tables are an emerging form factor with largely immature user interface design. Our research results, along with that of other researchers, set forth interaction techniques, user experiences, and design considerations that we will continue to expand as we exploit and explore the advantages of interactive tabletop systems.

Among our lessons learned so far is that, whenever we demonstrate our tabletop systems to actual users or potential customers, the most compelling moments occurred when the tables interoperated with vertical displays and other devices. This observation agrees with our previous finding that group interactions require supplemental vertical displays (Wigdor et al. 2006).

While the digital table provides a compelling focal point for group activity, we recognize the opportunity to augment it with additional computational resources and surfaces. We have thus begun exploring multi-surface table-centric interaction (Forlines et al. 2006, Wigdor et al. 2006), wherein all interaction occurs at a table, while ancillary surfaces provide coordinated and multi-view visualization and display space. This is different from previous interactive room research, in which displays and devices are generally independent.

There are many outstanding research issues in this area. In our view, two of the most fundamental open questions are: Does a large tabletop provide spatial and perceptual cognitive advantage in helping users accomplish their tasks? If so, under what circumstances does this cognitive assistance occur, and when does it break down? To fully examine these questions, we must step back and analyze basic human perception and cognition; evaluate not only our design artefact, but the cognitive prosthesis it might enable; and envision how people might use this externalization device to better represent, visualize, and express their ideas.

References

Esenther, A., and Ryall, K., 2006, "Fluid DTMouse: Better Mouse Support for Touch-Based Interactions," *Proceedings of the Working Conference on Advanced Visual Interfaces* (AVI), ACM Press, pp. 112–115.
Everitt, K., Shen, C., Ryall, K., and Forlines, C., 2005, "Modal Spaces: Spatial Multiplexing to Mediate Direct-Touch Input on Large Displays," *extended abstracts, Proceedings of the*

International Conference on Human Factors in Computing Systems (CHI), ACM Press, pp. 1359–1362.

Forlines, C., and Shen, C., 2005a, "DTLens: Multi-User Tabletop Spatial Data Exploration," *Proceedings of the 18th Annual ACM Symposium on User Interface Software and Technology,* ACM Press, pp. 119–122.

Forlines, C., Shen, C., Vernier, F., and Wu, M., 2005b, "Under My Finger: Human Factors in Pushing and Rotating Documents Across the Table," *Proceedings of the International Conference on Human–Computer Interaction* (Interact), LNCS 3585, Springer Verlag, pp. 994–997.

Forlines, C., Esenther, A., Shen, C., Wigdor, D., and Ryall, K., 2006, "Multi-User, Multi-Display Interaction with a Single-User, Single-Display Geospatial Applicatio," *Proceedings of the 2006 ACM Conference on User Interface Software and Technology,* (Montreux, Switzerland), ACM Press. pp. 273–276.

Hancock, M. S., Shen, C., Forlines, C., and Ryall, K., 2005, "Exploring Non-Speech Auditory Feedback at an Interactive Multi-User Tabletop," *Proceedings of the 2005 Conference on Graphics Interface,* Canadian Human–Computer Comm. Soc., pp. 41–50.

Hancock, M.S., Vernier, F.D., Wigdor, D., Carpendale, S., and Shen, C., 2006, "Rotation and Translation Mechanisms for Tabletop Interaction," *Proceedings of the 1st IEEE International Workshop Horizontal Interactive Human–Computer Systems* (TableTop), IEEE CS Press, pp. 79–78.

Kruger, R., Carpendale, S., Scott, S. D., and Greenberg, S., 2004, "Roles of Orientation in Tabletop Collaboration: Comprehension, Coordination and Communication," *Journal of Computer Supported Cooperative Work,* vol. 13, no 5–6, pp. 501–537.

Scott, S.D., Grant, K.D., and Mandryk, R.L., 2003., "System Guidelines for Co-located, Collaborative Work on a Tabletop Display," *Proceedings of the European Conference on Computer-Supported Cooperative Work* (ECSCW), Kluwer Press, pp. 129–178.

Scott, S. D., Sheelagh, M., Carpendale, T., and Inkpen, K. M., 2004, "Territoriality in Collaborative Tabletop Workspaces," *Proceedings of the ACM Conference on Computer-Supported Cooperative Work* (CSCW), ACM Press, pp. 294–303.

Shen, C., Everitt, K., and Ryall, K., 2003, "UbiTable: Impromptu Face-to-Face Collaboration on Horizontal Interactive Surfaces," *Proceedings of the 5th International Conference on Ubiquitous Computing,* LNCS 2864, Springer Verlag, pp. 281–288.

Shen, C., Vernier, F. D., Forlines, C., and Ringel, M. 2004., "DiamondSpin: An Extensible Toolkit for Around-the-Table Interaction," *Proceedings of the International Conference on Human Factors in Computing* (CHI), ACM Press, pp. 167–174.

Shen, C., Hancock, M. S., Forlines, C., and Vernier, F. D., 2005, "CoR2D: Context-Rooted Rotatable Draggables for Tabletop Interaction," *extended abstracts, International Conference on Human Factors in Computing Systems* (CHI), ACM Press, pp. 1781–1784.

Tse, E., Shen, C., Greenberg, S., and Forlines, C., 2006, "Enabling Interaction with Single User Applications Through Speech and Gestures on a Multi-User Tabletop," *Proceedings of the Working Conference on Advanced Visual Interfaces* (AVI), ACM Press, pp. 336–343.

Wigdor, D., and Balakrishnan, R., 2005, "Empirical Investigation into the Effect of Orientation on Text Readability in Tabletop Displays," *Proceedings of the 9th European Conference on Computer-Supported Cooperative Work* (ECSCW), Kluwer Press, pp. 205–224.

Wu, M., Shen, C., Ryall, K., Forlines, C., and Balakrishnan, R., 2006, "Gesture Registration, Relaxation, and Reuse for Multi-Point Direct-Touch Surfaces," *Proceedings of the 1st IEEE International Workshop Horizontal Interactive Human–Computer Systems* (TableTop), IEEE CS Press, pp. 183–190.

Wigdor, D., Shen, C., Forlines, C., and Balakrishnan, R., 2006, "Table-Centric Interactive Spaces for Real-Time Collaboration," *Proceedings of the Working Conference on Advanced Visual Interfaces* (AVI), ACM Press, pp.103–107.

Interpersonal Computers for Higher Education

Frédéric Kaplan, Son Do Lenh, Khaled Bachour, Gloria Yi-ing Kao,
Clément Gault, and Pierre Dillenbourg

An interpersonal computer is a computer on which several persons can interact at the same time, in the same place. Whereas personal computers' input devices (keyboard and mouse) and displays (individual screen) are adapted to a single user, interpersonal computers enable distributed control by multiple inputs and are equipped with public displays, where the result of a computation can be shared by a group of users. In this chapter, we explore the design and use of interpersonal computers for higher education through the discussion of two specific examples developed in our lab – a table and a lamp. In particular, we discuss how the introduction of these novel pieces of technology coherently complements the use of personal computers in an integrated learning scenario.

Keywords Collaborative co-located learning, Multi-user interfaces, Augmented furniture

1 Personal and *Interpersonal* Computers

Personal computers were introduced in educational environments with the hope that they would enhance learning particularly by reinforcing the autonomy of students, helping them create their own *individual* learning trajectories and fostering their ability to discover and explore by themselves (Pelgrum and Plomp 1991). Associated with a philosophy arguing that the teacher should remain in the background to permit more flexible and open learning scenarios, PCs were expected to radically change the way teachers teach and students learn. Indeed, as the number of PCs per students in school is constantly increasing, some educational practices have started to change. However, the overall impact is uneven. In many cases, integrating personal computers with existing classroom practices proved to be anything but easy (Rhodes and Cox 1990). Some reports argued that personal computers actually made teaching more difficult (Kerr 1991). Moreover, since PCs facilitated individual learning, some teachers had the impression they were no longer teaching (see for instance Sandholtz et al. (1990) report on the Apple Classroom of Tomorrow).

From an educational perspective, the power of the personal computer came from the fact that it was *individual* (each student could learn at his own pace). It can be argued that this was also its main weakness as many learning processes in educational environments can benefit from collaboration. Indeed, the art of class teaching can be viewed as the search for the proper equilibrium between individual and group activities. In higher education, collaborative learning itself can occur in a variety of contexts, ranging from formal to casual ones. Sometimes, collaborative learning can be proposed in highly structured environments where teamwork is regulated by a teacher. A team of students typically conducts experiments in a science lab, with specific tasks and deliverables assigned by the teacher, close regulation by assistants and a clear time structure. In other situations, collaborative learning is proposed in semi-structured contexts where students' activity is structured by tasks and deliverables, but where they are able to freely organize a collaborative process. Typically, a team of students has to sustain a project over a few weeks and are free to work together when and where they want. Collaborative learning also occurs in informal contexts, in situations where collaboration is not part of the course requirements. For instance, students often decide to study course readings side-by-side or to do course exercises together. Students define their own social organization according to their experience as well as the available resources and social norms of the place (e.g. speech volume in the library). Learning could also occur when students socialize during their free time while eating lunch, during sports, or other activities that are not pedagogically oriented.

Research has focused on potential relevant use of laptops or desktop machines in computer rooms in such collaborative learning scenarios. But several problems have been reported. Personal computers keep attention focused on human computer interaction at the expense of human-human interaction (Prante et al. 2004). In the case of several students working together on the same machine, collaboration usually ends up with one person controlling one computer or each person working alone on his computer (Shih et al. 2004). In short, personal computers are not necessarily the most efficient tools for learning together. To support co-located collaborative learning, they could be complemented with *interpersonal computers* (Fig. 1).

An interpersonal computer is a computer on which several persons can interact in the same place, at the same time. Personal computers have input devices adapted to a single user (e.g. keyboard, mouse), interpersonal computers enable distributed control by multiple users and must therefore introduce novel input tools (e.g. multi-touch screen, visual movement recognition, multi-modal interfaces). Personal computers are characterized by a personal display, interpersonal computers are characterized by the use of public display, where the result of a computation can be shared by a group of users. Whereas personal computers are adapted to personal focus on a personal task, interpersonal computers permit a shared focus on a common context during a collective task.

Current work on interpersonal computers is inspired by previous research on so-called "single display groupware", i.e. large displays to be used by several people at the same time (Stewart et al. 1998) and multiple-input devices, for instance computers equipped with two mice (Inkpen et al. 1999). Both approaches rely on

Fig. 1 The classical model of the computer classroom. Personal computers facilitate individual learning, but do not encourage collaborative processes

the adaptation of personal computers for interpersonal situations. In this chapter, we explore interpersonal computers, as artefacts originally designed for several users working face-to-face or side-by-side. Interpersonal computers can be used in many contexts, but here we address their use for collaborative activities in higher education. In the next section, we discuss how research in collaborative learning motivates the design of computers that scaffolds productive interactions. In short, students learn more when they verbalize knowledge that would otherwise remain tacit. Interpersonal computers must, therefore, be designed to foster fluid but lively exchanges including, in particular, argumentation episodes. Research in ubiquitous computing has been struggling for years to create artefacts that are sufficiently discreet to not act as obstacles during natural interactions but engaging enough to enrich people's awareness and possibility of actions. These two contradictory goals act as guidelines for designing efficient interpersonal computers. The rest of the paper discusses two specific examples developed in our lab, a lamp and a table that can be described as two different embodiments of interpersonal computers and offer a survey of the most interesting technologies currently available to create computers that can support simultaneous interactions by multiple users. In the future, interpersonal computers may be portable tools, like our lamp, or augmented furniture, like our table. We conclude by discussing how the introduction of these novel technologies coherently complements the use of personal computers in an integrated learning scenario.

2   Designing Computers that Scaffold Productive Interactions

Why would students learn better in groups? How could knowledge emerge from the interactions among them? Initial empirical studies have shown that collaborative learning is often more effective than learning alone, but not systematically (Slavin 1983). Task features, group size, group heterogeneity, medium features also certainly play a role in the effectiveness of collaboration (Dillenbourg et al. 1996). However, too many parameters need to be controlled in order to predict these effects. Moreover, these parameters interact with each other in a complex way. Therefore, more recent studies do not try to control the effectiveness of collaborative learning as if it was a black box but zoom in on the collaborative process in order to grasp which type of interactions produce learning and when these interactions occur. In other words, **the effects of collaborative learning depend on the quality of interactions during collaboration**. Several types of interactions have been studied such as the quality of explanations (Webb 1991), mutual regulation (Blaye 1988), argumentation (Baker 1999), and conflict resolution (Doise et al. 1975). What is common to all these interactions is that they all lead students to **verbalize knowledge** that would otherwise remain tacit.

Research in collaborative learning invites us to consider two key features for the design of interpersonal computers. Interpersonal computers should permit fluid interactions among group members and not act as an obstacle to natural collaboration. Interpersonal computers should also be designed to influence interactions by augmenting the frequency of conflicts, fostering elaborated explanations and supporting mutual understanding. **These two goals may seem contradictory**: how can the same tool be sufficiently transparent to foster natural interaction dynamics and sufficiently present to anticipate or actively shape group processes.

The type of dilemma we face in the design of interpersonal computer (shaping interactions without overwhelming them with inappropriate technological intermediaries) is at the heart of the research in ubiquitous computing. Since the late 90s, many projects in the field of ubiquitous computing have investigated how information technology could be incorporated into everyday objects and infrastructures (clothes, furniture, buildings, urban settings) (Weiser 1991, Norman 1998, Greenfield 2006). The central idea of this research is to go beyond what is possible with traditional computers by creating more **fluid ways of interacting with technology**. A main trend in this field consists in the development of "smart environments" or "roomware" (Prante et al. 2004, Cantarella and Guallart 2005).

As more researchers investigate this field, different perspectives on how such technologies should be implemented have arisen. Some researchers in ubiquitous computing have advocated for "calm technology" (Weiser and Brown 1997) and "proactive computing" (Tennenhouse 2000). In these views, technology literally has to disappear in order to not overburden our daily practices. Like doors in public spaces that automatically open when you walk towards them, proactive smart environments continuously sense what is going on and are designed to make appropriate automatic decisions depending on the context. Information and technological tools remain invisible most of the time and appear in the centre of our attention only when needed.

However, "calm technologies", because they imply context-awareness are intrinsically difficult to implement. Moreover, as they usually involve tracking and monitoring people, they also raise ethical and societal issues (Greenfield 2006). For these reasons, some researchers argue for moving from "proactive computing to proactive people" and for technologies that focus on "engaging rather than calming" people (Rogers 2006). For these researchers, the human must always be in the loop and the purpose of ubiquitous technologies is, first, to represent information relevant to the activity at hand using the most appropriate surfaces or devices and, second, to augment the possibility of action by providing novel adapted tools embedded in everyday objects. People must be able to understand these displays and tools sufficiently well in order to know how to control them and interact with them.

In the context of designing interpersonal computers for learning spaces, both "calm" and "engaging" approaches are appealing. On the one hand, hiding technology in walls, tables and chairs may indeed foster fluid and dynamic interactions (Bly 1988, Tang 1991, Prante et al. 2004, Shih et al. 2004). On the other hand, in most situations, the aim is to provide new tools and visualizations that could be used by learners in a proactive way. The NIMIS experience is interesting because, in some way, it embodies both approaches (Hoppe et al. 2000). Researchers developed an environment for learning to read by learning to write, a method used in some primary schools in Germany. They simply embedded touch screens in the kids' desks and put all computers in a separate room. This apparently minor difference (hiding the computers) had a large impact on the 'natural' richness of social interaction in the classroom. The NIMIS experience was run for several years in a real first year classroom with good learning outcomes. However, the hidden computers in the experience were still, in many ways, traditional personal computers. Learning was made efficient by suppressing the anti-social dimension of computer devices. We believe more can be done by creating novel hardware designed to explicitly support interpersonal interactions. Let us now consider two very different examples of interpersonal computers developed in our lab.

3 DOCKLAMP, A Portable Projector-Camera System

Why should a lamp produce only light? With the recent advances in LED projector miniaturization, now it is possible to consider lamps that could project not only light but also images and videos. DOCKLAMP can act not only as a lamp but also as a novel type of interface permitting augmented interaction on a tabletop. The lamp's head is equipped with a tiny projector and a camera and its base is a mini-pc, with a WiFi antenna (Figs. 2 and 3). In its closed position, the device looks like a long suitcase that can be easily carried using a handle. The projector lens and the camera are placed in a secured position. The suitcase can be opened with a simple gesture and transformed into a lamp. In its resting position, the projector box is automatically positioned in the appropriate vertical position, facing down at a height of 90 cm. The whole lamp can be easily rotated in order to project in the most adapted space of the table. Thus, the small dimensions of the projected image are compensated for by the simplicity of changing the position of the projection.

Fig. 2 First prototype of DOCKLAMP, a smart lamp that can not only act as a lamp but also as a novel type of interface permitting augmented interaction on a tabletop

One of the first software programmes we developed for this system permits sharing displays just by pressing one button on the lamp base. In a prototypical situation, six students work together on shared projects sitting around a table. They actively discuss a particular plan for the project presented by one of them. Instead of using a standard video projector, they use the lamp to project the presenter's laptop display. The image of the presentation is projected on the table. This type of projection fosters group discussion and prevents the feeling of passivity associated with projected presentations. As the discussion goes on, one of the students using his own laptop has just found a relevant resource on the Internet. Instead of turning his laptop around to show the information to the other participants, he just pushes the central button of the lamp to project his own laptop on the tabletop. This is a public gesture, understood by the others, as "I'm going to interrupt to show you something".

As the lamp is also equipped with a camera, we have explored novel ways of interacting with the projected image using a multi-finger detection system. This opens up the possibility for many augmented reality applications such as interaction with projected buttons, contextual pop-up menus, manipulation of projected images using several fingers, interaction with projected virtual characters, mixed reality games, etc. More specially, we are developing specific applications targeted to tasks relevant in higher education contexts.

One of the applications we are currently developing permits users to collectively sort multiple items such as images, formulas and documents). In a typical classification

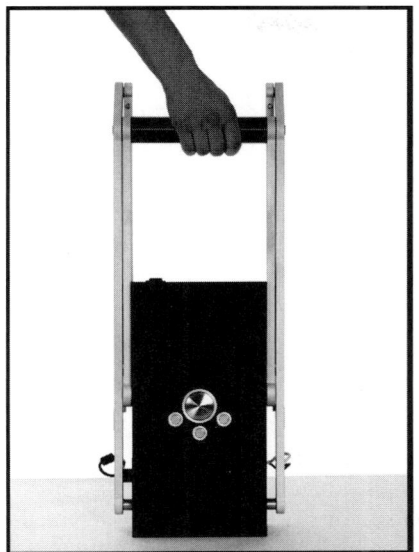

Fig. 3 Second "Portable" version of DOCKLAMP (Design: Martino d'Esposito). DOCKLAMP is organized into two separated aluminium "boxes". The first one contains a mini-PC equipped with a Wi-Fi antenna and electronics for the buttons and the power adapters for both the PC and the projector. The second box contains the projector and the camera. In its closed position, DOCKLAMP looks like a long suitcase that can be easily carried on using a handle. The projector lens and the camera are placed in a secured position. The suitcase can be opened with a simple gesture and transformed into a lamp. In its resting position the projector box is automatically positioned in the appropriate vertical position, facing down at 90 cm of height. The whole lamp can be easily rotated in order to project in the most adapted space of the table. Thus, the small dimension of the projected image is somehow compensated for by the simplicity for changing the position of the projection. In this sense, DOCKLAMP has to be viewed as an augmented desktop lamp rather than the substitute for a whole table projection system

task, a group of students receives a set of objects to be classified into different sets. The task may be deductive (the teacher defines the categories and students have to apply classification criteria) or inductive (the teacher provides examples and students have to define the categories). Inductive tasks can be mono-category (the teacher specifies which examples are positive and negative about the concept to be induced) or multi-category (students have to do clustering from a set of objects without knowing which or how many categories have to be formed).

Another application concerns the collective exploration of a large amount of data. A group of students receives a set of multidimensional data such as those collected from a geological survey, environmental monitoring, socio-economical indicators or physics experiments. These students have to explore the data in order to find relationships between parameters that reflect the phenomena to be modelled. The task may be deductive (the teacher provides the model that students have to apply), inductive (students explore data for finding patterns) or hypothetic-deductive (students express a hypothesis, verify it and refine it).

This system is likely to be relevant for other types of tasks like control and regulation of a complex system simulation or browsing through large sets of documents.

DOCKLAMP is an interpersonal computer because it is made to support interactions between different users. However, it is not meant to be used only as a standalone computer. Some applications make a relevant use of the fact that users that interact with the lamp also have their own personal laptop, like in the display switching scenario we have just presented. The goal of these applications is to permit efficient, easy exchanges between the personal spaces of the laptops and the shared display of the interpersonal computer.

4   REFLECT, A Conversation Board

REFLECT is a table that monitors, via embedded microphones, the conversation taking place around it. In the middle of the table, a matrix of LED display presents participants with a real-time visualization of the structure of their interaction. REFLECT can be scripted for different pedagogical usages. One application of the current prototype displays the relative amount of speaking time for each participant sitting around a table. We chose a simple visualization approach. Based on the notion that in conversations self-regulation of participation's contribution is important, we indicate on the board, territorial information, where the size of a participant's territory is related to how much that participant has spoken during the last 15 min. Around the location of each participant's position, a circle of illuminated LEDs grows and shrinks depending on his dominant role in the conversation, i.e. the amount of conversation time that the participant is taking up. In addition, to make the table more reactive, a short term visualization is also displayed. It is represented by a ring that grows when the participant is talking and shrinks when they are silent. This creates the effect of visually taking and ceding the floor. Figure 4 shows the current prototype in use.

As such, this metaphorical representation is not a normative one. Given the particular context of the meeting, it is maybe relevant that one of the participants keeps the floor for a longer time than the others (e.g. he reports about an experiment he just made). However, as we mentioned earlier, students who verbalize their knowledge the most, learn the most. The display has the same social function as a mirror: giving back a representation that may or may not lead to some regulatory feedback process (in the same way as looking at the mirror before going to work in the morning may or may not change our mind about what to wear) (Jermann 2004, Dillenbourg et al. 2002, Zumbach et al. 2002).

REFLECT shares several similarities with a project of Lira Nikolovska, a table with a one-dimensional LED array designed for conversation between two people (Nikolovska and Ackerman, this volume). In a sense, that table offers a minimal board, with just a single line. REFLECT is designed for larger groups and permits the exploration of complex forms of visual representations. DiMicco (2005) has explored a visualization system for observing various aspects of a group's conversation

Fig. 4 First prototype of REFLECT, a noise-sensitive table that plays the role of a group mirror permitting to visualization conversation dynamics

(participation level, turn-taking patterns, overlapping speech, etc.). These novel visualizations are presented on a separated computer screen, typically after the meeting and not in real-time during the group interaction. The research of Donath, Karahalios and colleagues on visualization of conversations is also relevant for this project (Donath et al. 1997, Donath 2002, Karahalios and Bergstrom 2006), and, more generally such kinds of systems are linked with research on shared display as group memory (Dillenbourg and Traum 2006).

REFLECT is an example of what we call a "mid-tech" approach to interpersonal computers based on simple, cheap and robust pieces of technology. We have deliberately chosen not to equip the table with a large and expensive hi-resolution tactile display. We believe that highly detailed feedback is likely to be counter-productive for the group self-regulation. In this particular case, students should not view these tables as a computer displays, but as furniture. Despite their interactive nature, these tables should be primarily used as normal tables.

5   Other Technologies for Interpersonal Computers

DOCKLAMP and REFLECT are just two examples of what can an interpersonal computer can be. To give a broader overview of the emerging field of "interpersonal computing", we will now review some of the recent advances in terms on input tools, public display and context-aware systems. Although the term "interpersonal computer" is not yet a common term in our research communities, many technologies relevant to interpersonal computers are currently being investigated. As mentioned, such devices call for novel input tools as well as public displays facilitating multi-user/multi-point interactions. In addition, technologies for context-awareness use in robotics research can also be relevant in this context, as they permit a device to track and monitor what is going on around it.

5.1 Input Tools

Input interfaces other than a single mouse have been explored for a long time, including eye gazes, head movements, multi-user physical objects/devices, voice, or human hand gestures. While eye gaze and head movements are not really natural to face-to-face multi-user interactions, the others can be considered to be applicable to interpersonal computers.

Multi-mice are the obvious solution to support more than a single user simultaneously interacting with the system. There has been much research in the literature dealing with this issue, allowing the plugging in of more mice, and controlling them all together: (Bier and Freeman 1991, Hourcade and Bederson 1999, Tse and Greenberg 2002, Pawar et al. 2006). Other methods using physical objects/devices involve joysticks (Wilson and Agrawala 2006) and tangible objects (Fitzmaurice et al. 1995, Ullmer and Ishii 1997, Berard 2003, Metoyer et al. 2003). Pens, such as optical/magnetic styli, are also widely used as an appealing and robust input device (Bandyopadhyay et al. 2001, Ashdown and Robinson 2005).

A broad spectrum of systems involves voice input and using the voice to control the computer. Some early attempts have been made in (Schmandt 1982, Bolt 1980, Weimer and Ganapathy 1989). Assuming that the voice/speech recognition cannot be 100% accurate, however, the authors exploited voice as a complementary channel to hand gestures, to control the interface. While recent works have shown that speech commands could be a potential input to standard graphical user interfaces (Gorniak and Roy 2003), we believe they are still far from providing a robust multi-user system permitting concurrent interactions based on voice input.

There is a large body of literature introducing an extensive list of interesting systems exploiting user's hands as an input method as they provide a simple, natural and direct mechanism for interactions. The technologies can be categorized into two approaches: hardware-based and vision-based approaches. The term "hardware", although not exact, is used here to refer to special materials needed during the installation of the system. Hardware-based systems make use of the materials like matrices of force-sensitive-resistors (Hillis 1982), capacity electrodes (Dietz and Leigh 2001, Rekimoto 2002) or digitizing tablets (Leganchuk et al. 1998). Vision-based approaches recognize user interaction by processing captured images from cameras and then using a projector to display feedback (Wellner 1993, Koike et al.

2000, Letessier and Bérard 2004, McDonald et al. 2004, Wilson 2004, 2005). Various techniques can be used to estimate depth using either stereovision (Malik and Laszlo 2004, Wilson 2004) or intensity level (Matsushita and Rekimoto 1997). There are some combinations of these two approaches such as the work of (Han 2005) which is based on the Frustrated Total Internal Reflection (FTIR) technique, or in (Kamiyama et al. 2005) where the use of markers embedded in deformable substrates is shown. Other technological routes are also explored based on laser detection for multi-finger detection or alternatively on temporal reversal of acoustic waves (Ing and Fink 1998) permitting to turn common objects into tactile screens. Commercial products already exist for these hand-based interfaces.

In sum, techniques that support simultaneous multi-user interactions are becoming more common, yet very few research studies currently address the issues of collaborative gestures that could be performed with such systems. One interesting exception is the work of Morris and co-workers on this subject (Morris et al. 2006). As an example of cooperative gesturing, they present the case of a deleting command that must be performed simultaneously by all the participants in order to be validated and of "photo passing actions" involving specific gesturing of two participants. Consensus, involvement, group cohesion and a greater sense of teamwork can be achieved and fostered by designing specific cooperative gestures. However, such kinds of rather rigid design result in overall lower performance efficiency. It is certainly possible to design systems that permit smoother transitions between simultaneous parallel actions to cooperative gesturing.

5.2 Public Displays

There have been two main trends in how to form the public display. One trend suggests large scale displays with the aim to augment discussions such as meetings, talks, etc. The others provide table-size situated displays supporting several users in collective co-located manipulation task, as is the case with interactive tabletops.

Various large scale displays have been used in different situations. The early system Tivoli (Pedersen et al. 1993) provided a pen-based electronic whiteboard for office meetings. Within the same context, the system in (Malik et al. 2005) allows users to interact with a wall-size display while remaining seated at a table with bare hands. The same scheme applies in the Dynamo (Izadi et al. 2003), a communal multi-user wall display which supports the sharing and exchange of digital documents. In the early 1990s, Hiroshi Ishii's ClearBoard realized a seamless shared drawing space in which eye-contact could be maintained between the different users (Ishii and Kobayahi 1992). Guimbretière and colleagues presented a pen-based large interactive display developed as a brainstorming tool (Guimbretière et al. 2001). Large displays are also used as a resource for shared awareness. The Notification Collage (Greenberg and Rounding 2001) provided community members with the means of indicating their presence by posting live video onto the public display or joining in the conversations of others. The Kimura system (MacIntyre et al. 2001) augments the user's awareness with a background of their past and current activities. Other uses of large display can be found in classrooms (Li et al. 2006), or together with mobile devices (Paek et al. 2004).

Interactive tabletops primarily serve as a mediated environment for co-located manipulation task in which multiple users interact shoulder-to-shoulder on the same interface. Stewart et al. (1999) suggested the notion of single display groupware (SDG) to refer to these systems. The main characteristic of interactive tabletops is the direct mechanism of interaction, i.e. the input and output visual spaces are superimposed onto the same surface. An increasing number of these novel interfaces have been developed recently (Ullmer and Ishii 1997, Koike et al. 2000, Dietz and Leigh 2001, Rekimoto 2002, Berard 2003, McDonald et al. 2004, Wilson 2005). Some experiments concerning the design and implementation of these displays have been conducted, resulting in guidelines for co-located collaborative work (Scott et al. 2003), and initial findings on the effects of group and table size on interactions around a tabletop (Ryall et al. 2004).

Vertical large-scale display and interactive tabletops can be used in very complementary manners as shown by the research conducted at Fraunhofer IPSI involving several roomware components such as the DynaWall, a large, touch-sensitive information display or the InteracTable, a touch-sensitive plasma display embedded in a tabletop (Prante et al. 2004).

5.3   Context-Awareness

Context-awareness technologies, investigated in the robotics and ubiquitous computing communities are also relevant to our concerns. Microphone arrays allow detecting user positions using frequency bands provided by a Fast Fourier Transform computation on the microphones streams (Lathoud and McCowan 2004). Laser-range finders and the cheaper IR distance sensors can be used to sense the presence of people or objects around a computer. Moreover, there now exists multiple ways to recognize who is currently interacting with the computer, either through active identification of the user (e.g. showing an RFID tag) or through passive monitoring (e.g. Bluetooth detection of cell phones ID). Eventually, using a combination of these techniques, an interpersonal computer can sense and assess how many people are interacting with it and who or where these people are. And this is just the beginning. By analyzing movement and voice features (i.e. prosody), researchers are now investigating how the computer could achieve finer grained context awareness, for instance, by identifying conversation episodes around a table or segment coordinated activity patterns in a room (Kaplan and Hafner 2006). All this contextual information can be used by the machines to make appropriate decisions but also to produce some interesting visualizations of the current state, actions and dynamics of the group.

6 Interpersonal Computers As Key Components for Integrated Learning

The famous slogan "From a sage on the stage to the guide on the side" has been misleading: reducing the amount of lectures does not mean reducing the salient role of teachers in the social process of learning. If technical constraints often reduce teacher's freedom to adapt his or her plan on the fly, we have to adapt the technology instead of reducing the teacher's freedom. Interpersonal computers can play a key role in the novel type of technology-enhanced teaching where the teacher is the *driver* who orchestrates the sequence of activities and may adapt the scenario in real time. We believe that interpersonal computers can play a key role in this novel form of integrated learning.

The design space for interpersonal computer is huge. A personal computer can be portable, like a laptop, fixed like a desktop or even integrated in a piece of furniture, like in an information kiosk. Likewise, interpersonal computers can be embedded in tables, walls, floors and ceilings and they can also be designed as portable devices, that a group can bring when it wants to work collectively (in the same way one would bring a projector or retro projector during a meeting).

Interpersonal computers are meant to be efficient tools that permit users to exchange and collectively organize data in a fluid and intuitive manner. They also can be used to shape interactions in ways that foster argumentation, mutual understanding, confrontation or any other means that may lead users to verbalize knowledge that would otherwise remain tacit. We believe this is maybe the beginning of a novel use of computers that permit natural collaboration and scaffold productive interactions. It is clear that most of the work remains to be done particularly in developing the right shape and features of these novel devices and set of relevant applications that goes with them. However, there may come one day when people will commonly refer to "IPCs" as relevant complementary tools to "PCs".

Acknowledgements The authors would like to thank former members of the CRAFT team, Jean-Baptiste Haué, Andrina Brun, Annick Plancherel, Guillaume Raymondon and Michael Ruflin who contributed at different stages of the projects discussed in this chapter.

References

Ashdown, M. & Robinson, P. (2005). Escritoire: A personal projected display. *IEEE MultiMedia* 12 (1), 34–42.

Baker, M. J. (1999). Argumentation and constructive interaction. In G. Rijlaarsdam & E. Espéret (Series Eds.) & Pierre Coirier and Jerry Andriessen (Vol. Eds.), *Studies in Writing: Vol. 5. Foundations of Argumentative Text Processing* (pp. 179–202). Amsterdam: University of Amsterdam Press.

Bandyopadhyay, D., Raskar, R. & Fuchs, H. (2001). Dynamic shader lamps (2001): Painting on movable objects. In *IEEE and ACM International Symposium on Augmented Reality (ISAR'01)* IEEE Computer Society Washington, DC, USA.

Berard, F. (2003). The magic table: Computer vision based augmentation of a whiteboard for creative meetings. In *IEEE International Conference in Computer Vision, Workshop on Projector-Camera Systems*. Nice, France.

Bier, E. & Freeman, S. (1991). Mmm: A user interface architecture for shared editors on a single screen. In *UIST'91* Proceedings of the 4th annual ACM symposium on User interface software and technology, Hilton Head, South Carolina, United States, ACM New York, NY, USA (pp. 79–86).

Blaye, A. (1988). Confrontation socio-cognitive et résolution de problèmes. *Doctoral dissertation*, Centre de Recherche en Psychologie Cognitive, Université de Provence, France.

Bly, S. (1988). A use of drawing surfaces in different collaborative settings. In *Proceedings of the 1988 ACM Conference on Computer-Supported Cooperative Work*, Portland, Oregon, USA The publisher is ACM New York, NY, USA (pp. 250–256).

Bolt, R. A. (1980). Put-that-there: Voice and gesture at the graphics interface. *SIGGRAPH Computer Graphics* 14 (3), 262–270.

Cantarella, L. & Guallart, V. (2005). *The media house project. The house is the computer, the structure is the network*. Actar

Dietz, P. H. & Leigh, D. L. (2001), Diamond Touch: A multi-user touch technology. In *ACM Symposium on User Interface Software and Technology (UIST'01)* ACM New York, NY, USA (pp. 219–226).

Dillenbourg, P. & Traum, D. (2006). Sharing solutions: Persistence and grounding in multi-modal collaborative problem solving. *Journal of the Learning Sciences* 15 (1).

Dillenbourg, P., Baker, M., Blaye, A. & O'Malley, C. (1996). The evolution of research on collaborative learning. In E. Spada & P. Reimann (Eds.), *Learning in Humans and Machine: Towards an Interdisciplinary Learning Science* (pp. 189–211). Oxford: Elsevier.

Dillenbourg, P., Ott, D., Wehrle, T., Bourquin, Y., Jermann, P., Corti, D. & Salo, P. (2002). The socio-cognitive functions of community mirrors. In F. Flückiger, C. Jutz, P. Schulz & L. Cantoni (Eds.), *Proceedings of the 4th International Conference on New Educational Environments*, Lugano, May 8–11, 2002.

DiMicco, J. (2005). *Changing Small Group Interaction through Visual Reflections of Social Behavior*. PhD thesis, MIT Media Laboratory.

Doise, M., Mugny, G. & Perret-Clermont, A.-N. (1975). Social interactions and the development of cognitive operations. *European Journal of Social Psychology* 5, 367–383.

Donath, J.(2002). A semantic approach to visualizing online conversations. *Communications of the ACM (SPECIAL ISSUE: Supporting Community and Building Social Capital)* 45 (4), 45–49.

Donath, J., Karahalios, K. & Viegas, F. (1997). Visualizing conversation. *Journal of Computer Mediated Communication* 2 (4).

Fitzmaurice, G. W., Ishii, H. & Buxton, W. (1995). Bricks: Laying the foundations for graspable user interfaces. In *Proceedings of the ACMSIGCHI Conference on Human Factors in Computing Systems (CHI'95)* ACM Press, New York, NY. (pp. 442–449).

Gorniak, P. & Roy, D. (2003). Augmenting user interfaces with adaptive speech commands. In *Proceedings of the 5th International Conference on Multimodal Interfaces,* November 05–07, 2003, Canada *(ICMI'03)* ACM Press, New York, NY, USA. (pp. 176–179).

Greenfield, A. (2006). *Everyware: The Dawning Age of Ubiquitous Computing*. Berkeley, CA: New Riders.

Greenberg, S. & Rounding, M. (2001). The Notification Collage: Posting information to public and personal displays. In *Proceedings of the SIGCHI Conference on Human Factors in Computing Systems (CHI'01)* ACM Press, New York, NY, USA (pp. 514–521).

Guimbretière, F., Stone, M. & Winograd, T. (2001). Fluid interaction with high-resolution wall-size displays. In *Proceedings of the 14th Annual ACM Symposium on User interface Software and Technology (UIST'01)* (pp. 21–30).

Han, J. (2005). Low-cost multi-touch sensing through frustrated total internal reflection. In *UIST'05*, October 23–27, Seattle, Washington, USA. Proceedings of the 18th annual ACM Symposium on User Interface Software and Technology, ACM Press, New York, NY, USA.

Hillis, W. (1982). A high resolution imaging touch sensor. *International Journal of Robotics Research* 1 (2), 33–44.

Hoppe, H. U., Lingnau, A., Machado, I., Paiva, A., Prada, R. & Tewissen, F.(2000). Supporting collaborative activities in computer integrated classrooms – the NIMIS Approach. In *Proceedings of the 6th International Workshop on Groupware, CRIWG 2000*. Madeira, Portugal: IEEE CS Press.

Hourcade, J. P. & Bederson, B. B. (1999). Architecture and implementation of a java package for multiple input devices (mid). Tech Report HCIL-99-08.

Ing, R. & Fink, M. (1998). Time-Reversed lamb waves. *IEEE Transactions on Ultrasonics, Ferroelectrics, and Frequency Control* 45, 1032–1043.

Inkpen, K. M., Ho-Ching, W., Kuederle, O., Scott, S. D. & Shoemaker, G. B. (1999). This is fun! We're all best friends and we're all playing: supporting children's synchronous collaboration. In C. M. Hoadley and J. Roschelle (Eds.), *Proceedings of the 1999 Conference on Computer Support for Collaborative Learning*, December 12–15, 1999, Palo Alto, California, (p. 31). International Society of the Learning Sciences.

Ishiii, H. & Kobayahi, M. (1992). ClearBoard: A seamless medium for shared drawing and conversation with eye contact. In *Proceedings of the SIGCHI Conference on Human Factors in Computing Systems* Monterey, California, United States, ACM Press, New York, NY, USA. (pp. 525–532).

Izadi, S., Brignull, H., Rodden, T., Rogers, Y. & Underwood, M. (2003). Dynamo: A public interactive surface supporting the cooperative sharing and exchange of media. In *Proceedings of the 16th Annual ACM Symposium on User interface Software and Technology (UIST'03)* ACM Press, New York, NY. (pp. 159–168).

Jermann, P. (2004). *Computer Support for Interaction Regulation in Collaborative Problem-Solving.*Unpublished Doctoral Dissertation, University of Geneva.

Kamiyama, K., Vlack, K., Mizota, T., Kajimoto, H., Kawakami, N. & Tachi, S. (2005). Vision-based sensor for real-time measuring of surface traction fields. *IEEE Computer Graphics and Application* 25 (1), 68–75.

Kaplan, F. & Hafner, V. (2006). Information-theoretic framework for unsupervised activity classification. *Advanced Robotics* 20 (10), 1087–1103

Karahalios, K., Bergstrom, T. (2006). Visualizing audio in group table conversation. In Tabletop, *Proceedings of the First IEEE International Workshop on Horizontal Interactive Human-Computer System*. IEEE Computer Society.

Kerr, S. T. (1991). Lever and Fulcrum: Educational technology in teachers' thought and practice. *Teachers College Record* 93 (1), 114–136.

Koike, H., Sato, Y., Kobayashi, Y., Tobita, H. & Kobayashi, M. (2000). Interactive textbook and interactive Venn diagram: natural and intuitive interfaces on augmented desk system. In *SIGCHI Conference on Human Factors in Computing Systems (CHI'00)* ACM Press, New York, NY, USA. (pp. 121–128).

Lathoud, G. & McCowan, I. A. (2004). A sector-based approach for localization of multiple speakers with microphone arrays. In *Workshop on Statistical and Perceptual Audio Processing SAPA-2004*, October 3, 2004, Jeju, Korea.

Leganchuk, A., Zhai, S. & Buxton, W. (1998). Manual and cognitive benefits of two-handed input: An experimental study. *Transactions on Human-Computer Interaction* 5 (4), 326–359.

Letessier, J. & Bérard, F. (2004). Visual tracking of bare fingers for interactive surfaces. In *ACM Symposium on User interface Software and Technology (UIST'04)* (pp. 119–122).

Li, W., Tang, H. & Zhu, Z. (2006). Vision-based projection-handwriting integration in classroom. In *Proceedings of the 2006 Conference on Computer Vision and Pattern Recognition Workshop* (June 17–22, 2006).

MacIntyre, B., Mynatt, E. D., Voida, S., Hansen, K. M., Tullio, J. & Corso, G. M. (2001) Support for multitasking and background awareness using interactive peripheral displays. In *Proceedings of the 14th Annual ACM Symposium on User interface Software and Technology (UIST'01)* ACM Press, New York, NY. (pp. 41–50).

Malik, S. & Laszlo, J. (2004). Visual Touchpad: a two-handed gestural input device. In *Proceedings of the 6th International Conference on Multimodal Interfaces (ICM'04)* (pp. 289–296). New York, NY: ACM Press.

Malik, S., Ranjan, A. & Balakroshnana, R. (2005). Interacting with large displays from a distance with vision-tracked multi-finger gesturual input. In *Proceedings of the 18th Annual ACM Symposium on User Interface Software and Technology,* Seattle, WA ACM Press, New York, NY. (pp. 43–52).

Matsushita, N. & Rekimoto, J. (1997). HoloWall: Designing a finger, hand, body and object sensitive wall. In *Proceedings of the 10th Annual ACM Symposium on User Interface Software and Technology (UIST 1997)* (pp. 209–210). New York, NY: ACM Press.

McDonald, C., Roth, G. & Marsh, S. (2004). Red-Handed: Collaborative gesture interaction with a projection table, In *Sixth IEEE International Conf. on Automatic Face and Gesture Recognition (FG'04)* (p. 773–778).

Morris, M. R., Huang, A., Paepcke, A. & Winograd, T. (2006). Cooperative gestures: Multi-user gestural interactions for co-located groupware. In *CHI 2006* Proceedings of ACM CHI 2006 Conference on Human Factors in Computing Systems 2006. pp. 1201-1210. ACM Press, New York NY. (pp. 22–27).

Norman D. (1998). *The Invisible Computer.* Cambridge, Mass.: MIT Press.

Paek, T., Agrawala, M., Basu, S., Drucker, S., Kristjansson, T., Logan, R., Toyama, K. & Wilson, A. (2004). Toward universal mobile interaction for shared displays. In Proceedings of the 2004 ACM Conference on Computer Supported Cooperative Work, CSCW 2004, Chicago, Illinois, USA, ACM Press, New York, NY. (pp. 266–269).

Pawar, U., Pal, J. & Toyoma, K. (2006). Multiple mice for computers in education in developing countries. In *International Conference on Information and Communication Technologies and Development* 2006.

Pedersen, E. R., McCall, K., Moran, T. P. & Halasz, F. G. (1993). Tivoli: An electronic whiteboard for informal workgroup meetings. In *Proceedings of the SIGCHI Conference on Human Factors in Computing Systems (CHI'93)* ACM Press, New York, NY. (pp. 391–398).

Pelgrum, W. & Plomp, T. (1991). *The Use of Computers in Education Worldwide.* Oxford: Pergamon Press.

Prante, T., Streitz, N. & Tandler, P. (2004). Roomware: Computers disappear and interaction evolves. *IEEE Computer,* 47–54.

Metoyer, R. A., Xu, L. & Srinivasan, M. (2003). A tangible interface for high-level direction of multiple animated characters. In *Proceedings of Graphics Interface 2003,* Halifax, Canada.

Rekimoto, J. (2002). SmartSkin: An infrastructure for freehand manipulation on interactive surfaces. In *CHI'02* Proceedings of the SIGCHI Conference on Human Factors in Computing Systems. ACM Press, New York, NY. (pp. 113–120).

Rhodes, V. & Cox, M.(1990). *Current Practice and Policies for Using Computers in Primary Schools: Implications for Training.* ESRC, University of Lancaster.

Rogers, Y. (2006). Moving on from Weiser's vision of calm computing: Engaging UbiComp experiences. In P. Dourish & A. Friday (Eds.), *Ubicomp 2006, LNCS 4206* (pp. 404–421).

Ryall, K., Forlines, C., Shen, C. & Ringel-Morris, M. (2004). Exploring the effects of group size and table size on interactions with tabletop shared-display groupware. In *ACM Conference on Computer Supported Cooperative Work (CSCW)* ACM Press, New York, NY. (pp. 284–293).

Sandholtz, J. H., Ringstaff, C. & Dwyer, D. C. (1990). *Teaching in High-Tech Environments: Classroom Management Revisited: First-Fourth Year Findings.* Cupertino: Apple Computer Inc.

Schmandt. C. (1982). Voice interaction: Putting intelligence into the interface. In *Proceedings, IEEE International Conference on Cybernetics and Society,* IEEE, Seattle, WA.

Scott, S. D., Grant, K. D. & Mandryk, R. L. (2003). System guidelines for co-located collaborative work on a tabletop display. In *Proceedings of European Computer-Supported Cooperative Work (ECSCW 2003)* Springer (pp. 159–178).

Shih, C. C., Crone, M., Fox, A. & Winograd (2004). T. Teamspace: A simple, low-cost and self-sufficient workspace for small-group collaborative computing. In *CSCW 2004 Interactive Poster,* Chicago, IL, ACM Press, New York, NY. USA.

Slavin, R. E. (1983). *Cooperative Learning*. New York: Longman.

Stewart, J., Raybourn, E. M., Bederson, B. & Druin, A. (1998). When two hands are better than one: Enhancing collaboration using single display groupware. In *Proceedings of CHI'98* Proceedings of the SIGCHI Conference on Human Factors in Computing Systems. ACM Press, New York, NY. (pp. 287–288).

Stewart, J., Bederson, B. & Druin, A. (1999). Single display groupware: A model for co-present collaboration. In *Proceedings of CHI 1999* (pp. 286–293).

Tang, J. (1991). Findings from observational studies of collaborative work. *International Journal of Man-Machine Studies* 34 (2), 143–160.

Tennenhouse, D. L. (2000). Proactive computing. *Communication of the ACM* 43 (5), 43–50.

Tse, E. & Greenberg, S. (2002). Sdgtoolkit: A toolkit for rapidly prototyping single display groupware. In *CSCW'02*, ACM Press, New York, NY. November 2002.

Ullmer, B. & Ishii, H. (1997). The metaDESK: Models and prototypes for tangible user interfaces. *ACM Symposium on User interface Software and Technology (UIST'97)* ACM Press, New York, NY, USA. (pp. 223–232).

Webb, N. M. (1991). Task related verbal interaction and mathematical learning in small groups. *Research in Mathematics Education* 22 (5), 366–389.

Weimer, D. & Ganapathy, S. K. (1989). A synthetic visual environment with hand gesturing and voice input. In K. Bice & C. Lewis (Eds.), *Proceedings of the SIGCHI Conference on Human Factors in Computing Systems: Wings For the Mind CHI'89* (pp. 235–240). New York, NY: ACM Press.

Weiser, M. (1991). The computer of the 21st century. *Scientific American* 94–104.

Weiser, M. & Brown, J. S. (1997). *The Coming Age of Calm Technolgy, Beyond Calculation: The Next Fifty Years*. New York: Copernicus.

Wellner, P. (1993). Interacting with paper on the Digital Desk. *Communications of the ACM* 36 (7), 87–96.

Wilson, A. (2004). TouchLight: An imaging touch screen and display for gesture-based interaction. In *Proceedings of the 6th International Conference on Multimodal Interfaces, ICMI'04* (pp. 69–76). New York, NY: ACM Press.

Wilson, A. D. (2005). PlayAnywhere: A compact interactive tabletop projection-vision system. In *ACM Symposium on User Interface Software and Technology (UIST'05)* ACM Press, New York, NY, USA. (pp. 83–92).

Wilson, A. D. & Agrawala, M. (2006). Text entry using a dual joystick game controller. In R. Grinter, T. Rodden, P. Aoki, E. Cutrell, R. Jeffries, and G. Olson (Eds.), *Proceedings of the SIGCHI Conference on Human Factors in Computing Systems (CHI'06)* ACM Press, New York, NY. (pp. 475–478).

Zumbach, J., Mühlenbrock, M., Jansen, M., Reimann, P. & Hoppe, H. U. (2002). Multi-dimensional tracking in virtual learning teams: An exploratory study. In G. Stahl (Ed.), *Computer Support for Collaborative Learning: Foundations for a CSCL Community* (pp. 650–651). Mahwah, NJ: Lawrence Erlbaum Associates.

Exploratory Design, Augmented Furniture

On the Importance of Objects' Presence

Lira Nikolovska and Edith Ackermann

This chapter explores the poetics of everyday objects, and their abilities to elicit meaningful interactions. Our focus is on a special kind of everyday objects: a chosen set of "augmented" chairs and tables, especially designed to gently disrupt usually associated emotional/social responses, and to shake habitual ways in which people interact with – and through – furniture. We address the physical, relational, and cultural qualities of these objects in terms of the objects' "presence" and "personality", and we discuss their abilities to engender amusing incongruities. We conclude by speculating on the need of using exploratory, non-mainstream design methods as a means to understanding and thinking through innovations in human-computer interaction. Several cases of augmented furniture will be presented to illustrate the raised points: i) therapeutic furniture (*Robotic Massage Chair* and *Squeeze Chair*) and ii) furniture that mediates human transactions and aides self-reflection (*Conversation Table*, *Stealing Table* and *Table Childhood*).

Keywords Interaction design, Furniture, Tangible interactions, Small moments

1 Introduction

From third-generation mobile phones (with embedded cameras) to smart cars (with built-in navigational systems), and from iPods and TiVos to robotic massage chairs we are surrounded by hybrids and quasi-objects (Latour 1993). Yet, not all hybrids and quasi-objects (generally referred to as "augmented" devices) are equally engaging, or vivid as relational "partners" (Kaplan 2005). Some draw us in while others keep us at a distance. Some are obedient while others seem to have a mind of their own. Some are tiny and accompany us as we transit between places while others, big and bulky, keep us grounded, posted, or even boxed in: they require that we position ourselves with respect to them.

This chapter addresses a particular kind of everyday objects: furniture with embedded technologies, or "augmented furniture". Of particular interest to the authors are the evocative, transformative, and mediating powers of slightly "incongruous"

P. Dillenbourg et al. (eds.), *Interactive Artifacts and Furniture Supporting Collaborative Work and Learning*,
DOI: 10.1007/978-0-387-77234-9_9, © Springer Science + Business Media, LLC 2009

tables and chairs, i.e., their abilities to amuse and delight. We characterize such tables and chairs as *uncanny* everyday objects[1] (Freud 1925) or *strangely familiar* objects (ref. familiar strangers[2]). Their main "relational" quality is that they surprise while, at the same time, evoking the familiar. While tapping into the habitual, they gently disrupt expectations.

In the sections below, we explore the poetic qualities, or presence, of such artefacts, i.e., their abilities to mediate and alter the social and emotional responses of people who interact with, and through, them. The focus is on every day, non-instrumental scenarios of interaction (e.g. dinner at a table, conversation with a friend) that we qualify as *small moments* (de Certeau 1984). Lastly, we address some methodological issues for the study of poetic "augmented" furniture.

2   The Poetics of Everyday Objects, and Their Abilities to Elicit Meaningful Interactions

While each person experiences and appropriates cultural artefacts in very personal ways – depending upon interests, experience, and background – it is also the case that objects and places set their own constraints on the ways we engage them. In other words, not all artefacts are good enough projective materials![3] Some are clearly better suited to foster meaningful and delightful encounters.

2.1   The Beauty in the Eyes of the Beholder?

All forms of human imagination – from fantasy play to musing about incongruities – are based on a unique mental process that the writer Arthur Koestler called "bisociation"

---

[1] The German word for uncanny is *unheimlich*, the opposite of *heimlich* (homely) and *heimish* (native), the opposite of what is familiar. We are tempted to think that the uncanny is frightening precisely because it is not known and familiar. Yet not everything that is new and unfamiliar is frightening. We can only say that what is novel holds the potential of being frightening. In this paper we use the world "uncanny" as a non-frightening incongruity, or gentle "disruption". In Freud, S. *The Uncanny.* 1925.

[2] The *Familiar Strangers* research project (Intel Research, Berkeley) explores often ignored yet real relationships with familiar strangers. Experiments and studies derived from Milgram (1972) have lead to the design of a personal, body-worn device called *Jabberwocky*. Retrieved on 20 April 2006 from http://berkeley.intel-research.net/paulos/research/familiarstranger.

[3] It seems essential for designers, say of learning toys, to take responsibility for their products by not assuming – to caricature the constructivist's stance – that, no matter the external form, people will use it as Rorschach stains and project their own experience, or alternatively that the intent of the author is what prevails through a design. Any creations, once launched, may well speak to others in ways not intended. It too takes on a life of its own.

and which consists of "perceiving a situation or idea in two self-consistent but habitually incompatible frames of reference" (Koestler 1964, page 94). While some form of unexpected, surprising, or incongruous relation is always present in play, poetry, or humour, the presence of incongruity won't suffice to create humour, delight, or playfulness. Instead, incongruity can be perceived in any of three ways: interest, fear, or amusement, depending upon the context. For an incongruous event or object to engender amusement or delight it needs to be taken seriously in its *unreality*, which in turn requires a person's ability to operate on make-believe ground, or do as-if – what psychologists refer to as *suspension of disbelief.*[4]

A person who laughs at jokes, amused when pretending or observing incongruous events, acknowledges the "unreality" (the impossibility or absurdity) of the imagined events: events are humorous *because* they are at odds with reality. Suspension of disbelief is the one single most important quality of human imagination.

A child's abilities to pretend sets in at a time when she most needs them – developmentally speaking – because she enters in the process of individuation, and builds a fragile sense of self. Through pretend and fantasy play, a 2-year-old gets a chance to *dramatize* many intriguing events, sometimes changing the original event's outcome, which helps the child to come to grips with the hardships that identity-formation entails. Piaget noted, for example, that at 23 months of age, his daughter Jacqueline "put a shell on the table and said *"sitting"*, then put another shell on top of the first, adding delightedly: *"sitting on the potty"*. Quite an enactment! Through exaggerations and nonsense, the child distances herself from the seriousness of everyday life, while capturing its essence through fictionalizing (Piaget 1962). Her use of humour cleverly relieves some of the tension from what might be a stressful situation (in this case toilet training). Isn't it why we all like comedy and slapstick humour, for it injects a sense of levity or ridiculousness into many otherwise too serious, painful, or untenable situations?

2.2   Objects' Presence?

The poetics of everyday objects speak to an artefact's abilities to evoke incongruous yet amusing associations while at the same time, uncovering otherwise veiled "truths" or "dangerous" ideas. We refer to this as "object's presence" and we explore the potential of opening up new mental venues, or possibilities, often *possibilities within* – i.e., re-digesting or reverberating deeply felt human experience.

---

[4] Early manifestations of suspension of disbelief appear in a child's fantasy or pretend play, and in her urge to invent/converse with imaginary companions. They also appear in the ability to tease and joke.

3 Designing Objects with a "Presence" and "Personality": Physical, Relational and Cultural

Donald Norman introduced the term "affordance" to refer to an object's ability to signal its potential uses (Norman 1988). Examples of objects with poor affordances include a lamp that doesn't tell the location of its "on" switch and a doorknob that doesn't communicate whether the door should be pushed or pulled[5]. While affordance speaks to an artefact's clarity to signal its whereabouts, something more is needed to sustain interest, produce delight, or enchant. This "something more", in the case of augmented furniture is the surprising blend of autonomy and responsiveness alluded to before: a clear invitation to play and dance!

3.1 Characteristics of Furniture

Furniture has unique physical[6] and relational characteristics. Material properties, such as shape, scale as well as temporal immobility and stability fall into the category of physical characteristics of furniture. "Relational" characteristics include different functional and symbolic characteristics, as signalled/perceived within accepted cultural conventions or "scripts that guide the sequence of behaviour" (Norman 1988). We review the following issues unique to furniture:

- Scale, the body and the engagement of senses
- Temporal personalization and shared use
- Stability of furniture
- Cultural conventions
- Relations between shape and arrangement of furniture, and its meaning

3.1.1 Scale, the Body and the Engagement of Senses

We interact in different ways with small hand-held objects than we do with furniture, cars, rooms or spaces, simply because the scale of the objects is different.

---

[5] Ultimately, even a mundane doorknob could be delightful if, beyond getting us through a doorway, it could retain our attention, suspend our breath and – why not? – slow down our steps. It too could evoke feelings about passages and thresholds, and enrich our experience of moving between places. It too could speak a language that reaches our inner most aspirations.

[6] John Gloag (1966) states that "[n]early all articles of free-standing furniture are variations of two basic shapes: a platform or a box. Stools, benches, chairs, couches, beds and tables are platforms elevated on feet or legs or underframing, on which you sit, lie, or put things; chests, cupboards and wardrobes are boxes for storing anything from linen and clothes to food, wine, drinking vessels, documents or money." (pp. 3–4)

Mobile: Hand-helds and wearables are small and light, and are designed to be held or worn. We carry them along, and they become a part of our "nomadic" selves.

Grounding: Buildings, parks and rooms are habitats that provide shelter and places to live and rest. This is true even of habitats in motion, as in the case of a car. The capsule may move and get us places yet it is still a shelter (a mobile "home"!)

Holding: Furniture, lastly, keeps us settled. Chairs, beds and benches provide body-sized "zones" to rest. Tables bring friends and families together supporting us either socially (to dine or converse with others) or physically (to rest, sleep or sit). The seats in a car, train, or airplane (moving capsules) keep our bodies immobile while we are on the go. Horizontal surfaces offer a fit terrain for placing objects.

3.1.2 Temporal Personalization and Shared Use

We often share furniture, appropriating and sometimes personalizing it temporarily, both at home and in public spaces. We often settle and become temporarily immobile as we sit on a chair or bench, eat at a table, or lie on a bed. Occasionally, the inability to move around or shift our positions relative to the furniture (location or distance) results in peculiar social situations – from the conversations at long holiday dinners, to uncomfortable silences during social events.

3.1.3 Stability of Furniture

Unlike consumer electronics products, augmented furniture is inherently stable. When a cell phone breaks, we cannot use it until it is fixed or we replace it with a new one. When tables with embedded screens and a robotic massage chair is out of power, the objects maintain their core functionality. In other words, they keep their integrity as holding devices that allow us to eat, read, converse with others, sit or relax. This stability of augmented furniture is a critical feature that lends it much of its instrumental and evocative powers.

3.1.4 Cultural Conventions

Accepted cultural conventions and "scripts" guide the sequence of people's behaviour (Norman 1988). Such conventions include behaviours at or around tables, chairs, etc. Table manners are one such set of culture-specific "rules" of behaviour. In the West, proper use of dining utensils is expected. In contrast, in many other countries it is considered perfectly appropriate table manners if fingers are used instead of dining utensils. Another example of culture specific behaviour is illustrated in a report about 19th century Hindu craftsmen (Cranz 1998). The squatting of these blacksmiths, carpenters, and masons while at work was interpreted as uncivilized by their English employer who tried to force the workers to sit on chairs and work on a table, only to find them on the following day working while squatting on the top of the table (page 24). Cranz indicates that "… the reason[s] for sitting on the floor, on mats, on carpets, platforms, Chinese *k'angs,* or stools stem from cultural traditions rather than economic development" (page 26). According to Csikszentmihalyi and Rochberg-Halton, "…the notion that chairs and tables are more comfortable [than, say, sitting on the floor] is not true in absolute sense; they are so only within a pattern of cultural habits and expectations" (Csikszentmihalyi and Rochberg-Halton 1981, page 58). In fact, traditional Japanese or Hindu homes do not have much furniture.

3.1.5   Relations Between Shape and Arrangement of Furniture, and Its Meaning

The following two examples illustrate the interweaving of physical, symbolic and cultural meanings embedded in an object.[7]

Example 1: The knights and the round table The circle is a shape that has an infinite order of symmetry and can be split into an infinite number of equal parts. The legendary King Arthur gave his knights an equal place at the table and, therefore, an equal right to speak. Today the term "roundtable" is synonymous with the terms for committee or assembly. The shape itself symbolizes fairness and equality in group conversations.

Example 2: "Roundtables" for peace talks? One of the most "graphic and politically important instances of deliberately manipulating the shape and symbolism" (Herdeg 1983, page 27) of a piece of furniture for a "round table" occurred in Paris in the late 60s during the peace talks between the United States, South Vietnam, North Vietnam, and the National Liberation Front (NLF).[8] The parties involved could not agree about the organization of the conference, and, in particular, the shape of the conference table. The North Vietnamese and the NLF preferred a square table to stress equality between the parties (Fig. 1 left) while the US and South Vietnam proposed a rectangular table that did not provide an equal amount of space for all of the parties (Fig. 1 right). After numerous iterations of proposals and rejections, the Soviet ambassador in Paris proposed a giant, round table with two smaller rectangular tables located at two opposite sides of the round table (Fig. 2). After ten weeks of deadlock in the negotiations due to the table's shape, everyone agreed. Herdeg comments that the negotiating parties never disagreed about the meaning of the proposed shapes of tables and "… both recognized and cherished the political symbolism implied in form" (page 27).

---

[7] According to Csikszentmihalyi and Rochberg-Halton, "[o]bjects are not static entities whose meaning is projected on to them from cognitive functions of the brain or from abstract conceptual systems of culture. They themselves are signs, objectified forms of psychic energy (page 173).

[8] Thanks to Mark Meagher for pointing out this example during the CAIF 2005 workshop.

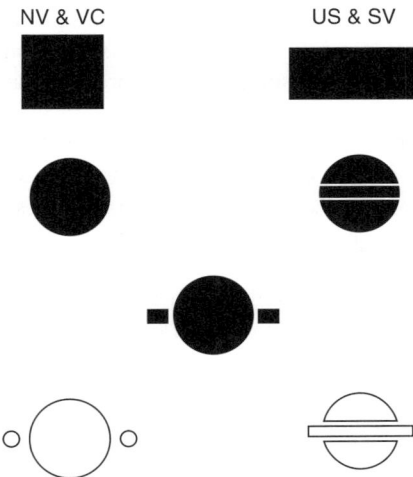

Fig. 1 Diagrams with proposals for the shape of the conference table. From The Decorated Diagram (Herdeg 1983, page 28)

Fig. 2 The giant table and the signing of the peace agreement in Paris on 27 January 1973. Image retrieved in March 2006 from http://www.gruntonline.com/TheWar/peace_accord1.htm

4 Augmented Furniture: Incongruous Chairs and Tables Designed to Elicit "Small Moments"

In *Practice of Daily Life,* the French philosopher Michel de Certeau distinguishes two types of daily activities, *strategic* and *tactical*, and stresses that each has their own modes of production and consumption. According to de Certeau, formally acknowledged social activities such as classroom-based school work, working in a job, having a meeting, or playing in the (local) football team are *strategic* in their character. By contrast, many marginal, everyday practices such as talking, reading, walking in the city, shopping, cooking, are *tactical* in their characters. Marginal social activities are important for the social development of the members of the community, but are not acknowledged as such in a formal way.

Designing for work-related activities or scenarios implies focusing on efficiency, productivity, relationships between clients and providers, etc. This approach is *rational* and *programmatic*, implying "air-tight", "wind tunnel" tested objects – furniture, domestic appliances, mobile phones, user interfaces – that will not fail nor allow any unplanned ambiguities when engaged by users. The instances of reviewed augmented furniture in this paper are not driven by work themes. Rather, they explore the theme of *small moments,* everyday, noninstrumental interaction scenarios (e.g. dinner at a table, conversation with a friend, walking on the street, relaxing, reading a newspaper) that may appear marginal but are in fact the very glue of our daily lives.

4.1   Therapeutic Furniture: Robotic Massage Chairs and Squeeze Chairs

Robotic Massage Chairs have a precise functionality: they give massage. They also capture our imaginations in a deeper ways because they deliver mediated touch. The chairs interpret the topography of a person's body and match it to a fixed repertoire of motions. A pair of rollers ("a contoured tracking system") located in the back panel of the chair first "scans" the back of the user by moving along their spine. The same rollers can then create a variety of massage patterns. The user can choose a duration and specific type of massage (rolling, kneading, compression or percussion) using a remote control. Models of robotic massage chairs may include i-Pod docking station, built-in speakers, subwoofers and beverage-holder, to "blend music and massage into the ultimate relaxation experience".

An advertisement for the *Ijoy™ Robotic Massage Chair®* describes their patented *Human Touch Technology®* as "wrists and arms" that behave as the "hands" of a trained massage professional (Fig. 3):

> Meet your new, best friend. The science of comfort. Inside every iJoy™ Robotic Massage® Chair are the "hands" of a trained massage professional, just waiting to provide you with a soothing back massage. But don't take our word for it. Sit down in one. Human Touch Technology® starts with a patented mechanism that works like "wrists and arms," we added "hands" – massage rollers that move three-dimensionally on a straight track. The result is a Robotic Massage® that feels remarkably human. (Retrieved on 28 April, 2006 from www. abtelectronics.com/product/16957.html)

While the rhetoric used in the advertisement refers to the embedded technologies as the "hands" of a human, the advert actually sells mediated touch. This topic was

Fig. 3 Panasonic EP3202 Real Pro robotic massage chair provides "Swede-atsu" massage. Image retrieved on 28 September 2004 from http://www.sharperimage.com

researched by Rachel Maines in her work on early 20th century therapy for female hysteria using small electric appliances. Maines found that: "the idea that technologies are deliberately shaped for social purposes is now widely accepted, but the phenomenon of camouflage is less familiar" (Maines 2001, page 117). The word "camouflage", according to Maines, means that the advertising rhetoric of products conveys what the item offers without endorsing all of their possible uses.

Although robotic massage chairs do not have "clandestine" advertising needs (they are still chairs!), the variety of audio, etc. peripherals, seem to obscure the core use of the object. Paradoxically, the more functions are added to the chair, the more precise these functions become. When Baudrillard talks about gadgets or thingamajigs, he states: "[s]o precise is the function proposed, in fact, that … such objects are *subjectively* functional, that is to say, obsessional"[9] (Baudrillard 1996, pp. 113–114).

Arguably, these chairs *are* functional, "declare their own existence" and remain stable even if technology fails. Although the ambition to optimize the experience of the object has pushed the "experience to the prosaic" (Dunne 1999, page 14), these strange, fascinating objects with many purposes still serve us. As Baudrillard puts it, "… like all obsessions … this particular variety has its poetic side" (page 114).

---

[9] Baudrillard continues by stating that the same obsession exists for the opposite, aesthetic approach to designing objects: "As for the opposite, 'aesthetic', approach, which omits function altogether and exalts the beauty of pure mechanism, this ultimately amounts to the same thing. For the inventor of the Concours Lépine, the creation of a solar-powered boiled-egg opener or some other equally dotty gadget is merely an excuse for obsessive manipulation and contemplation." (Baudrillard 1996, page 114)

The *Squeeze Chair* by Wendy Jacob provides another example of therapeutic furniture addressing mediated touch. In the mid 1990s, Wendy Jacob, faculty at the MIT Visual Arts program, read a *New Yorker* interview with Temple Grandin, a renowned American animal scientist best known for designing livestock facilities that restrain and calm animals before they are killed. Grandin, herself autistic, writes:

> From as far back as I can remember, I always hated to be hugged. I wanted to experience the good feeling of being hugged, but it was just too overwhelming. It was like a great, all-engulfing tidal wave of stimulation, and I reacted like a wild animal. Being touched triggered flight; it flipped my circuit breaker. … Many autistic children crave pressure stimulation even though they cannot tolerate being touched. It is much easier for a person with autism to tolerate touch if he or she initiates it. When touched unexpectedly, we usually withdraw, because our nervous system does not have time to process the sensation. (Grandin 1995, page 62)

Through a series of self-experiments conducted since her teen years, Grandin discovered that physical pressure stimulation on animals and autistic people produces similar results – a calming sensation (page 83). Based on her experiences in designing squeeze machines for livestock, Grandin designed a human squeeze machine for lessening hypersensitivity and anxieties of autistic people. Her goal in designing the machine was "… to enhance the feeling of being embraced" (page 80).

Jacob was "intrigued with this idea of taking something as emotionally complicated as an embrace and reducing it to something mechanical" (Jacob 2000). She carried out a series of conversations with Grandin, and the outcome of this collaboration was *The Squeeze Chair* (Figs. 4–5), an armchair designed to soothe people. The armchair has two curved arms that can inflate to embrace the person sitting in the chair. The arms inflate using an attached foot pump. The pump is activated either by the person who sits in the chair or by an outside observer. Regulating the amount of air increases or reduces the strength of the arms' embrace. Those who used this armchair identified the experience as soothing and relaxing, as if one received a giant, firm hug.

Fig. 4 Wendy Jacob, Squeeze Chaise Lounge, 1998. Red mohair, wood, pneumatic system with pump and hoses

Fig. 5 Wendy Jacob, Child Squeeze Chair, 2001

4.2 Mediating: Conversation Table, Stealing Table and Table Childhood

Conversations often take place at tables, either among colleagues in a business meeting, or between family members that come together for an everyday meal or special celebration. As we have seen, each of these occasions carries own set of accepted cultural conventions.

The *Conversation Table* by Nikolovska was inspired by such situations (Figs. 6–7). The goal of the project was to offer a commentary on power dynamics as they occur during conversations. The table, made from cardboard, was designed for two people, each seated at one end of the table. Two microphones placed at each end below the surface of the table, capture the initiation, duration and volume of speech at regular intervals. The captured signals trigger the lighting of an array of LEDs (light emitting diodes), going from the person who speaks to the person who listens. The animation of the LEDs provides a visual representation that mirrors the conversational dynamics between the people seated at the table.

Interaction between dyads of users at the table was observed. These dyads knew each other well (friends, spouses, colleagues). Each dyad was asked to complete a sequence of simple tasks (conversation about a specific topic, daily chore or a personal object). The table, inert at first, was switched on half way through their interaction, and the influence of this "intrusion" was observed. From having a conversation and having a mutual awareness of each other, users of the *Conversation Table* suddenly became aware of the table's unusual "responsiveness." Most users referred to it as a third participant in their interaction. For more information see Nikolovska (2006).

The *Stealing Table*, another project by Nikolovska, was an example of a kleptomaniac or a magician table (Figs. 8, 9, 10). Acts of disappearance can be interpreted as stealing, borrowing, storing or even cleaning. Disappearance can also be interpreted as magic, suspension of disbelief, and understanding of a situation as something out of one's immediate control. Magicians have mastered the art of illusion,

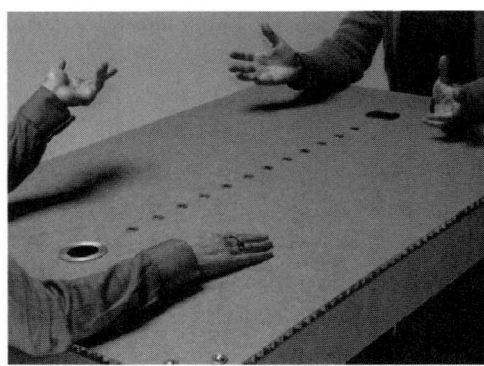

Fig. 6 The Conversation Table. Gemma Shusterman and Lira Nikolovska (left) and Kelly Dobson and Susanne Seitinger (right) at the Conversation Table. Left photo by Kate Kunath, 2005

Fig. 7 The Conversation Table. Gemma Shusterman and Lira Nikolovska (left) and Kelly Dobson and Susanne Seitinger (right) at the Conversation Table. Left photo by Kate Kunath, 2005

Fig. 8 Student playing with the Stealing Table during the Four Tables exhibit at MIT Rotch library in October 2005

Fig. 9 Custom-made aluminium parts are attached to servo motors and load cells. Red plexiglas parts connect the servos with the planks

offering optical illusions such as floating ghosts and oracles, vanishing elephants or ladies sawn in half. Cabinets equipped with angled mirrors give the illusion that whoever was inside, disappeared (Steinmeyer 2003). The audience often knows that the whole event is an illusion, but is unable to figure out how the trick was done. This table was designed to examine our relationships with objects placed at tables, specifically, what happens when objects disappear. The table, in this case, is the symbolic thief or the magician, and it is a selective one because it absorbs only small and light object placed on it.

Half a year after it was made, the behaviour of the table became unpredictable. The honeycomb cardboard weakened due to the frequent transport of the table and the weight of the hardware components. As a result, the plywood, the plexiglas planks and the sensors became misaligned. The planks on the tabletop continued to sense and absorb objects, but started to open and close spontaneously, surprising (and even pinching!) users who tried to predict the pattern of behaviour. This table was also evaluated by pairs of users that knew each other. Its behavioural quirks triggered gamut of responses and emotions, from amusement to discomfort. For additional information see Nikolovska (2006).

Table Childhood by Max Dean and Raffaello D'Andrea is an example of "inquisitive" furniture (Fig. 10). This autonomous robotic table "resides" in an enclosed room in a museum or gallery. Its name refers to its child-like abilities to learn and develop relationships with museum visitors. The table selects one of the visitors, and attempts to start a "conversation". The development of the "conversation", or "dance" is based on the motion of the visitor. If she is timid, the table becomes inquisitive and pursues the visitor around the enclosed room. If the visitor is assertive, the table may either run away or become unfriendly. D'Andrea pointed out that the table is not a technologically complicated device but it appears to behave in a complicated manner because the people who engage with it behave in complicated ways. As the table chooses whom to pursue, the visitor *becomes* the selected object of attention and, ultimately, she becomes artwork. The roles of visitor and artwork reverse.

Fig. 10 A museum visitor interacting with the Table Childhood (1984–2001) by Max Dean and Raffaello D'Andrea. Collection of The National Gallery of Canada, Ottawa. Photos by Robert Keziere

The table moves with four motors and wheels located at each leg. A computer vision system with a camera mounted on the ceiling of the room enables real-time tracking of the selected person in the room in relationship to the table, and controls the table's movement.

5 Taxonomy of Augmented Furniture: Functional, Relational and Poetic

5.1 Functional

A first, very basic dimension, or continuum, refers to the **functionality** of augmented furniture (Nikolovska 2006). The augmentation can be *relative* to the existing functions (for example, when a recliner becomes a massage chair or a work chair with built in computing peripherals). In this case the core functionalities are extended and the object becomes a *hyper object*. Examples of *hyper objects* include *Robotic Massage chairs, Squeeze Chair, and Conversation and Stealing Tables*. At other times the augmentation can be *unrelated* (for example, when a recliner or a chair acquires built-in speakers or built-in refrigerator). In this case, the functionalities are tangential to the core use of the object and the object becomes *an alien object*. Examples of *alien objects* include *The Table Childhood*.

5.2   *Relational*

A second dimension, or continuum, refers to the degree of **autonomy**[10] of augmented furniture. Elsewhere, Ackermann (2005) has explored the "relational" qualities of artificial play-partners, or "animates," grouping instances of animated/robotic toys along the following continuum: "good slaves" (malleable and obedient), "inner driven" (stubborn) and "good dancers" (autonomous yet responsive). In another study, Nikolovska (2006) has investigated augmentation of furniture along a passive to autonomous continuum. One observation is that augmentations are more like gradients rather than clear-cut categories because even autonomous objects are passive at times. For this chapter, we propose the following continuum:

- "PRETTY" YET INERT (ORNAMENTED AND PASSIVE): These objects remain stable within a certain state – they are either switched on or off. Numerous examples of passive augmented furniture use light (from fluorescent light to LEDs and electroluminescent wires) as a decorative element that offers new kind of ornamentation possibilities. Examples of passive furniture are the *Eudora chair* by Critz Campbell, a translucent fibreglass chair internally illuminated with fluorescent light, and the *LED Table* by Ingo Maurer where over 200 miniature LEDs are encased between two layers of glass.
- "GOOD SLAVES" (MALLEABLE AND OBEDIENT): "Push their buttons" and they obey (execute your orders)! These objects can sense and respond by exhibiting branched behaviours, but have no mind of their own. Examples of "good slaves" include the *Robotic Massage chair*, and the *Squeeze Chair*. In the example of the *Squeeze Chair*, the more air one pumps into the chair, the more the chair squeezes. If someone else is pumping, the chair's "blind tendency" to hug or let go is out of the user's control, in which case the chair may be perceived by the user as being autonomous, with a mind of its own.
- "INNER-DRIVEN" (STUBBORN): These objects keep their bearing without paying much attention to anything else. They optimize their performance along some predetermined dimension, and they do so no matter what. Most importantly, they will not flinch, no matter how hard users try to engage them! They may have sensors, yet their sensors are blind to users' solicitations. Examples of stubborn objects include, ironically, many self-orienting devices, such as compasses, gyroscopes, or levers. They are referents precisely because they do not "compromise". Examples of inner-driven augmented furniture may include devices that know when their battery is low and automatically seek their cradle to recharge.
- "GOOD DANCERS" (AUTONOMOUS YET RESPONSIVE): These objects are ideal relational partners that share control and engage in dialogic gives-and-takes. They are not only autonomous and empathetic, they also have personality. The *Table-Childhood* by Dean and D'Andrea falls in this category. The table chooses a viewer and attempts to establish a relationship with them: this table "likes" a good dance!

---

[10] An autonomous object is self-governing, independent, not ruled by external law or force. For detailed discussion on autonomy see Winner (1977).

5.3   Poetic

A third dimension, poetic, has emerges from a conscious **design strategy.** Projects like *Robotic Massage chairs* are designed in a programmatic way: a clear, rational programme of input and outputs drives the design of the object. By contrast, projects such as Jacob's *Squeeze Chair,* Dean and D'Andrea's *Table Childhood* and Nikolovska's *Conversation* and *Stealing Tables* are designed to allow the emergence of incongruous or surprising responses to people's solicitations. This poetic approach emphasizes the emergence of *small moments* and, incidentally, enriches the relational qualities with two new categories which we call MEDIATORS and MISCHIEVOUS.

- MEDIATORS (THE EYE OF THE PSYCHOANALYST): The *Conversation Table* is an embodiment of what an "intelligent" listener role may be – the psychoanalyst's eye. Without being intrusive, and if one pays attention, this table reveals otherwise unspoken aspects of the dynamics of interaction between its users.
- MISCHIEVOUS (THE THIEF): The stealing table is an embodiment of naughty and curious troublemaker. It is the quintessence of an "uncanny" piece of furniture! When least expected, this table intrudes and asserts its own presence.

6   What Kinds of User Evaluations are Appropriate?

When asked about the role of end users in innovation, Henry Ford responded: "If I had asked people what they wanted, they would have said faster horses."[11] In a less cynical way, Brenda Laurel makes a similar point in her book *Utopian Entrepreneur:*

> Asking people to choose their favourites from among all the things that already exist doesn't necessarily support innovation; it maps the territory but may not help you plot a new trajectory. On the other hand, most people are not very good at inventing *new objects of desire.* If you asked someone in 1957 what new thing they would like to play with, chances are they would not have asked for a plastic hoop that they could rotate around their hips. Somebody had to invent the Hula Hoop. (Laurel 2001, page 37)

While essential to refining the use of a product, traditional user studies are not necessarily the best candidate when it comes to envisioning the future, or designing innovative concepts/products.

One approach used to remedy this problem is what is known as *co-creation*, or *designing with users.* In this approach, designers work together with users, immersing both users and themselves in the projected uses of a product. Another approach used by design consultancies to evaluate "visions of the future" projects is known as *expert evaluation studies.* The idea here is to bring experts who know the field intimately, and to interview them about the issues potentially important for the projects. As Deasy states, it is important to "...be broad in your definition of expert;

---

[11] Thanks to Dana Cho from IDEO for pointing out this example during the CAIF 2005 workshop.

for example, teens make great experts when you are investigating instant messaging." (2003, page 173). Experts can be brought in any phase of the project. The goal is that designers get enough critical support without "killing" the seeds of ideas that seem uninteresting or irrelevant early on.

Research by Höök et al. (2003, page 1) suggests that methods for evaluating human-computer interaction (HCI) are "...useful for improving the design of inter-active systems, yet may be rejected by non traditional technology disciplines such as media art". Indeed, when it comes to usability, the arts and HCI are often at odds! Both disciplines have elected different evaluation methods and perspectives. HCI evaluation strategies are routinely applied to find out how and where to improve the performance of products or systems. HCI researchers use ethnographic observa-tions or quantitative-scientific/user studies. Art projects, on the other hand, are evaluated either by art critics, professionals skilled in placing the work in a specific socio-cultural context, or by the actual audiences. The interpretation is subjective and, in the mind of the artist, users should derive their own conclusions or interpre-tations of the work they observe and experience[12].

How to bridge the gap? In the paper *Sense and Sensibility: Evaluation and Interactive Art* Hook, Sengers and Andersson discuss evaluation techniques that have been used in two Royal College of Arts (London) projects, *Presence* and *Placebo*. In *Presence*, a European Union (EU) project, the evaluation included informal reflections by authors Dunne and Gaver about the installation process and on-site use of augmented benches by people in a neighbourhood in Amsterdam (Sengers and Gaver 2005). In *Placebo,* a project by Dunne and Raby (2001), a small number of people were interviewed and recruited to "adopt" one of the eight placebo objects. These people lived with the objects in their homes for a short period of time after which the designers interviewed them about their experiences with the objects. These interviews are transcribed verbatim in the book about the project, and as the authors state, the authors offer no analysis or conclusions and leave all the thinking to the readers. In contrast, ethnographic research and user study evaluations were continuous throughout other EU projects, such as the *Living Memory*[13] project (from the same project cluster as *Presence*). *Living Memory* was developed among project partners from industry and academia. The evaluation of the interaction scenarios in *Living Memory* was embedded with the design work.

Arguably, much of the interactive media artwork can benefit from critical HCI insights about its usability. We are already seeing a new genre of art critics emerge, ones grounded in HCI. In the end, it will be the users that will have the final word.

---

[12]Michael Mateas writes about the differences between cultural production in the arts and artificial intelligence (AI). Whereas the arts rely on poetics, audience perception, specificity and artistic abstraction, the focus in AI is task competence, objective measurements, generality and realism. (page 149) Mateas, Michael. *Expressive AI: A hybrid art and science practice.* In *Leonardo: Journal of the International Society for Arts, Sciences, and Technology* 34 (2), 2001. 147--153.

[13]One of the Living Memoryproject partners was the Communications Department at the Queen Margaret College from Edinburgh, UK. They closely worked with human factors specialists from Philips Design in Eindhoven.

7 Concluding Remarks

What is it that "poetically" links people and "augmented" furniture? How can such a link, or rapport, form and evolve? What thoughts and feelings draw people to certain artefacts? What qualities of the artefacts themselves may lead to engaging or amusing interactions?

People are born into a world of signs, symbols and human-made artefacts, and as they grow older, they appropriate these objects, recreating and interpreting their meanings through the lenses of their interests and experience. Cultural artefacts, on the other end, go beyond affordances. They exhibit relational and poetic qualities best described in terms of objects' *presence* and *personalities*.

As a way of conclusion, a few words on people, things, and the poetics of playful interactions, or small moments, follow.

7.1 On People

In the first part of this paper, we have shown that the understanding of beauty depends on the individual's perception. Without suspension of disbelief, that is, we would not be able to engage in play, or appreciate a joke or a work of art. Like imagination itself, pretend play and joking are non-literal. They are about make-believe. Both pretence and humour allow a person to step back occasionally from the seriousness of everyday life and approach it with a "grain of unreality." Symbolic replays, through dramatization or humour, are not confusing, even to young children, provided the context is safe. Likewise, fantasy play is not an escape from reality. Rather, it helps people to better understand reality.

7.2 On Things

If beauty ultimately relies on perception ("eyes of the beholders"), not all objects are equally good projective materials. As a way to capture the *hidden qualities* of artefacts that enable meaningful encounters – and sustain engagement over time – a useful heuristic has been to "ask" the object itself a host of questions relative to *its' relational abilities to draw in people and keep them engaged.* The following relational vocabulary presents a means to capture many essential qualities, usually left unexamined by instrumental or rational approaches to object's affordances:

- *Holding power:* A concept's ability to engage person's attention and sustain her interest long enough for a meaningful relation to take place (play it again).
- *Transformative power:* A concept's ability to *let* the person *in*, i.e. to encourage her initiative, both physical and mental (do, transform).

- *Evocative power:* A concept's ability to bring about rich associations and thus to unleash a person's imagination (be transported, inspired).
- *Mediating power:* A concept's ability to facilitate the expression, communication, and negotiation of feelings and ideas (say it with...).
- *Reflecting power:* A concept's ability to open up a space for reflection and contemplation (stop and think).

7.3   On the Poetics of Playful Interactions, Or "Small Moments"

As mentioned earlier, designing for work-related activities or scenarios implies focusing on efficiency, productivity, and transactions between clients and providers. This approach is deliberately *rational* and *programmatic* and the goal is that "products" will not fail nor allow unplanned ambiguities when used by end users. In this paper, we have instead explored the theme of *small moments,* everyday, non-instrumental interaction scenarios between people or between people and artefacts. Although these interactions may appear marginal, they represent the very glue of our daily lives. Much of the information technology developments in the last decades have enabled work, pleasure and leisure activities of daily lives to intersect (Mitchell 2003). Rather than designing for these intersections, or creating a design strategy for addressing small moments in a rational way (the dominant HCI approach), the chosen approach of the examined projects is best described as a *poetic.*

Acknowledgements Special thanks to Simon Schiessl for technical consulting (programming and electronics) for the *Stealing Table* project. The making of the *Stealing Table* was funded in part by a grant from the MIT Council for the Arts.

References

Ackermann , Edith. *Playthings that Do Things: A Young's Kid's "Incredibles"!* In IDC 2005, June 8–10 2005, Boulder, Colorado.
Baudrillard, Jean. *The System of Objects.* London & New York: Verso, 1996.
Cranz, Galen. *The Chair: Rethinking Culture, Body, and Design.* New York: W. W. Norton & Company, 1998.
Csikszentmihalyi, Mihaly and Rochberg-Halton, Eugene. *The Meaning of Things: Domestic Symbols and the Self.* Cambridge, UK: Cambridge University Press, 1981.
de Certeau, Michel. *The Practice of Everyday Life.* Berkeley and Los Angeles: University of California Press, 1984.
Dunne, Anthony. *Hertzian Tales: Electronic Products, Aesthetic Experience and Critical Design.* London: Royal College of Arts CRD Research Publications, 1999.
Dunne, Anthony and Raby, Fiona. *Design Noir: The Secret Life of Electronic Objects.* Basel: Birkhäuser Publishers, 2001.
Freud, Sigmund. *The Uncanny.* Penguin Classics, 2003.
Gloag, John. *A Social History of Furniture Design from B.C. 1300 to A.D. 1960.* New York: Crown Publishers, Inc., 1966.

Grandin, Temple. *Thinking in Pictures*. New York: Vintage Books, 1995.

Herdeg, Klaus. *The Decorated Diagram: Harvard Architecture and the Failure of the Bauhaus Legacy*. Cambridge: MIT Press, 1983.

Höök Kristina, Sengers Phoebe, and Andersson, Gerd. *Sense and Sensibility: Evaluation and Interactive Art*. Proceedings of CHI 2003, April 5–10, 2003, Ft. Lauderdale, Florida, USA.

Intel Research Labs, Berkeley. *Familiar Strangers* research project. Retrieved on 20 April 2006 from http://berkeley.intel-research.net/paulos/research/familiarstranger.

Jacob, Wendy. *Squeeze Chair. Creative Capital Channel web site, 2000*. Retrieved on 11 February 2006 from http://channel.creative-capital.org/project_311.html

Kaplan, F. *Poupées: Des enfants qui apprivoisent des robots. In Machines Apprivoisées*. Paris Editions Vuibert, 2005. Chapter 13, pages 219–241.

Koestler, Arthur. *The Act of Creation*. New York: Dell, 1964.

Laurel, Brenda. *Utopian Entrepreneur*. Cambridge: MIT Press, 2001.

Latour, Bruno. *We Have Never Been Modern*. Cambridge: Harvard University Press, 1993.

Maines, Rachel. *The Technology of Orgasm: "Hysteria," the Vibrator, and Women's Sexual Satisfaction*. Baltimore & London: The John Hopkins University Press, 1999.

Maines, Rachel. *Socially Camouflaged Technologies: the Case of the Electromechanical Vibrator* (pages 117–143). In Pursell, Carol (editor). American Technology. Malden: Blackwell Publishers, 2001.

Mitchell, William J. *ME + +* . Cambridge: MIT Press, 2003.

Nikolovska, Lira. *Physical Dialogues with Augmented Furniture, PhD dissertation*. Cambridge: MIT School of Architecture and Planning, June 2006.

Norman, Donald. *The Design of Everyday Things*. New York: Basic Books, 1988.

Piaget, Jean. *Play, Dreams, and Imitation in Childhood*. N.Y.: W. W. Norton and Company, 1962.

Sengers, Phoebe and Gaver, Bill. *Designing for Interpretation. In Proceedings of Human-Computer Interaction International Conference*, 2005.

Steinmeyer, Jim. *Hiding the elephant: How Magicians Invented the Impossible and Learned to Disappear*. New York: Carroll & Graf Publishers, 2003.

Winner, Langdon. Autonomous *Technology: Technics-out-of-Control as a Theme in Political Thought*. Cambridge: MIT Press, 1977

Author Index

Subject Index

Printed in the United States of America